DEFENDANT RIGHTS

A Reference Handbook

Other Titles in ABC-CLIO's
CONTEMPORARY
WORLD ISSUES
Series

Books in the Contemporary World Issues series address vital issues in today's society such as genetic engineering, pollution, and biodiversity. Written by professional writers, scholars, and nonacademic experts, these books are authoritative, clearly written, up-to-date, and objective. They provide a good starting point for research by high school and college students, scholars, and general readers as well as by legislators, businesspeople, activists, and others.

Each book, carefully organized and easy to use, contains an overview of the subject, a detailed chronology, biographical sketches, facts and data and/or documents and other primary-source material, a directory of organizations and agencies, annotated lists of print and nonprint resources, and an index.

Readers of books in the Contemporary World Issues series will find the information they need in order to have a better understanding of the social, political, environmental, and economic issues facing the world today.

DEFENDANT RIGHTS

A Reference Handbook

Hamid R. Kusha

**CONTEMPORARY
WORLD ISSUES**

A B C ❧ C L I O

Santa Barbara, California
Denver, Colorado
Oxford, England

Library of Congress Cataloging-in-Publication Data is available from the Library of Congress.

08 07 06 05 04   10 9 8 7 6 5 4 3 2 1

This book is also available on the World Wide Web as an eBook. Visit abc-clio.com for details.

ABC-CLIO, Inc.
130 Cremona Drive, P.O. Box 1911
Santa Barbara, California 93116-1911

This book is printed on acid-free paper ∞.
Manufactured in the United States of America

Contents

Preface

Defendant Rights: A Reference Handbook gives to a lay audience a synopsis of the legal milestones and important people in the development of defendant rights in criminal prosecution. In particular, the Anglo-American notion of these rights is investigated and is discussed throughout the text. The desire to defend one's basic liberties against charges of criminality is a universal one. Thus throughout history different cultures have come up with quasi-social and legal mechanisms for protecting criminal defendants. For example, in some ancient tribal societies a council of elders would act collectively in the capacity of a tribunal in determineing the guilt or innocence of the accused. With the passage of time, tribal societies created villages and small cities with different forms of government. With the gradual emergence of settlement under a central authority, kingdoms emerged in different parts of the Middle East, North Africa, and Asia, and legal authority became more centralized under a ruling power. Later, some of these smaller kingdoms merged with one another to create empires. These developments led to the rise of more complex social and legal relationships. This complexity also led to the gradual reforming of the ancient tribal legal systems, including the manner in which criminal defense and prosecution was practiced.

It was only in the modern legal systems of the twentieth and twenty-first centuries that defendant rights have reached their current level of complexity. One reason is that modern legal systems have developed in democratic societies with free-market economic systems. Such free-market systems operate in their optimal capacity only when civil liberties are protected and all social groups are positively engaged in economic activities. Full participation in economic activities is only possible when legal equality is maintained in society. One of these modern legal systems is the Anglo-American tradition, which has spread to the majority of English-speaking countries, such as Australia, Canada, and New Zealand.

The U.S. legal system evolved from the British common law, which is one of the oldest systems of conflict resolution in the world. It began in England in medieval times, and then many of its doctrines, practices, and devices were passed on to colonial America with the pilgrims. Its stated purpose is to resolve civil and criminal conflicts based on the ideals of equity, fairness, and justice. The development of defendant rights is an expression of this ideal of justice in the Anglo-American legal tradition. Legal scholars have argued that the Anglo-American legal system has produced the most comprehensive set of rights for criminal defendants, which this book outlines for the lay audience, including recent changes in response to events such as the terrorist attacks of 11 September 2001.

Hamid R. Kusha
Texas A&M International University
Laredo, Texas

1

History

This chapter provides a brief historical background of defendant rights in the U.S. criminal justice system. In this book, the term *defendant rights* refers to a set of legal procedures that the U.S. justice system guarantees to those accused of violating criminal laws, beginning with their arrest and proceeding throughout the duration of their prosecution and—if they are found guilty—their eventual sentencing and appeals they may bring.

Defendant Rights Defined

The rights of defendants hold a cherished place in the American legal tradition. Their origins date back to the English Magna Carta (or "Great Charter"), signed by King John in the year 1215 after his army was defeated in battle by English barons who fought his abuse of power. The Magna Carta contained sixty-three clauses, some of which dealt with crime and criminal prosecution. The clauses set out rules whereby members of the English nobility accused of crimes could defend themselves in the king's court. Certain of these found their way in some form into the Fourth, Fifth, Sixth, and Eighth Amendments to the U.S. Constitution, in the section known as the Bill of Rights. The provisions in these amendments form the legal basis of defendant rights in U.S. legal tradition.[1]

In a U.S. criminal trial, the party accused of a crime is known as the defendant. The Constitution guarantees defendants the right to contest the charges against them in a court of law. When a criminal defendant pleads "not guilty," it becomes the legal responsibility of the prosecution to prove "beyond a reasonable doubt" that the charges are valid and that the defendant is indeed the culprit. It is noteworthy that legal wrongs can be divided into categories such as crimes and torts, which have different remedies. For example, breach of contract constitutes a tort wrong, which is tried in civil, rather than criminal, court. In civil proceedings, the guilt of a defendant can be established through the so-called preponderance of evidence, meaning that the weight and thrust of the evidence are against the defendant. In criminal proceedings, the guilt of the defendant is established "beyond a reasonable doubt," which is a much more stringent criterion than the preponderance of evidence.

Defendant Rights in the U.S. Constitution

The U.S. Constitution is a very important legal document that assures citizens a set of basic rights, freedoms, and implied responsibilities. The first ten amendments to the Constitution are known collectively as the Bill of Rights. These amendments were ratified by three quarters of the states and declared part of the U.S. Constitution by Congress in 1791, and have played an important role in the operational dynamics of the U.S. criminal justice system ever since. Most importantly, the Fourth, Fifth, Sixth, and Eighth Amendments protect those accused of crimes from arbitrary or abusive treatment by the federal government. The Fourteenth Amendment extends most of these same protections to defendants prosecuted by state governments. Thus, these amendments protect citizens against potential abuses of both federal and state governments and their agents. For example, no government agency with law enforcement powers is authorized to arrest, search, or interrogate citizens and/or legal aliens without probable cause or appropriately issued warrants.[2]

Altogether these amendments, as interpreted by the courts throughout U.S. history, set the minimum standards for *due process of law* for criminal defendants. Due process of law mandates that a defendant receive a certain legal process before punishment may apply. Simply put, due process of law means that a criminal case has to go through certain steps of the legal process before a final verdict is reached as to whether the defendant is guilty or innocent of the charges. These steps start with the arrest of a suspect, and continues until a verdict of guilt or innocence is reached by a court of law.

Discretionary Power and Defendant Rights

U.S. police officers have what is known as *discretionary power* to investigate, arrest, and interrogate suspects based on probable cause that a crime was committed or that a crime is in progress. However, there are limits to this discretion. Police officers may be held liable in a civil court if they knowingly violate a person's constitutionally protected rights—an issue to be discussed in this chapter. Prosecuting attorneys and judges also have a wide range of discretionary powers they regularly exercise in criminal cases. To minimize the abuse of discretionary powers given to the officials of the criminal justice system, the Founding Fathers of American democracy adopted many procedures that had developed in the common law of England as well as those stated in the Magna Carta. In addition, the colonial period saw the development of some checks on the authority of prosecuting officials. These, too, became enshrined in the Bill of Rights. A synopsis of the protective clauses of the Fourth, Fifth, Sixth, and Eighth Amendments follows.

A Dual Court System

In the United States, criminal defendants are prosecuted in either state or federal courts, depending on whether a state or federal law is alleged to have been broken. If the act at issue violates a federal law, the defendant is prosecuted under the jurisdictional authority of the federal government and in the federal court system. If the act violates a state code, jurisdiction shifts to the respective state's government and its court system. Thus, the U.S. court system has a dual hierarchy.

The term *jurisdictional authority* means the legal right state and federal courts have to prosecute a crime that has taken place in their respective areas of authority. Federal crimes are those acts that violate federal criminal laws. For example, if a person threatens the life of the U.S. president, or resists arrest by murdering an agent of the federal government, that person would be prosecuted under federal court jurisdiction. State crimes, on the other hand, are those acts that violate state criminal laws. If a person speeds on a state highway, that person will be prosecuted in a state court. In both court systems criminal defendants are entitled to legal defense.

The Adversarial Nature of the U.S. Court System

A U.S. criminal proceeding is adversarial in nature. This means that two opposing sides—the defense and the prosecution—present their differing evidence and arguments before an impartial jury in a trial presided over by a neutral judge. The two opposing parties are entitled to contest each others' arguments and evidence during the course of the proceedings so that the guilt or innocence of the criminal defendant may be determined. This contrasts with an inquisitorial system, typical of many other countries, in which the judge takes an active role along with the prosecutor in interrogating the defendant in an effort to determine the truth.

The Fourth Amendment Rights

The Fourth Amendment provides criminal defendants with two sets of basic rights in relation to (1) searches and (2) seizures by the police and other governmental agencies.[3] The intent of the Fourth Amendment is that a person's home, possessions, and communications are generally beyond the reach of government prying.

The Right to Protection from Unreasonable Search

The right against unreasonable search prevents the police or governmental agencies from violating the privacy of citizens in their homes unless they have a compelling reason to do so. This reason must be convincing enough to allow the issuance of a search warrant by a judge or a magistrate. This right to privacy, and against unreasonable search, extends to one's personal effects and papers as well. This means that not only a person's house is secure against illegal intrusion by the police and other governmental agencies, so are the contents of the house. The key term here is "unreasonable search," implying that law enforcement agencies do have the right to search a person's home as long as there is a legally valid basis for doing so. What are some of these valid bases?

One basis is known as the probable cause criterion. Probable cause is generally defined as possessing sufficient information to convince a reasonably prudent person that evidence of a crime is likely to be found in a stated location. For example, if police were tipped off that a large number of sealed containers were regularly being ferried in and out of a house in a certain neighborhood known for its illicit drug-smuggling activities, there might be probable cause to believe that the house was being used for drug-smuggling purposes. Therefore a search of those premises would be reasonable. When probable cause exists, law enforcement authorities must generally obtain warrants for either arrest or confiscation, unless exigent circumstances exist; for example, when the police believe that evidence will be destroyed because they hear a toilet flushing when they announce their presence at a house they believe to be used for drug purposes.

Another basis is known as the plain view doctrine. This holds that police may seize any evidence of criminal activity that is in "plain view" and, hence, obviously not within the reasonable expectation of privacy of the owner. Moreover, the finding of such evidence in plain view may provide the probable cause for searching a premise further. For example, a police officer stops a motor vehicle for a traffic violation. As the officer approaches the driver and asks for a driver's license and/or registration documents, he or she sees drug paraphernalia on the seat of the car in plain view. At this point, the officer is legally allowed to conduct a further search of the vehicle and to confiscate whatever other incriminating evidence is in the car. In the above example of the house used for drug-smuggling purposes, once a warrant for search of the premises is obtained, the police may also search for other incriminating evidence left in plain view. In other words, once in the house, if the police officers were to come across drug paraphernalia, drug containers, or names and addresses of the accomplices lying around in plain view, such may also be confiscated as evidence.

Other places where an individual has a reasonable expectation of privacy are, for example, his or her automobile along with its glove compartment and trunk, and the contents of briefcases or purses. As a general rule, police officers are not allowed to conduct illegal search and seizure activities. However, in the general climate of anxiety over international terrorism since 11 September 2001, U.S. judges and prosecutors have begun allowing more leeway to police officers as they conduct search, seizure, and surveillance activities. The rationale is that law enforcement has to exercise vigilance against a wide range of factors that may help agents of terrorism achieve their goals, a view that has led conservative judges and prosecutors to a more restrictive interpretation of civil liberties.

For example, in some jurisdictions police officers are allowed to make full arrests for minor traffic violations so that officers can conduct a comprehensive search of vehicles without need for a probable cause, as happened in the case of *Atwater v. City of Largo Vista* (2001). Historically, it has not been clear whether it is constitutional for police to arrest citizens for minor offenses not punishable by prison or jail time. The *Atwater* case has set a precedent, because although the defendant was arrested for not wearing a seat belt, which is a minor offense punishable by fines and not jail, the U.S. Supreme Court did not concur with her argument that the arrest was unconstitutional.

The Right to Protection from Unreasonable Seizure

The right against unreasonable seizure prevents police and other law enforcement agencies from arresting persons or seizing property incident to investigating criminal activity unless they have a warrant to do so. Police officers seeking a warrant must take an oath before the judge or magistrate issuing such warrant. The practice is known as taking an oath of affirmation. The purpose of an oath of affirmation is to ensure that the police officers are not being motivated by personal vendetta, malice, or other ulterior motives against the suspect, but that they sincerely believe that probable cause exists necessitating the issuance of warrants for arrest or search and seizure activities. In most jurisdictions, a false oath of affirmation by the police is perjury, which is a felony and carries a prison sentence for those convicted.

A warrant (for arrest, or search and seizure activities) is a carefully drafted legal document. It is issued by a court authority (e.g., a judge or a magistrate). It specifies (1) who is to be arrested,

(2) the place to be searched, and (3) what property or which documents are to be seized. The warrant must officially be served on the party to whom it is addressed. The server of the warrant is usually a law enforcement agent who could belong to local, state, or federal police agencies (e.g., the municipal police, the sheriff, the FBI, the DEA, the ATF, and so on). The warrant must clearly specify the purpose of the action, to whom the warrant is addressed, and what will happen if the legal injunctions of the warrant are ignored. For example, a warrant to "show cause" informs the subject that he or she must appear before a certain court at a specified time in order to demonstrate why he or she is not guilty of the charges specified in the warrant.

Police officers are allowed to enter a residential home without a warrant if the residents voluntarily allow the police to do so. This allowance, however, does not mean that the police can ransack the premises in search of incriminating evidence. Most citizens usually allow the police to enter their homes if the police officers ask for such permission. However, one is under no obligation to allow the police to enter one's premises without a valid search warrant.

Police officers may legally enter residential premises when they believe in "good faith" that a crime is being committed there. This is known as the crime-in-progress exception. In such cases, the police have the discretionary power to enter the premises in order to investigate the crime in progress and to arrest suspects without warrants. Later, the police may let the suspect(s) go free if it turns out that they were not involved in the commission of crime. The exception also applies when police are in "hot pursuit" of a suspect. In hot pursuit cases, the officers may without a warrant arrest and search a person they believe to have just committed a crime. They are allowed to follow such suspects into buildings, particularly if they have reason to believe that evidence of the crime will be destroyed before they can get a warrant.

Police officers are also authorized to enter a house or a place of work without a warrant if they believe that there is imminent danger to life or to property. For example in the case of a hostage situation, fire, or when a 911 call is made asking for the police to be dispatched to a home where the residents face such imminent dangers, no warrant is required. The rationale for these exceptions, supported by the case law, is that life is too precious to let it be lost. If one were to choose between a warrantless intervention by the police to save life or time lost obtaining warrants in order to intervene, the first course of action is preferable. In other words, in exceptional cases where imminent danger to life and/or to property exists, police are not required to obtain a warrant to enter residential premises.

Police officers are also authorized to stop and frisk (pat down) suspects in streets, to ask questions, and to take the suspect(s) to the police station provided that probable cause exists. (Technically speaking, arrest of a person in the street is a form of seizure.)

Search and Seizure under Public Scrutiny

Search and seizure activities of the police have been subjected to public scrutiny in recent years. A good number of cases have reached the U.S. Supreme Court, a subject to be dealt with in more detail in Chapter 2.[4] One reason for this scrutiny has to do with the fact that until the rise of the civil rights movement in the 1960s, the public perceived the main function of the police as enforcing criminal laws to control street crime. By and large, the public believed that those who committed street crimes belonged to the lower echelons of the working class. It was a general perception then that those who committed street crimes were either not decent, hard-working members of society, or that they were afflicted with social malaise.

The civil rights movement of the 1960s and 1970s, in conjunction with other social protest movements, changed the overall U.S. perception of crime commission, of the police, and of the rationale of law enforcement. From the 1980s to the early twenty-first century law enforcement agencies have gone through much rethinking as to what constitutes the essence of policing. This rethinking has been greatly influenced by what the United States had become by the last decades of the twentieth century: a rich multicultural and heterogeneous society.

The Fourth Amendment is a very important promoter of defendant rights. The protective clauses of the Fourth Amendment prohibiting unreasonable search and seizure have forced U.S. law enforcement agencies gradually to recognize the fact that citizens of this country are entitled to privacy in their homes and in their places of work. Unlike undemocratic societies in which police agencies have free rein to deprive citizens of their basic right to privacy, such is not the case with U.S. law enforcement—

thanks to the protective clauses of the Fourth Amendment. Therefore, U.S. police agencies, at both state and federal levels, have gradually moved to organize their search and seizure activities in a manner to ensure that these clauses are not violated.

To achieve these goals, police agencies have adopted codes of professionalism in their law enforcement activities. Through such standards, police agencies have also tried to protect themselves against civil liability suits. Civil liability suits that allege police misconduct can have devastating financial consequences for both the individual officer and the police department.[5] For example, the cost to local governments defending police departments against civil liability suits was estimated to be $780 billion by 2001, according to the International Association of the Chiefs of Police (IACP).[6] Because of the high costs involved in either litigating such cases or settling them out of court, police agencies have become very cautious in their search and seizure activities, especially in urban areas and in dealing with minority groups.

The Fifth Amendment Rights

The Fifth Amendment provides criminal defendants with four basic rights as follows: (1) the right to a grand jury (for federal law violations), (2) the right against double jeopardy, (3) the right against self-incrimination, and (4) the right to due process. Each of these rights is discussed below.

The Right to a Grand Jury

In the United States, except for in times of war or other emergencies, only a grand jury is legally allowed to accuse a person of violating federal law in the commission of capital (or *infamous*) crimes. Other violations of federal law do not require grand jury indictment. The definition of infamous crimes is not a consistent one; it has changed through time, and so has the severity of punishment applied to such crimes. This is known as the indictment power of the grand jury. Nineteen states follow this model and allow criminal indictments for state law violations to issue only from grand juries in relation to capital crimes. In the rest of the states, district attorneys are also empowered to initiate prosecution.[7]

The size of a grand jury varies. In some states the grand jury is composed of six jurors, in others sixteen, and in yet others twenty-three jurors make up the panel. These are ordinary citizens who are randomly selected from among registered voters residing in a prospective jurisdiction, from tax returns, or from telephone directories. However, jury selection is still subject to the Equal Protection Clause of the Fourteenth Amendment, which ensures that fair racial representation is maintained in the pool.

The grand jury is empowered to listen to the evidence of criminality that federal or state prosecuting authorities may have compiled against citizens. If the evidence is compelling, the grand jury indicts the suspects. The indictment opens the way for formal criminal prosecution. Otherwise, if the grand jury finds the evidence weak, or insufficient, it dismisses the case and no further legal action is taken against the accused. The following facts apply to grand jury indictments and deliberations:

- Any federal offense that may result in the imposition of the death penalty must be prosecuted by indictment of the grand jury. This applies to the nineteen states that keep the grand jury rule.
- Any federal offense that may result in incarceration of the criminal defendant in prison, or at hard labor, must be prosecuted by indictment of the grand jury. This applies to the nineteen states that keep the grand jury rule.
- A grand jury indictment determines the scope of the charges against a defendant.
- A presiding judge is bound by the scope of the indictment as determined by the grand jury, which means that the judge can't instruct the jury to go beyond the scope of the indictment in determining the guilt of the defendant.
- Grand jury deliberations take place in secrecy, without the prior knowledge of the subject(s) of the investigation.
- Grand jury deliberations are not to determine the guilt or innocence of the defendant, but to determine if sufficient evidence exists to indict (accuse) a defendant of criminality.

- Grand jury deliberations are not of an adversarial nature and therefore the rules of evidence and other procedural rights are not applied.
- A grand jury has the power to subpoena anyone to testify during its deliberations.
- Witnesses found in contempt by a grand jury may face fines or imprisonment as a form of punishment.[8]

The right to a grand jury was included in the U.S. Constitution because the framers wanted to limit the power of the government to maliciously prosecute its citizens. To indict a person of good standing in any community, the prosecutor has to convince a grand jury that enough evidence exists to indict the accused despite his or her reputation and standing. This is not an easy task because not only does it take much time, energy, and expense to put together a viable case, the grand jury has the power of refusing to indict (known as *no bill*). Thus, prosecutors do not initiate grand jury proceedings lightly, and citizens are protected, to some extent, from frivolous prosecution.

In practice, however grand jury proceedings have some disadvantages. One disadvantage is that the accused does not know of the proceedings and thus cannot be present during the indictment phase. Because the secret proceedings are not for the purpose of determining the guilt or innocence of the accused, only the prosecuting authorities appear before the grand jury to present their evidence. The grand jury has the authority to subpoena witnesses, who are entitled to legal counsel prior to the actual initiation of the grand jury proceedings. In essence, the witness is legally entitled to consult and confer with his or her defense lawyer before appearing in front of the grand jury to testify, but the witness is not allowed to be accompanied by defense lawyer(s) during the testimony.

Another disadvantage is that the rules of evidence do not apply to grand jury proceedings. For example, hearsay can be presented as evidence. Witnesses subpoenaed by a grand jury are allowed to invoke the Fifth Amendment privilege against self-incrimination provided that the witness has not been granted immunity from prosecution by the government. However if a witness has immunity and still refuses to testify, he or she can be cited for contempt and sent to jail or fined, or both. These are known as the subpoena, contempt, and immunity authorities of the grand jury.[9]

The Right to Protection from Double Jeopardy

The right against double jeopardy mandates that no person be subjected to criminal prosecution twice for the same offense. The right not to be placed in double jeopardy is one of the most complex and confusing provisions of the Fifth Amendment. Simply put, the double jeopardy clause means that once a disposition is reached in a criminal case—either an acquittal or a conviction—the defendant may not be tried again for the same offense. This applies to cases that are decided on guilty pleas as well as set aside on appeal for insufficiency of the evidence. Numerous rationales for the double jeopardy clause have been advanced, including protecting individuals from ongoing harassment by prosecutors, providing a sense of closure to both the defendant and the public in criminal matters, saving both the defendant and the state time and money, and preserving the integrity of jury verdicts.

The double jeopardy clause does not apply when there is a hung jury or a mistrial is declared. A hung jury means that the jury could not reach a decision on the guilt or innocence of the defendant or was not unanimous in its opinion in jurisdictions that require unanimity. A mistrial may be declared by a judge for any number of reasons, usually when some occurrence has rendered the process irreparably unfair, as for example, when a juror is discovered to have been bribed or threatened. Double jeopardy also does not apply when a court of appeal returns the case back to the trial court for reconsideration due to procedural errors.[10]

In addition, a defendant whose offense violates both federal and state criminal codes may be prosecuted under both federal and state laws without violating the double jeopardy clause of the Fifth Amendment. The U.S. Supreme Court has affirmed this view in *United States v. Lanza* (1922). It was only in 1969 that the double jeopardy clause was recognized to apply to state trials. The U.S. Supreme Court in *Benton v. Maryland* (1969) held that the Fifth Amendment's right against double jeopardy applied to state trials because it was "fundamental" to the American notion of fairness and right.[11]

The greatest source of confusion regarding the right against double jeopardy concerns the definition of "same offense." For example, may a defendant acquitted of burglary of a home be tried for criminal trespass on the same premises stemming from the same incident? Generally, the rule is that if the evidence necessary to convict on one charge is exactly the same as that necessary to convict on the other charge, disposition of one will bar prosecution for the other.

The Right to Privilege against Self-Incrimination

The right against self-incrimination protects any person from compulsion to testify against himself or herself. The right applies to anyone in police custody or who has been called before a court of law, a federal or state grand jury, or essentially any representative or agency of government at whatever level. In such situations any person may refuse to answer questions that would tend to implicate him or her in illegal activity.

Historically, it was in the year 1537 that the issue of self-incriminating testimony was addressed in English common law, to which the Fifth Amendment (including its section on the right against self-incrimination) is traceable. This development involved the century-old case of John Lambert, a heretic who objected to the fact that his trial was based on self-accusatory statements extracted from him through torture. Although Lambert's objection was overruled by the ecclesiastical court, which subsequently burned him on the stake, it took the English another century to establish the legal principle that no one should be subjected to trial based on self-accusation. The framers of the Bill of Rights adopted this principle in the Fifth Amendment because they wanted to ensure that the U.S. legal system remain of an adversarial rather than inquisitorial nature.

In a modern example, in the financial demise of the Houston-based energy company Enron in 2001, the chief executive officer and other members of the top management of the company appeared before a congressional committee formed to investigate whether fraud and insider trading played a part in the company's collapse. Enron's managers refused to testify, citing their Fifth Amendment right against self-incrimination. Once they invoked this right, the congressional committee could no longer press them for information on that topic. The case has since been taken up by the federal authorities for criminal prosecution.

The right against self-incrimination is not absolute. A person may not refuse to answer questions when subpoenaed if doing so would simply subject him or her to embarrassment or discomfort not involving criminal prosecution. Moreover, a person may not refuse to testify on the grounds that doing so may incriminate someone else. Also, a witness who has been granted immunity from prosecution must answer questions when subpoenaed to do so. In addition, a defendant who chooses to take the witness stand at his or her trial has waived the right against self-incrimination. On the witness stand, the defendant is subject to cross-examination by the prosecution, a process that may produce incriminating evidence.

It is noteworthy that the right to self-incrimination cannot be reclaimed after voluntary disclosure of incriminating evidence by the defense.[12] That is why experienced defense lawyers don't put their clients on the witness stand unless the direction of the proceedings forces them to do so. But over time, the range and the scope of "testimony" has expanded beyond its anecdotal base because incriminating evidence may be obtained by examining a wide range of records such as business and personal papers, blood and DNA samples, "breathalyzer" tests, or even mug shots taken in a police station during booking. Whether any of these evidentiary instruments, if compelled from a person in the course of an investigation, should fall under the purview of the Fifth Amendment's right against self-incrimination is as yet an unsettled issue. The thrust of the case law is that testimony must be of an oral nature for the right against self-incrimination to apply.

The right against self-incrimination also protects against the government's use of force, such as corporal punishment or torture, to extract confessions from criminal suspects—a practice that is widespread in many undemocratic societies. As a general rule, from the moment a person is "compelled" to reveal to a police officer or to any government official, whether during arrest, questioning, or arraignment, evidence that may be used to levy criminal punishment, the right against self-incrimination is invoked. This right also applies to police interrogation of suspects at the police precincts. Police are not allowed to use physical or mental coercion on the suspects in order to extract incriminating confessions from them. Logically speaking, compulsion starts once a person is in police custody being interrogated. What transpires during interrogation (i.e., methods, tone, body language, and actual words used during interrogation, including the length of it) constitutes both the content and the context of compulsion. For example, a suspect may not know that he or she is not supposed to be coerced into self-accusation, just as a police officer may be ignorant of the fact that he or she is not supposed to verbally or psychologically abuse a suspect in custody.

What constitutes compulsion? The intent of the Fifth Amendment is that no person shall be compelled in any criminal case to be a witness against himself. However, it has been observed that "the issues that arise with police interrogation and coerced confessions were long avoided by the Court until the Fifth Amendment was applied to states in *Malloy v. Hogan* (1964)."[13] Prior to this landmark case, the Court applied the Fourteenth Amendment's Due Process Clause in relation to the rights of the accused in police custody. However, until the application of the Fifth Amendment to states, the Supreme Court used the "totality of the circumstances" test to determine whether police had violated suspects' Fourteenth Amendment rights. This meant that if the "circumstances" warranted compulsion, the Fifth Amendment did not apply.

Prior to the application of the Fifth Amendment's right against self-incrimination in *Miranda v. Arizona* (1966), suspects in state police custody were routinely subjected to coercion that included manhandling and even torture as in *Brown v. United States.* The application of the Fifth Amendment (in conjunction with the Sixth Amendment) to states restricted a wide range of unsavory interrogation methods that the state police could and did utilize under the litmus test of the "totality of the situation."

Once the police have acted in good faith and determined that probable cause existed for executing an arrest, a suspect is subjected to booking. Booking consists of finger printing, taking photographs of the suspect (the "mug shot"), and checking to see if prior criminal records of the suspect exist. Subsequent to arrest, and within twenty-four to forty-eight hours in most jurisdictions, the booked suspects have to be brought before a magistrate or judge for what is known as the first appearance. If enough evidence exists pointing to the possible involvement of the suspect in crime, he or she may be detained and transferred to a local jail for formal arraignment. If such evidence does not exist, the suspect is released. Depending on the conditions surrounding the case, a suspect may also be released on his or her own recognizance or on bail posted on his or her behalf. In either case, the defendant has to appear before a court at a later date for formal arraignment.

May a court draw an inference of guilt from a defendant's assertion of the right to remain silent? Historically speaking, although silence in the face of accusation has been interpreted socially as a sign of probable culpability, the Fifth Amendment implies that the court may not infer guilt if one invokes his or her right to remain silent, a subject also addressed by the U.S. Supreme Court in *Miranda v. Arizona* (1966). The rationale behind the right against self-incrimination is that in the U.S. criminal justice system, the so-called burden of proof rests with the prosecution. This means that the state is legally obligated to prove the validity of the charges leveled against the defendant, rather than the defendant proving his or her own innocence. The defendant is not legally obligated to provide any incriminating evidence to the prosecution, an act that would logically work against one's best interests.

Miranda Rights

Miranda rights emerged after the 1966 U.S. Supreme Court decision of *Miranda v. Arizona*. The case involved the interrogation of Ernesto Miranda by the Arizona state police while in custody. During police interrogation, Miranda was not informed of his constitutional right against self-incrimination. The entire interrogation took place while he was effectively cut off from the outside world. The confessions obtained by the police were admitted in Miranda's trial and led to his conviction. The case reached the U.S. Supreme Court and the conviction was overturned on the grounds that incriminating confessions had been obtained from Miranda through violation of his Fifth Amendment right against self-incrimination.

The *Miranda* decision instituted the requirement that police inform detainees of their rights to

- remain silent during the entire custodial interrogation unless the suspect voluntarily decides otherwise;
- be informed, prior to any interrogation, that the suspect may remain silent if he or she wishes to do so and that anything said will be used against him or her in a court of law;
- consult with a lawyer and to have a lawyer present during the entire interrogation process;
- to have a lawyer appointed in case the suspect is financially indigent.[14]

In addition, the *Miranda* decision mandates that a suspect in custody is entitled to invoke his or her Fifth Amendment rights at any time during the course of interrogation. For example, if after initially responding to police officers' questions the suspect decides to remain silent by invoking his or her *Miranda* rights, the police interrogator(s) must immediately stop questioning. If it is established at trial that the defendant's *Miranda* rights have been violated by the police, the defense may make the motion for the dismissal of the case altogether. The defendant may also ask the court to exclude the incriminating evidence that has been obtained by such deliberate disregard of *Miranda* rights by the police.

Miranda has been extensively criticized in recent years by those who argue that it gives too many procedural rights to suspects, making it very difficult for the police and the prosecution to perform their duties effectively. Some aspects of this issue are discussed in Chapter 2.

The Right to Due Process

The right to due process mandates that criminal defendants shall not be deprived of their basic rights that are defined in the U.S. Constitution. To refresh our memory, the Constitution has characterized as basic the rights to life, liberty, and property. The right to due process mandates that no criminal defendant can be deprived of such basic rights unless all the procedural amenities recognized by the Bill of Rights have been observed during prosecution. For example, if a defendant is found guilty of a crime without the benefit of legal counsel (e.g., not allowed to be represented by a defense lawyer), he or she has effectively been deprived of one of the basic rights to due process.

Another example relates to the rules of evidence. If police officers obtain incriminating evidence through unethical and/or illegal means such as duress, threat of bodily harm, or torture, such evidence, no matter how important it may be to a case, is subject to exclusion from the proceedings. This is one of the most controversial issues to be discussed in Chapter 2.

The right to due process has been affirmed by such U.S. Supreme Court landmark decisions as *Powell v. Alabama* (1932), *Moore v. Dempsey* (1923), *Brown v. Mississippi* (1936), and *Rogers v. Richmond* (1961).[15] For example, in *Powell v. Alabama* the defendant's constitutional right to legal counsel was affirmed by the

Court. In *Moore v. Dempsey* the overall fairness of the trial atmosphere was taken up by the Court, which held that due process required trial proceedings to be free of mob-based intimidation tactics. In *Brown v. Mississippi,* the Court declared that due process as stated in the Fourteenth Amendment did not allow states to convict defendants based on coerced confessions, which was reaffirmed in *Rogers v Richmond.*

The Sixth Amendment Rights

The Sixth Amendment provides defendants with (1) the right to a speedy trial; (2) the right to an open and public trial; (3) the right to a jury trial; (4) the right to be informed of the charges against one and to confront one's accusers; and (5) the right to legal counsel. A synopsis of each of these defendant rights is presented below.

The Right to a Speedy Trial

The right to a speedy trial mandates that criminal prosecutions proceed expeditiously. In Anglo-American legal thinking, the basic belief is that justice delayed is in essence justice denied.

The speed of criminal trials in the United States is affected by the necessity of meticulously observing the procedures that secure defendant rights. Different steps that are taken by legal authorities as they prepare a criminal case can be itemized as:

- pretrial activities
- jury selection
- opening statements (first by the prosecution followed by defense)
- presentation of evidence (first by the prosecution followed by defense)
- closing arguments
- judge's charge to the jury
- jury deliberations
- verdict.[16]

These sequential activities are time-consuming and yet necessary, because the circumvention of even one of these steps may open the case to appeal on the grounds that the prosecution has not followed the legal procedure and therefore has deprived the defendant of his or her right to due process.

Although the U.S. Supreme Court has reaffirmed that a speedy trial is a basic constitutional right of criminal defendants, the Court has nonetheless cautioned that there are other criteria that have to be taken into consideration in preparing cases for trial. For example, in *Smith v. United States* (1959) the justices observed that: "While justice should be administered with dispatch, the essential ingredient is orderly expedition and not mere speed."[17]

It is important to expeditiously bring the case to trial because a defendant whose case is pending before a court goes through much mental anguish—especially those who cannot post bail and must remain in jail. In addition, delay often makes it harder to mount a defense; witnesses' memories may fade or they may become unavailable to testify, or physical evidence may deteriorate or become lost. It is therefore only just to expedite the process in order to lesson the period of anxiety and maximize the effectiveness of defense efforts.

In the past, if criminal defendants did not assert this basic right with regard to the pace of the prosecution they would suffer the consequence of their failure to do so. Criminal defendants could be detained in the local or county jail waiting for the commencement of the prosecution. By and large, this situation did not apply to those defendants who were represented by competent defense lawyers who would have their clients out on bail. However, indigent and uneducated defendants are often unaware of this basic right, or are not able to pay for the services of competent defense lawyers. A competent defense lawyer handling a case of long undue incarceration would consider making a motion to the trial court asking for the dismissal of the case without prejudice on the grounds that a basic constitutional right of the defendant has been denied.

To prevent such delays, the U.S. Congress passed the Speedy Trial Act in 1974, giving the federal district courts 100 days to initiate trials. Most states have enacted similar legislation. The Speedy Trial Act of 1974 has been altered through the years in order to accommodate inevitable delays that may arise as pretrial activities are under way to prepare the case. However, in most cases charges can be dismissed at both the state and federal levels if it can be shown by the defense that the speedy trial provisions have deliberately been violated by the prosecution. If delays are due to the illegal actions of the defendant (e.g., escape from detention centers, failure to appear at trial, skipping bond, fleeing the jurisdiction, etc.), the Speedy Trial Act's provisions for dismissal do not apply to such cases.

The U.S. Supreme Court has dealt with different legal issues in relation to the right to speedy trials in cases such as *Smith v. United States* (1959), *Klopfer v. North Carolina* (1967), *Dicky v. Florida* (1970), and *Barker v. Wingo* (1972), which I will discuss in chronological order.

First, in *Smith v. United States*, the Court ruled that the essential ingredient in the expeditious disposition of cases is not mere speed but orderliness, in order to protect defendants' rights. In *Klopfer v. North Carolina*, the right to speedy trial was applied against states. North Carolina had a law that allowed the prosecutor to indefinitely postpone criminal prosecution without dismissal of the indictment. Although the defendant would not actually be incarcerated, this law allowed the prosecutor to reinstate the charges against him or her any time the prosecutor decided to do so. The Court found this law unconstitutional in that it violated defendants' right to a speedy trial as articulated by the Sixth Amendment.

In *Dicky v. Florida*, the Court examined what constitutes "speedy" in relation to length of time in any particular jurisdiction. The Court ruled that because it had taken eight years for the State of Florida to initiate trial despite the fact that the defendant was in continuous residency in state jurisdiction, it had violated Dicky's right to speedy trial. During the long period that elapsed between the initial indictment and trial, a number of material witnesses had died or become unavailable, making it impossible to conduct a fair trial.

In *Barker v. Wingo*, the Court opined that, whereas in none of the previous cases brought before it were any attempts made "to set out the criteria by which the speedy trial right is to be judged. . . . This case compels us to make such an attempt."[18] The case involved the arrest of two suspects, Willie Barker and Silas Manning, by the Christian County police of the state of Kentucky. The police believed that the two had been involved in the murder of an elderly couple. The evidence against Manning was stronger and therefore the prosecution sought to get a statement from him implicating Barker. Through this strategy the prosecution believed that it could convict Barker. However, Manning did not comply, rightly assuming that such a statement against Barker would incriminate himself as well.[19]

While Willie Barker was kept in jail awaiting his turn, Manning was tried six times. This unusual situation came about because the first two trials ended with hung juries, the next two trials resulted in convictions that were reversed on appeal, the fifth trial resulted in Manning's conviction for one murder, followed by the sixth trial that convicted him for the other one. Meanwhile, the prosecution had made more than twelve motions for continuances before it could bring Barker to trial. Finally, the defense made a motion to the court asking that all charges against Barker be dismissed on the grounds that his constitutional right to a speedy trial had been violated. Nearly a year had passed since Barker's arrest. Upon a threat by the presiding judge that the motion would be granted unless trial proceedings commenced in the next session, Barker's trial was initiated, resulting in a conviction that carried a life sentence.

The case was granted certiorari (a document by means of which the U.S. Supreme Court orders a case tried at the lower court to be sent to the Court for reconsideration). After deliberations, the Court affirmed the trial court's decision, arguing that although the right to speedy trial was guaranteed by the Sixth Amendment, the ten-month delay in Barker's case did not constitute a deliberate and malicious violation of this right by the Commonwealth of Kentucky.

Going through the reasons for delay, the justices observed that: (1) there are "generic" differences between the right to speedy trial and other constitutional rights; (2) delay is inevitable when a defendant is unable to make bail as in the case of Barker and therefore is kept in jail; (3) a defendant's right to speedy trial is "vague" when compared with other procedural rights enunciated in the Constitution for the protection of the accused; and (4) that Barker had not asserted his right to speedy trial.[20]

One could argue that when Barker's attorney made a motion to the court to dismiss the case, it was in effect an assertion of Barker's right to speedy trial. However, the counterargument is that the U.S. Supreme Court has historically given much leverage to state courts in relation to their speed in bringing a case to trial. That is why the Court in Barker used a tripartite test to consider "speediness." The very use of the test is an indication that the Court was reluctant to apply a uniform standard to the issue of speediness despite the fact that in *Klopfer v. North Carolina*, the justices had ruled that the right to a speedy trial was an explicit right expressed in the Sixth Amendment that applied to states through the Fourteenth Amendment.

In sum, the Supreme Court has upheld the right to a speedy trial is an important constitutional right, but the application of this right is dependent on a number of factors that make a uniform definition of speed difficult. Some cases may take longer than others, not because the legal authorities want to deprive criminal defendants of this basic right, but because individual cases may necessitate procedures that make delay inevitable.

The Right to an Open and Public Trial

The Sixth Amendment mandates that the prosecution of adult defendants takes place in courts that are open and public. The legal implication of this right is simple: criminal prosecutions are not to take place in secrecy. All deliberations of the court and all verdicts reached by the juries belong to the public domain and therefore are to be accessible to the public. The only exceptions are those cases that involve juvenile offenders brought before juvenile courts.

The purpose of open and public trials is to ensure that the government and its agents do not violate the provisions of due process in the prosecution of criminal defendants, including such basic rights as the right to legal counsel, the right to confront one's accuser(s), the right to cross-examine witnesses, and so on. These constitute the backbone of the Anglo-American notion of a fair trial.

Legal scholar Louis Fisher observed that "the Anglo-American distrust of secret trials has been traced to the Spanish Inquisition, the English Star Chamber, and the French *lettre de cachet*."[21] In the Spanish Inquisition (which commenced in 1480 during the reign of King Ferdinand V and Queen Isabella and continued until 1838), the determination of the guilt or innocence of a defendant accused of sin, or of crime, took place in secrecy and without the presence of a defense lawyer who could contest the charges. Especially during the sixteenth century various forms of corporal punishment, including torture, were utilized to extract confessions from the accused. Such coerced confessions would subsequently be used as proof of the guilt of the accused.[22]

To bring under control these types of abusive practices, the Sixth Amendment mandated the use of open and public trials. Judges, however, have closed criminal proceedings to the public under extraordinary circumstances as in *Levine v. United States* (1960).[23]

As previously mentioned, cases involving juvenile offenders are closed to the public because the philosophy of the U.S. juvenile justice system is grounded on protection of juvenile offenders from the stigma of being identified in a public trial. Juveniles, so the thinking goes, should be given some leeway to make mistakes and correct them without having the opprobrium of a criminal record follow them into adulthood and diminish their chances of becoming productive citizens. Nonetheless, juvenile cases that are transferred to adult courts are open to the public. The justification is that a juvenile who commits serious adult crime is no longer a juvenile per se, but an adult criminal who does not deserve the legal niceties that the juvenile system extends to juvenile offenders.

Other Sixth Amendment issues include the role of the press in public trials, pretrial publicity and its threat to a fair trial, the use of cameras in the courtroom, and the circumstances under which trials may be closed. Under certain circumstances, the trial proceedings may be closed to the public. The court may also impose prior restraints on information in cases that otherwise would create much public anxiety. These are generally cases involving issues related to national security (for example, *New York Times v. United States* [1971]); law enforcement investigations (for example, *Florida Star v. B. J. F.* [1989]); privacy (for example, *Sinatra v. Kelley* [1983]); and obscenity (for example, *Ashcroft v. Free Speech Coalition* [2002]).

A free press is the main vehicle through which the public is informed of trial proceedings, results of jury deliberations, and verdicts. In addition, the press, through its editorials and guest opinion sections, educates the public about the many controversial legal and procedural points raised during the course of a trial. An active, informed, and free press can effectively check the abusive practices that could creep into trials that take place in secrecy.

A fair trial is supposed to take place unencumbered by preconceived notions of guilt and in front of an impartial judge and jury. However, some cases raise the public ire due to the nature of the criminal act. By reporting the details of the crime act, the press may inadvertently cause pretrial prejudice against the accused and thus jeopardize his or her right to a fair trial. This creates a conflict between the guarantees of the Sixth Amendment and those of the First Amendment (freedom of expression). Both of these freedoms may shape a court's decision to impose restrictions on press access. A defendant can request a "closed trial" on the grounds that the pretrial publicity surrounding the case has made it impossible for the impanelment of an impartial jury.

The issue of pretrial publicity was addressed in *Sheppard v. Maxwell* (1966) when the U.S. Supreme Court overturned a twelve-year-old conviction of Dr. Sam Sheppard for murdering his wife. The Court ruled that the conviction of Sheppard had taken place in a highly publicized trial in which the trial judge had failed to maintain proper courtroom decorum conducive to the Sixth Amendment guarantee of a fair trial. During the course of the trial, the press had been given total access to the proceedings in such a manner that the attending journalists could even overhear the conversions that took place between the defendant and his attorneys. In short, the judge had failed to strike a balance between the Sixth Amendment guarantee of fairness and the First Amendment guarantees of freedom of the press. Different aspects of the fair trial versus free press conflict, including the issue of access, have been addressed in *Nebraska Press Association v. Stuart* (1976), *Gannett Co. v. DePasquale* (1979), *Richmond Newspapers v. Virginia* (1980), *Globe Newspaper Co. v. Superior Court for the County of Norfolk* (1982), *Press-Enterprise Co. v. Superior Court of California* (1986), and *Mu'min v. Virginia* (1991).[24]

In *Nebraska Press Association v. Stuart*, the U.S. Supreme Court addressed the constitutionality of a trial judge's order prohibiting the media from publishing or broadcasting certain pretrial information it had obtained about Edwin Charles Simon, the suspect in the murder of six members of the Henry Kellie family in Sutherland, Nebraska. The trial judge's prior-restraint order was intended to ensure Simon's right to a fair trial. The Nebraska Press Association appealed to the state supreme court challenging the constitutionality of the trial court's restraining order on the grounds that it violated the right to freedom of the press as stipulated in the First Amendment. The state supreme court partially agreed with the appellant and modified the trial court's original order, which covered five areas, reducing it to three areas. The

Nebraska Press Association then appealed to the U.S. Supreme Court, which granted certiorari and subsequently struck down the entire prior restraint order. The Court ruled that the trial court's prior-restraint order was not justified because the trial judge could use alternative means to ensure a fair trial. The Court stated that the judge had restrained free speech in a way that "freezes it at least for the time."[25]

In *Gannett v. DePasquale,* the issue raised before the U.S. Supreme Court was whether members of the press or public had a constitutional right to access to pretrial proceedings that had been closed by a trial judge's exclusionary order. Although the prosecutor did not raise any objections to the closure of the proceedings, a member of the press objected to the exclusionary rule and asked the judge to set it aside. Upon his refusal, the case went to the U.S. Supreme Court. The Court ruled that the trial judge's order to close the pretrial proceedings had not violated the First Amendment rights of the press or of the public.[26]

In *Richmond Newspapers v. Virginia,* the U.S. Supreme Court addressed another aspect of access to trial proceedings. The defendant in this case asked for his trial to be closed to the public, having been previously tried for a murder that ended up in conviction but was reversed on appeal, and two other trials that ended in mistrials. No objection was raised by the prosecution and thus the judge ordered the closure of the proceedings. A member of the press objected to the closure and asked the judge to rescind the closure order. The judge refused and the case went to the U.S. Supreme Court. The Court ruled that unlike in *Gannett v. DePasquale,* in this case the judge's order arbitrarily closed the trial, violating the long tradition of open public trials in the United States. Thus the closure did in fact violate the First Amendment guarantees of speech and freedom of the press, concluded the Court.[27] The Court's decision was reaffirmed in *Globe Newspaper Co. v. Superior Court for the County of Norfolk.*[28]

In *Press-Enterprise Company v. Superior Court of California,* the U.S. Supreme Court addressed the issue of constitutionality of the closure of a preliminary hearing for murder. A nurse, Robert Diaz, allegedly had committed twelve counts of murder according to a complaint the State of California filed against him on December 23, 1981, seeking the death penalty. The gravity of the alleged crimes led to national notoriety. On commencement of the preliminary hearing, Diaz moved to exclude the public from the proceedings, citing a section of the California Penal Code that allows for the closure of the proceedings if the publicity surrounding a case reaches a point that endangers the defendant's right to a fair trial. The judge agreed and closed the proceedings, which lasted forty-one days, during which scientific evidence, witnesses, and Diaz's testimony were recorded. At the end of the preliminary hearings, the *Press-Enterprise* asked for the release of the records of the proceedings. The magistrate refused and instead sealed the records. The case reached the U.S. Supreme Court, which ruled that the closure was not necessary on the grounds that "a qualified First Amendment right to access attaches to preliminary hearings."[29] The Court in essence agreed that reason for the closure did not measure up to the test of a "reasonable likelihood of substantial prejudice" as required by the California Penal Code.

The question as to whether the presence of television cameras in court impacts, one way or another, the dynamics of the trial proceedings has been discussed at some length in academia and among criminal justice practitioners. The main concern is that broadcasting of the trial proceedings may alter the natural course of the proceedings as the prosecutors, judges, and defense lawyers find themselves being heard or watched by a much larger national audience especially during controversial trials. Historically speaking, both English and U.S. courts have been open to the public, and therefore so-called professional courtroom actors (judges, prosecutors, defense lawyers, and bailiffs) have carried out their duties under the gaze of an audience.

The U.S. public has followed controversial criminal cases from colonial times to present. Examples of such controversial cases have been given above. However, it was in *Estes v. Texas* (1965) that the intertwined issues of "telecasting, radio broadcasting, and news photography" of the trial proceedings was addressed by the U.S. Supreme Court. Taking into consideration the massive pretrial publicity surrounding the case (which involved a Texas grand jury indictment against the petitioner for swindling), the Court reversed the trial court's verdict on the grounds that the petitioner's constitutional right to a fair trial, guaranteed by the Due Process Clause of the Fourteenth Amendment, had been violated.

The importance of *Estes v. Texas* stems from the fact that the Court gave a kind of road map as to when and under what circumstance access to a trial can be denied or circumscribed. The precedent cautions against situations when: (1) a case is highly publicized to the effect that it gains national notoriety; (2) a high degree of publicity creates an atmosphere of condemnation rather than of fairness toward the accused; (3) the freedom of the press interferes with the "absolute fairness in the judicial process" and thus deprives the defendant's right to a fair trial; and (4) the broadcasting distracts the judge, jurors, and prosecutors from giving their utmost attention to the case, or unfairly prejudices them against the defendant. *Estes v. Texas* has been cited extensively in other landmark cases such as *Waller v. Georgia* (1984), *Holbrook v. Flynn* (1986), *Lockhart v. McRee* (1986), *Darden v. Wainwright* (1986), *Brecheen v. Oklahoma* (1988), *Coy v. Iowa* (1988), *Crawford v. Georgia* (1989), *Swindler v. Lockhart* (1990), *Mu'min v. Virginia* (1991), and *Kelly v. Whitely* (1995).

The Right to a Jury Trial

A jury is a fact-finding body usually composed of twelve persons who are citizens of the community in which the alleged crime took place. The jurors are randomly selected from a larger pool of prospective jurors to hear a case and decide the guilt or innocence of the defendant(s).

The right to a jury trial has its historical origins in the English Magna Carta of 1215. The Magna Carta forbade sentences of imprisonment, fines, exile, or death unless imposed by a jury composed of the defendant's peers. This provision of the Magna Carta gradually led to the enhancement of the jury as a fact-finding body in the English common law legal tradition.[30]

In colonial America, the jury played a significant role in the prosecution of alleged criminals before a court of law. In fact, in colonial America the jury seems initially to have had more power than the presiding judge in a criminal court. Because of this initial power differential between the jury and the judge, the whole institution of the jury had to be reformed. Legal scholar Melvin Urofsky observes that "in theory, at the time of the Revolution juries judged both the law and fact in criminal cases, and the memory of local juries thwarting arbitrary royal power remained strong for a number of years."[31] It was the arbitrariness of the jury decisions that led to a reform that "involved the slow transfer of power from juries to judges."[32]

The right to a jury trial is specified in Article III, Section 2 of the U.S. Constitution as well as in the Sixth Amendment of the

Bill of Rights. (The Seventh Amendment extends the right to a jury trial to civil cases.) However, it was not until 1968 that this right, which had been observed in federal prosecutions, was extended to state prosecutions. In other words, it took more than 150 years for this important constitutional right to be applied to state-initiated criminal prosecutions. Of course, many states had already included the right in their own constitutions to varying degrees before that time. Important cases that have reached the U.S. Supreme Court concerning the issue of the right to jury trials in state prosecutions are *Duncan v. Louisiana* (1968), *Baldwin v. New York* (1970), and *Blanton v. City of North Las Vegas* (1989).[33] It is noteworthy that in the U.S. legal system the right to a jury trial does not apply to all criminal proceedings; for example, crimes that are considered petty in nature. Louis Fisher, citing the cases of *Cheff v. Schnakenberg* (1966), and *District of Columbia v. Clawans* (1937), states that "the right to a jury trial depends on the potential penalty, not the category of offense."[34] The general rule is that any offense that carries a sentence of six months imprisonment or more entitles the defendant to a jury trial.

Duncan v. Louisiana (1968) involved the prosecution of Gary Duncan, a nineteen-year-old African American youth who got into a fight with a white juvenile in Plaquemines Parish of Louisiana in 1966. Duncan was arrested, tried, and acquitted of the charge of cruelty to minors. However, he was rearrested and accused of battery for the same incident, a crime that carried a sentence of two years in prison. The defense asked for a trial by jury, citing the Sixth Amendment and arguing that the severity of the penalty made it imperative for Duncan to be tried in front of a jury composed of his peers. The presiding judge rejected the defense's motion. Duncan was convicted of the crime of battery, which was upheld by the Louisiana Supreme Court. Upon appeal to the U.S. Supreme Court, the case turned into a test examining the question of whether the Sixth Amendment's right to trial by an impartial jury applied to state prosecutions through the Due Process Clause of the Fourteenth Amendment.[35] The Court agreed with Duncan, and from then on the right to be tried by one's peers became a basic right of criminal defendants in state courts.

The question of what makes a jury of one's "peers" has also been the subject of litigation. Ideally, members of a jury should have some social and economic similarities with the criminal defendant in order better to judge factors involved in the criminal case under consideration. The reality, however, has been quite different. Before the rise of the civil rights movement in the 1960s, the jury was a very powerful instrument of repression against African Americans in the South. Harsh punishments were meted out to African American defendants charged—often falsely—with victimizing whites. To make matters worse, African Americans were legally excluded from serving on juries.[36] Various pretexts were used, such as exclusive reliance on voter registration lists before blacks had suffrage and voir dire (challenges for cause and peremptory challenges).

Choosing Jurors from Voter Registration Lists

Voter registration lists contain the names, addresses, gender, and other identifying characteristics of voters. These lists have been used as a tool for compiling the larger jury pools from which trial jurors are chosen to hear criminal cases. Naturally, those who do not vote are not included in the voter registration lists, and therefore are automatically excluded from the larger jury pool.

To exclude blacks from voting, Southern states came up with all kinds of preventive schemes such as poll taxes, literacy tests, and racial gerrymandering, which is defined as "the practice of drawing election district boundary lines in order to dilute or eliminate any concentration of black voting strength in a single district."[37]

These practices ran against both the letter and spirit of the Fifteenth Amendment to the Constitution ratified in 1870. The Fifteenth Amendment has two sections of which Section 1 is related to the issue of voting rights and reads: "The right of citizens of the United States to vote shall not be denied or abridged by the United States or by any State on account of race, color, or previous condition of servitude."[38] It was only after the civil rights movement in the 1960s that African Americans started moving in the direction of gaining their voting rights and privileges. This premise, of course, does not mean that African American communities have gained their full voting rights. Although important legislative gains were made through the passage of the Civil Rights Act of 1964 and Voting Rights Act of 1965, numerous lawsuits have been filed by African Americans regarding disenfranchisement, including one in the year 2000 after many African Americans were turned away from the polls in Florida.

Voir Dire

Voir dire is a French term that means "to speak the truth." The term refers to the oath a prospective juror takes to answer questions truthfully about his or her background, knowledge, or prejudices to determine his or her suitability to sit on a jury. The term also refers to the hearing in which this oath is taken and the questions that are put to the prospective jurors to aid in choosing an impartial panel. The voir dire allows the defense counsel, the prosecuting attorney, and sometimes the judge to question prospective jurors and to eliminate those who display obvious bias toward the defendant or the prosecution. However, the process can be, and has been, abused to exclude African American jurors.

Voir dire is used first to eliminate from jury participation those who do not meet statutory requirements, which include age, citizenship, lack of felony convictions, and basic mental competence. In addition, a prospective juror can be eliminated if it can be established that he or she has racial, ethnic, gender, religious, or any other prejudices for or against the defendant, the victim of the alleged crime, or the state, including antipathy toward the police or other officials involved. In addition, a juror's acquaintance with any of the trial participants, including the judge may be grounds for his or her exclusion. Also, jurors' attitudes towards crime and its prosecution in general or in regard to specific types of crimes (e.g., drug use) are examined. In capital cases, jurors' attitudes toward the death penalty are often considered relevant.

The defense attorney and the prosecutor each have a set number of "challenges" that they may use to strike prospective jurors from the panel. Challenge for cause requires the attorney to state why he or she wishes to eliminate a particular person from serving on the jury. The stated reason should relate to a particular finding of impermissible bias on the juror's part. Unlike challenges for cause, which require explanations as to why a certain juror should be excluded, so-called peremptory challenges allow the two sides to eliminate a certain number of jurors from impanelment without stating any reason at all. Both the prosecution and the defense counsel rely on their experience and intuition as they use their peremptory challenges to shape the jury to their advantage. Unfortunately, peremptory challenges have often been used to exclude people from jury service based solely on their race or gender. In *Batson v. Ken-*

tucky (1986) the U.S. Supreme Court ruled this practice unconstitutional. This case was followed eight years later by the ruling in *JEB v. Alabama ex rel. TB* (1994) that outlawed gender bias
in jury selection.

Even though racial and gender bias are not supposed to figure in selection of U.S. juries, the anonymous nature of the
peremptory challenge makes it difficult to be sure that this is not
the case in practice. If the above-mentioned practices are abused
regularly in the selection and impaneling of the jury, minority
defendants would be deprived of one of the most important features of due process of the Anglo-American system of criminal
prosecution: to be tried by a fair and impartial jury of their peers.
Racial discrimination in jury selection has been allowed to occur
in U.S. courts for more than one hundred years.

Studies of criminal cases in the South have shown that prior
to the civil rights movement, all-white juries overwhelmingly
convicted those black defendants accused of crimes against
whites (whether male or female). Serious crimes against whites,
such as murder or rape, were routinely punished by death.[39] On
the other end of the spectrum, when the victims were black and
the alleged perpetrators whites, the verdict would usually be not
guilty, or if guilty, result in a suspended sentence.

One of the most notorious cases was the Scottsboro Trial of
1931 to 1937. The case involved nine African American youths
accused of the rape of two white teenage girls. The boys were
arrested in Scottsboro, Alabama, after one of the girls, Ruby
Bates, told the police that she and her friend had been gang raped
by the defendants as all were riding a freight train across the
state—a common mode of travel for unemployed people in the
Depression years. The case was brought to trial on 6 April 1931.
Within a span of several days, and despite the fact that no corroborating evidence of rape surfaced, eight of the nine defendants were convicted of the charges by an all-white jury and sentenced to death in the electric chair. The case against one of the
black defendants, Roy Wright, who was only twelve years of age,
ended in a mistrial.[40]

The case owes its notoriety to Alabama's almost wanton disregard for due process in the prosecution of the Scottsboro defendants. For example, the court-appointed attorney for the defendants, Stephen R. Roddy, from Tennessee, admitted he was not
familiar with Alabama law. A local attorney who offered to help
the defense found Roddy "already inebriated at 9:00 a.m."[41] on

the day the trial commenced. The defendants were in effect deprived of the right to legal counsel. Put together, there were many factors that could provide reasonable doubt in the mind of any fair-minded jury, but the all-white jury in Scottsboro, far from the homes of any of the defendants, hardly qualified as a jury of their "peers." The Alabama Supreme Court upheld the convictions of the eight defendants, despite the obvious denial of due process, which the U.S. Supreme Court decried as it ordered a new trial.

The historical significance of the Scottsboro trial has been summarized by one scholar who observes that "No one knows how many cases like Scottsboro occurred in Southern states before this one—with its large number of defendants, their youth, their brief and almost cursory trials and severe sentences—demanded national attention."[42] None of the Scottsboro defendants were executed. They went through several trials and retrials. Every time they were found guilty of the same charges. This was despite the fact that many changes had taken place in the trial scene and personalities involved in the process since the first trial.

The main issue today is the manner in which jurors are selected to represent the social, economic, and ethnic-racial composition of the communities in which trials take place. Through the so-called scientific jury selection, the two sides try to create a jury that is most sympathetic to their side of the case. In scientific jury selection, attempts are made to analyze different moral standards, personalities, consumption patterns, and likes and dislikes of the prospective jurors to come up with a psychological profile of each juror. When these profiles are assembled, a team of experts analyze them and advise the defense or the prosecution lawyer which jurors should be included or eliminated from the panel so that the most sympathetic jury can be impaneled. It is a long, arduous, and expensive process that only financially well-off defendants are capable of using to their advantage. Scientific jury selection has led to criticism that juries are losing their presumed objectivity, a point explored in some detail in Chapter 2.

In sum, it can be argued that the importance of jury selection stems from the following factors:

- The jury involves the community in the application of the judicial process.

- The jury, as a fact-finding institution whose purpose is to determine the guilt or innocence of the defendant, represents the Anglo-American ideal of jurisprudential fairness in prosecution.
- The jury verdict, ideally speaking, is representative of the communal norms and values.
- The jury, through its power of nullification, has become an effective legal device against the government's abuse of the prosecutorial powers.[43]

The Right To Be Informed of Charges and To Confront Accusers

The right to confront one's accuser is fundamental to the Anglo-American notion of a fair trial. Although the idea dates back as far as ancient Roman and Hebrew law, its first expression in the Anglo-American world was probably in the English Magna Carta of 1215 in Clause Thirty-eight, which states that, "in the future no bailiff shall upon his own unsupported accusation put any man to trial without producing credible witnesses to the truth of the accusation."[44] Later attempts by the crown to try subjects by use of written affidavits whose authors were not required to appear in court for questioning caused such public outrage that the right personally to confront one's accusers was well established in English common law by the sixteenth century.

In the United States this right is enshrined in the Sixth Amendment provision that reads, "In all criminal prosecutions, the accused shall enjoy the right . . . to be confronted with the witnesses against him [and] to have compulsory process for obtaining witnesses in his favor." Today all fifty state constitutions contain similar provisions. However, it was not until 1965 that the Supreme Court extended the so-called confrontation clause to the states via the Due Process Clause of the Fourteenth Amendment in the case of *Pointer v. Texas*.

In spite of the absolute language of the amendment that "in all criminal prosecutions" the defendant has a right to confront witnesses, in reality there are many exceptions to this rule. The federal rules of evidence as well as evidence codes in the fifty states all allow for hearsay testimony under limited circumstances. The general rule for allowing evidence from a source who does not appear in the courtroom for questioning is that the source is unavailable (i.e., dead, outside the reach of a subpoena, incompetent, etc.) and the circumstances of the creation of the evidence indicate that it is likely to be reliable. For example, routine business records required by law to be kept may be entered into evidence without calling the person who made them because a business would be unlikely to falsify them. Other traditional hearsay exceptions include dying declarations (people about to die generally have no reason to lie); so-called excited utterances (made contemporaneously with a traumatic event such that there was no time to fabricate a response); statements against penal interest (statements incriminating the speaker are more likely to be true); or scientific data compiled for purposes other than the trial. In recent times controversy has raged over the propriety of allowing videotaped testimony from child victims of crime to protect them from the trauma of having to see the person who allegedly abused them. Sometimes judges allow testimony via closed-circuit television so that the accused and the court can see the witness, but he or she cannot see the court. In these cases, defense counsel usually questions the witness remotely or goes to the location of the witness to question him or her there.

The Right to Legal Counsel

The rationale for the right to legal counsel has perhaps stemmed from the fact that law is an extremely complex subject. Legal codes have many procedural nuances that are difficult to understand unless one is trained in the legal profession. In criminal prosecutions, defense lawyers play a central role in building viable defense strategies for defendants who retain their services. Defense lawyers study the charges leveled against their client, prepare the case by referring to their state criminal code, or in case of federal prosecution, to the Federal Code and Procedure. In addition, experienced defense lawyers also study the case law in the event that they lose the case in trial court and have to appeal the case to the appellate court for procedural reconsideration. As a general rule, defense lawyers maintain a cordial and professional relationship with the judges, the bailiff and the prosecuting attorneys no matter what the outcome of a case.

Criminal defendants may waive their right to legal counsel and represent themselves in the court, a right recognized by the

Supreme Court in *Faretta v. California* (1975). This is a rather risky endeavor. Indeed, the old joke that one who represents himself has a fool for a client is often apt. The main responsibilities of criminal defense lawyers include the following:

- Advising defendants of their legal rights in the criminal prosecution
- Vigorously defending their clients charged with the commission of a crime in a court of law
- Examining the evidence against their clients and questioning its credibility
- Ensuring that the police have followed due process in the arrest, search and seizure, and interrogation activities in relation to the case
- Making proper and timely motions and objections during the criminal trial
- Presenting direct and/or circumstantial evidences, alibis, and witnesses to testify on behalf of their clients
- Advising defendants on the advantages and disadvantages of a plea bargain
- Bargaining with the prosecution to reduce the charges in exchange for a guilty plea if this is agreed to by and in the best interest of the client
- Planning for alternative defense strategies if the initial strategy seems not to be proceeding to the advantage of their clients
- Preparing an appeal in case the defendant were to be found guilty.

The above list gives us an idea about the importance of access to trained legal council in criminal prosecutions. The question arises, what happens if a criminal defendant is unable to pay for the services of a trained lawyer? Due process requires that the state provide a lawyer to any criminal defendant who is unable to afford one. A growing problem is how to fund this service. To resolve this problem, most states have provided financial assistance for such purposes. This state-sponsored legal defense mechanism is known as indigent defense funds. States have also required law firms to provide free of charge, or so-called *pro bono,* legal services for indigent defendants.

The states have also provided operating funds for the organization and administration of public defenders' offices. State funds have also been appropriated for what is known in many states as court appointed attorney services for indigent clients. Even at this level, a certain gender, race, and ethnicity-based disparity in the quality of defense for indigent clientele has been observed by legal scholars. For example, some feminist scholars have observed that in the U.S. legal tradition a certain degree of legal paternalism towards female criminal defendants persists. The term *legal paternalism* means a fatherly attitude and perception among judges and prosecutors towards female defendants whose cases are brought before the bench. In the same manner that a father shows empathy to his daughter's delinquent acts, judges and prosecutors show the same empathy to female criminality. Simply put, female criminality is not taken seriously, nor the outcome of a female defendant's case.[45]

Because of legal paternalism, the task of the legal defense of indigent female defendants is usually given to court-appointed attorneys. These are usually young, inexperienced, and idealistic attorneys who have to handle a relatively large number of indigents' cases appointed to them. In contrast, the task of the legal defense of male indigent defendants is usually handled by the public defenders' office. The public defenders' office is much more competent than court-appointed attorneys. It has considerable resources at its disposal and is quite experienced in the pre-trial plea bargaining process. In other words, even at the level of indigence, prejudice enters the process of the dissemination of justice.[46]

The Eighth Amendment Rights

The Eighth Amendment is very concise, but it constitutes a very important basic right. It states that "Excessive bail shall not be required, nor excessive fines imposed, nor cruel and unusual punishments inflicted." Despite its shortness, the Eighth Amendment has played a significant role in giving a rather humanitarian face to the Anglo-American notion of justice.

What is bail? Bail is a legal document ordered by a judge to be purchased by the accused promising the state and/or the federal authorities that the defendant will appear before the specified court of law at the specified time to stand trial.

There are two general categories of bail. One category, known as the cash bond, consists of a certain amount of cash that must be deposited by the defendant as ordered by the judge. The bail money is returned to the accused once he or she makes the required appearance before the court. The other category, known as property bond, consists of real estate collateral posted by the defendant as the surety. Again, upon appearance before the court, the collateral is returned. If the defendant does not appear (known as *jumping bail*), the judge may order the state to keep the bail, be it cash or real estate.

Bail procedures vary depending on the nature and seriousness of the crime under consideration as well as the legal jurisdiction and community involved. For example, a judge may release the accused without bail if it can be established that he or she is not a flight risk. This is known as *release on recognizance*, which usually occurs when the accused does not have a prior criminal record, has a discernable interest and standing in the community (e.g., family, property, and business), and thus is not a flight risk. In other cases, the judge orders bail as a form of surety. However, the judge may deny the option of bail if it is a capital case or if the accused is a repeat offender likely to flee the jurisdiction.

Bail decisions are made during an initial appearance in court, which usually takes place twenty-four hours after arrest. In bail decisions, judges take into consideration the facts of the case, such as the seriousness of the crime. The more serious the crime, the higher the bail amount and the more likely the defendant is to forfeit bail. The judge also takes into consideration the prior criminal record of the accused. The more full the prior record, the higher is the likelihood the judge will deny bail. In addition, the judge asks the suspect questions in order to gauge his or her level of honesty. However, most bail decisions are made on incomplete information entailing risk assessment of whether a defendant will jump bail or commit additional crimes while on bail.

Bail has a discernable impact on jail overcrowding and case disposition. First, it allows defendants to better prepare themselves for pretrial activities, the most important of which is retaining the services of a competent criminal defense lawyer. In addition, the accused can seek financial help (from friends and family members) in order to afford the additional costs of expert witnesses or appeal. Finally, those on bail are spared the psychological trauma of waiting for trial in jail. The literature on bail argues that, by and large, pretrial release secured through bail positively impacts the outcome of cases for the reasons cited above.

Excessive bail puts much financial stress on the defendant. Excessive bail may deprive the accused of potential benefits if the accused is unable to come up with the amount. Due process advocates have raised objections against the bail system on the grounds that forcing the accused to remain in jail until the commencement of trial goes against the presumption of innocence, which is the cornerstone of justice in the Anglo-American criminal justice system. Crime control advocates, though, argue that bail plays an important function in protecting society against potential repeat criminals.

In addition to the issue of reasonableness of bail, the Eighth Amendment stipulates fines as a form of punishment. As previously mentioned, the Magna Carta, in its clauses numbered Twenty, Twenty-one, and Twenty-two, articulated the meaning of "reasonable fines," which applied to offenses committed by members of different social classes. For example, in medieval England a baron had high social standing. If a baron committed an offense, he would be tried in a court of law. If he were found guilty, his punishment consisted of a certain amount in fines that he had to pay to the plaintiff. The amount of the fine was set according to a scale that rated offenses in terms of their severity, yet took into account the social standing of the perpetrator. The amount of the fine could not be so high as to ruin the noble convict's economic or social standing. On the other hand, a person of lower social standing who committed the same offense could face harsher penalties, especially if he or she could not hire the service of a trained lawyer or a professional orator to plead the case. Thus, although it seems as if the Magna Carta provided for legal and social equity, since not all members of different social classes could pay fines, in practice the system of punishment inscribed class prejudice.

Following the Magna Carta's rationale of fines as punishment, in the United States a defendant's financial situation is taken into consideration by the courts. A fine is a form of restitution usually imposed for crimes of a petty nature such as shoplifting or traffic violations. In addition, fines can also be imposed for offenses characterized as victimless crimes, such as illegal gambling, cock fighting, or prostitution. However, because a fine is a form of punishment inherently related to one's economic viability, its utilization raises the issue of justice. For example, if most crimes were to carry fines as punishment, the rich would fare better than the poor who engage in those crimes. In addition, if the amount of a fine was excessive, it would make it much more difficult or even impossible for indigent defendants to post bail. Thus, the intention of the Eighth Amendment is that neither excessive amount of bail nor fines shall apply. In other words, the two are complementary to one another.

Some objection has been raised about the utilization of fines for too many crimes on the grounds that it dilutes the just deserts principle of American penology. The just deserts principle maintains that applying proper punishment to those who violate the law or commit a crime serves as a deterrent to crime. By overreliance on fines, they argue, the U.S. justice system allows the rich to get away with a wide range of infractions while disproportionately penalizing the indigent who can't pay the amount of the fines and thus end up in jail. This state of affairs has been maintained and even perpetuated through so-called indeterminate sentencing structure.

Indeterminate sentencing is the system by which judges, in determining sentences and punishments such as fines or imprisonment, are allowed discretion to find the most appropriate and just sentence for a given crime. The mitigating or aggravating factors judges are allowed to consider include the nature and severity of the crime perpetrated; the harm inflicted on the victim; the weapon(s) used; the age, prior record, demeanor, educational and economic standing of the accused; and the defendant's degree of remorse and cooperation with the authorities during the investigation phase.

In the 1970s, conservative legislators and legal practitioners started raising objections against indeterminate sentencing, arguing that it gave judges too much latitude in using inappropriate measures such as fines, community service, probation, and suspended sentences for a range of repeat offenders who commit crimes knowing full well that the system will penalize them lightly. For example, the actual time spent in prison is dependent upon inmates' good behavior, which can facilitate early release. Prisoners can be furloughed due to overcrowding or placed in halfway houses, provided that their crime was not of a serious nature. Critics of indeterminate sentencing propose that jurisdictions ought to move toward mandatory sentencing in which convicts have to stay in prison for the total length of a term as specified in the incarceration sentence.

Unlike indeterminate sentencing, which leaves much to the discretion of judges, mandatory sentencing is of a more structured nature. Its main objective is to create a uniform sentencing schedule whereby for each category of crime a set punishment (whether fines or incarceration) is specified. Once sentenced to a punishment, the convict must endure the full length of incarceration, which is not subjected to any changes. Under determinate sentencing, the convict has to bear the full brunt of the sentence in terms of its duration and severity.

Since the 1970s, many states have adopted determinate sentencing models. Instead of the maximum/minimum criteria used in indeterminate sentencing, judges use specific numbers of years as the duration of penalties. Parole release based on the discretion of parole boards has been abolished in those states. In some states the incarceration rate has increased, in some others it has either stayed the same or has decreased. In some states the length of sentences increased, and in others it either stayed the same or decreased.

In sum, if we make a comparison between indeterminate and determinate sentencing, the following applies:

• Indeterminate sentences are more likely to contribute to inequality in sentencing by subjecting the process to factors such as economic, gender, race, and ethnic differences.
• Indeterminate sentencing decisions are more likely to be influenced by judicial personality and social characteristics of the defendants.
• Defense attorneys are capable of manipulating the system to appear before judges who are known for their lenient sentencing decisions and patterns for certain crimes.
• Indeterminate sentencing can produce disparity and even dishonesty in sentencing.
• Time served under indeterminate sentencing is subjected to a good behavior qualifier that generally reduces the time indicated on the initial sentencing records.
• The problems with indeterminate sentencing led many states to revise their sentencing codes and structures.
• States that adopted mandatory sentences were concerned that three fundamental sentencing principles—equity, proportionality, and social debt—were being ignored by indeterminate sentencing.

Although the Eighth Amendment prohibits the imposition of cruel and unusual punishments on a criminal culprit, punishments such as public hanging, lynching, quartering, and flogging were applied in colonial America. This prohibition has yet to apply to the death penalty, which some consider the most cruel and unusual form of punishment. Worse yet, studies have shown that the death penalty, by and large, applies to poor and racial minorities disproportionately.[47]

In U.S. legal literature, it has become customary to consider the following statement of Chief Justice Earl Warren as the benchmark for determining what is cruel and unusual punishment:

> The basic concept underlying the Eighth Amendment is nothing less than dignity of man. While the State has the power to punish, the Amendment stands to assure that this power is to be exercised within the limits of civilized standards. Fines, imprisonment and even execution may be imposed depending upon the enormity of the crime, but any technique outside the bounds of traditional penalties is constitutionally suspect. . . . The Court [has] . . . recognized that the words of the Amendment are not precise, and that their scope is not static. The Amendment must draw its meaning from the evolving standards of decency that mark the progress of a maturing society.[48]

Conclusion

In the Anglo-American legal tradition, everyone is equal before the law and everyone is entitled to justice. In the past, however, such was not the case. In medieval England, the birthplace of the Magna Carta, a person who sought justice would go to the king's place of residence and plead for justice. This practice made the king's court the official place for hearing cases, which came to be known as common pleas. The Magna Carta, through its various clauses, changed this situation. Instead of the king's court, the Magna Carta designated public courts for hearing of common pleas. This was an important change that gradually led to the development of the English court system.

Later, in colonial America, the English common law system was adopted. With the creation of the United States, the U.S. Constitution and its Bill of Rights gave recognition to a number of basic rights and liberties, among which defendants' rights occupies a prominent place. The U.S. Constitution, through the Bill of Rights, made justice an orderly process, giving a number of important procedural and substantive rights to criminal defendants. Under the Constitution it was the court system, rather than the personal likes and dislikes of the government and of its authorities, that started to play a central role in the application of the justice process.

Notes

1. Dick A. E. Howard, *Magna Carta: Text and Commentary*, rev. ed. (Charlottesville: University of Virginia Press, 1998), p. 40.

2. Georg C. Edwards III, Martin P. Wattenberg, and Robert L. Lineberry, *Government in America: People, Politics, and Policy*, 3rd ed. (New York: Longman, 1997), pp. 328–329.

3. Louis Fisher, *American Constitutional Law: Constitutional Structures*, 3rd ed. 2 vols. (Durham, NC: Carolina Academic Press, 1999), p. 538.

4. Angelo DeLeon and Gary H. Weddle, *A Summary of U.S. Supreme Court Decisions for the Criminal Justice Community* (Flushing, NY: Looseleaf Law, 1998), pp. 46–47.

5. Dean J. Champion, *Police Misconduct in America: A Reference Handbook* (Santa Barbara, CA: ABC-CLIO, 2001).

6. Roy R. Roberg, Jack Kuykendall, and Kenneth Novak, *Police Management*, 3rd. ed. (Los Angeles: Roxbury, 2002), p. 355.

7. David W. Neubauer, *America's Court and the Criminal Justice System* (Belmont, CA: Wadsworth, 2002), p. 249.

8. Fisher, p. 723; Neubauer, pp. 259–261; George E. Rush, *The Dictionary of Criminal Justice*, 5th ed. (Guilford, CT: Dushkin/McGraw-Hill, 2000), p. 155.

9. Rush, p. 155.

10. Joan Biskupic and Elder Witt, *The Supreme Court and Individual Rights*, 3rd ed. (Washington, DC: Congressional Quarterly Press, 1997), p. 213.

11. Fisher, p. 738.

12. Biskupic and Witt, p. 197.

13. David M. O'Brien, *Constitutional Law and Politics, Vol. 2, Civil Rights and Civil Liberties*, 3rd ed. (New York: W. W. Norton, 1997), p. 925.

14. DeLeon and Weddle, pp. 46–47.

15. Fisher, pp. 718–719.

16. Frank Schmalleger, *Criminal Justice Today*, 6th ed. (Upper Saddle River, NJ: Prentice Hall, 2001) pp. 340–341.

17. Fisher, p. 736.

18. *Ibid.*

19. Lloyd L. Weinreb, *Leading Constitutional Cases on Criminal Justice* (Westbury, NY: Foundation Press, 1995), pp. 919.

20. *Ibid.*, pp. 920–921.

21. Fisher, p. 736.

22. Jason L. Slade, "The Spanish Inquisition," cited online at http://www.bibliotopics.com/biblestudy/64.htm, pp. 1–6. *See also* Jean Plaidy, *The Spanish Inquisition* (New York: The Citadel Press, 1967).

23. Fisher, p. 736.

24. O'Brien, pp. 575–587.

25. *Ibid.*, p. 581.

26. Joseph J. Hemmer, Jr., *Communication Law: The Supreme Court and the First Amendment* (Lanham, MD: Austin Winfield, 2000), p. 284.

27. *Ibid.*, pp. 284–285.

28. *Ibid.*, p. 285.

29. *Ibid.*, p. 285.

30. Howard, p. 42.

31. Melvin I. Urofsky, *A March of Liberty:* A Constitutional History of the United States (New York: McGraw-Hill, 1988), p. 156.

32. *Ibid.*

33. Gary Rabe and Dean J. Champion, *Criminal Courts: Structure, Process, and Issues* (Upper Saddle, NJ: Prentice Hall, 2002), pp. 156–183.

34. Fisher, p. 725.

35. O'Brien, pp. 331–332. See also Biskupic and Witt, pp. 171–172.

36. Elder Witt, *Congressional Quarterly's Guide to the U.S. Supreme Court* (Washington, DC: Congressional Quarterly Press, 1979), p. 483.

37. *Ibid.*

38. Cited in Urofsky, p. A22.

39. See for example Paul Butler, "Racially Based Jury Nullification: Black Power in Criminal Justice," pp. 325–347 in Shaun L. Gibbidon, Helen Taylor Greene, and Vernetta D. Young, eds.,

African American Classics in Criminology and Criminal Justice (Thousand Oaks, CA: Sage, 2002).

40. Edward W. Knappman, ed., *Great American Trials, From Witchcraft to Rodney King* (Detroit, MI: Visible Ink Press, 1994), pp. 351–356.

41. *Ibid.*, p. 352.

42. *Ibid.*, p. 351.

43. O'Brien, p. 1017.

44. Howard, p. 43.

45. Gregg Barak, Jeanne M. Flavin, and Paul S. Leighton, *Class, Race, Gender, and Crime* (Los Angeles: Roxbury, 2001), pp. 129–185.

46. *Ibid.*

47. See for example Robert M. Bohm, *Death Quest: An Introduction to the Theory and Practice of Capital Punishment in the United States* (Cincinnati, OH: Anderson, 1999), pp. 143–148.

48. Witt, p. 575.

2

Issues and Controversies

The main purpose of this chapter is to familiarize the reader with the complexity of U.S. criminal law. In particular this chapter focuses on the following controversies surrounding the application of defendant rights in the U.S. system of criminal prosecution:

- Scope of defendant rights in criminal prosecution
- "Law and order" versus "due process" advocates
- Exclusionary rules
- Actual guilt versus legal guilt
- Adversarial nature of U.S. criminal prosecution
- Discretionary powers of prosecutors
- "Beyond a reasonable doubt" standard
- Burden of proof
- Defendant rights versus victim rights
- Defendant rights and the USA PATRIOT Act

Opposing viewpoints are presented when possible to ensure a balanced perspective on the issues.

Scope of Defendant Rights in Criminal Prosecution

In the final decades of the twentieth century, a number of highly publicized and controversial criminal trials took place in the United States. Examples include the trials of Claus Von Bulow

45

(1982 and 1985), Oliver North (1989), Leona Helmsley (1989), Jim Bakker (1989), Charles Keating (1991–1993), William Kennedy Smith (1991), O. J. Simpson (1995), and Kobe Bryant (2004). Because of the controversial nature of these cases, some legal scholars have raised objections to the manner in which the U.S. system of criminal prosecution operates. For example, some of these critics argue that criminal defendants enjoy an inordinate number of procedural rights, as illustrated in the O. J. Simpson trial in 1995. These procedural rights may allow legal technicalities to result in mistrials or outright dismissals of cases in which the evidence is otherwise soundly incriminating.

However, many legal scholars, practitioners, civil rights leaders, and community activists defend the numerous rights that the U.S. legal tradition provides for criminal defendants. They reject the reasoning of those who are critical of the breadth of defendant rights and believe that defendant rights must be zealously protected. As one scholar observes, "The rights of the accused often mean very little because they are ignored by the police, prosecutors, and even judges."[1] The advocates of the two camps can be categorized as the law and order and the due process advocates. A synopsis of each camp's argument is presented below.

"Law and Order" versus "Due Process" Advocates

In U.S. criminal justice literature, the term *law and order* denotes an authoritarian approach to law enforcement. Those who advocate this philosophy believe that the primary function of law is to maintain social order at any cost even if strict enforcement has the potential of violating civil liberties. These advocates argue that because the main function of any criminal justice system is to ensure that the prevailing social order is maintained, the strategic priority should be given to enforcement rather than to the maintenance of every conceivable procedural right that the U.S. legal tradition provides to those suspected of criminal activity.

The "law and order" advocates further argue that the main function of the police is to control crime through effective law enforcement activities. However, the U.S. system of criminal prosecution prevents law enforcement agencies from achieving this goal. The system has provided too many procedural rights for criminal defendants. As observed by one critic, "The law effectively surrendered to the criminals when courts forced cops and prosecutors to fight with one arm held behind their backs."[2] This position implies that law enforcement agencies should be allowed to conduct their enforcement activities free of such restrictions that have been imposed on the police by due process rules. As already discussed at length in Chapter 1, these include *Miranda* warnings and police adherence to rules of professional conduct, as well as the exclusionary rules discussed in this chapter.

The advocates of the "law and order" viewpoint argue that although due process is important, when police are forced to meticulously follow these rules, their ability to conduct effective arrest, search, seizure, surveillance, and interrogation activities is restricted. If we want to effectively neutralize those who commit crimes and victimize society, we have to let the police do their jobs the way they see most appropriate, is the gist of the their position. The advocates of law and order also maintain that these restrictions negatively impact the prosecuting attorneys' range of actions as they prepare criminal cases for prosecution. However, they concede that the restrictions imposed by these rules on prosecuting attorneys are not as onerous as those imposed on the police.

In particular, the advocates of law and order are critical of exclusionary rules. Exclusionary rules are an important part of the rules of evidence applied to both state and federal systems of criminal prosecution. The rules of evidence define (1) what constitutes evidence, and (2) describe the manner in which evidence is introduced in a court of law. To elaborate on these issues, we have to briefly discuss the pre–civil rights movement era of law enforcement.

Prior to the rise of the civil rights movement in the 1960s, the state and local police had almost a free hand in their search and seizure activities. It is through these activities that the police gather the bulk of the incriminating evidence against a suspect. In the past, the idea that suspects had constitutionally protected rights was accepted only in theory. In practice, police agencies followed the "law and order" philosophy in an authoritarian manner. This style of law enforcement gave the police much leverage, and they gathered information on suspects any way they considered to be the most efficient.

The pre–civil rights movement era advocates of law and order earnestly believed that an efficient crime-control strategy bore fruit only when police officers were allowed to vigorously enforce criminal law with almost absolute impunity. This free style of law enforcement led to much police misconduct, corruption, and outright miscarriage of justice against indigent whites or racial minorities, especially in the South.

Police Misconduct

The history of U.S. police agencies is often tainted by misconduct scandals. "Police misconduct," observes one scholar, "is any inappropriate behavior on the part of any law enforcement officer that is either illegal or immoral or both."[3] Based on this definition, the following have been identified as police misconduct:

1. Accessing police records for personal use
2. Abusing sick leave
3. Lying to supervisors and managers
4. Perjuring on reports and in court
5. Committing a crime
6. Falsifying overtime records
7. Using excessive force
8. Drinking while on duty
9. Being involved in off-duty firearms incidents
10. Failing to complete police records
11. Accepting gratuities
12. Providing recommendations for an attorney, towing service, or bail bond service
13. Failing to report misconduct of a fellow officer
14. Failing to inventory recovered property or evidence
15. Sleeping on duty
16. Cheating on promotional examinations
17. Sexually harassing suspects or performing other such improprieties.[4]

The above list is not new. In fact, U.S. police departments have a long history of abusive practices. These abusive practices have forced the local, state, and federal authorities to investigate. From early 1930 to 2004, the following investigative commissions have studied police misconduct and corruption:

- Wickersham Commission, 1931
- Seabury Commission, 1932

- Knapp Commission, 1972
- Christopher Commission, 1991
- Mollen Commission, 1994
- Commission of Police Integrity in Chicago, 1997.[5]

These investigatory commissions have come up with different proposals to curb police misconduct. Some of these measures have worked, and some others have not been effective. Another form of unsavory police behavior is known as "street justice" among police officers.

Street Justice versus Legal Justice

Street justice is the logical outcome of overreliance by the police on the authoritarian "law and order" philosophy and style of the past. Street justice is different from the kind of "legal justice" police academies teach or legal scholars idealize in their writings. Street justice is what its advocates consider a "no nonsense" approach to fighting street crime. For the hard-core "law and order" advocates, fighting crime is the one and only real mandate of the police. It is through vigorous crime-fighting activities that the police serve and protect U.S. communities and our national borders, argue the advocates of street justice.

Street justice is not a reaction to but a reflection of the tough realities that the police routinely face as they patrol cities, highways, and borders of this country. As observed by one scholar, street justice can be looked upon as a rather brutal form of reminding the "wannabe" streetwise guys who is in charge of law and order in the streets. These are "teaching techniques," whose format differs depending on the situation.[6] These can range in mildness from giving a moral lecture to the average person who has been involved in some minor altercation in the public, to a wide range of punitive actions that the police can apply against unruly and disrespectful citizens.[7]

The civil rights movement constitutes an important era in U.S. social and political history. As a movement, it was initiated over the issue of voting rights and civil liberties. The advocates of the movement argued that the civil liberties recognized by the U.S. Constitution should apply to all citizens regardless of race, ethnic background, or religious affiliation. In particular, it was the African American communities that suffered from discrimination in relation to civil liberties. Therefore, the prominent leaders of the movement such as Dr. Martin Luther King Jr. advocated a nonviolent, nationwide movement for the realization of civil liberties. The purpose of the movement was to force the federal government to recognize African American citizens' civil rights. Another demand of the movement was to put an end to stark inequalities that came through segregation.

The civil rights movement gained momentum when Earl Warren was appointed chief justice of the U.S. Supreme Court in 1953 by President Dwight Eisenhower. The Supreme Court has played an important role in determining the manner in which U.S. police agencies operate. The Supreme Court is the highest authority as to what is legal or illegal from the standpoint of the U.S. Constitution. It was during the Warren Court (1953–1969) that law enforcement agencies started to conform their operations to due process rules.

The Warren Court is known for what has been termed "due process activism" that resulted from a strategic shift in the Court's legal philosophy. It was during this period that law enforcement agencies' evidence-gathering (i.e., search and seizure) activities came under close scrutiny at both state and federal levels.

"Due process" advocates argue that the police must recognize that the real aim of the U.S. Constitution is to protect citizens and communities against illegal and immoral conduct of the government. Police departments at any level are among the most powerful governmental agencies. Police agencies must therefore abide by high standards of professionalism as they carry out their activities. This is especially expected in a country that boasts a model democratic government built on an elaborate system of checks and balances. Therefore, the police and the prosecuting attorneys should not be tempted by the rationale of the advocates of street justice to ignore suspects' rights. Neither should these agencies be tempted to circumvent the procedural laws in the name of fighting crime.

The Warren Court made a number of important landmark decisions in relation to law enforcement practices, most of which related to tactics of the street-justice variety. The Warren Court was especially scrutinizing of police search and seizure because the bulk of police misconduct takes place during these evidence-gathering activities. Thus emerged the exclusionary rules, whose purpose was to discourage unconstitutional search and seizure activities by rendering evidence garnered by such methods inadmissible in court. In 1969, President Richard Nixon appointed Warren Earl Burger chief justice of the Supreme Court. Under Burger's tenure (1969–1989), a more conservative agenda was set in motion. The Court this time leaned more toward the "law and order" philosophy. This conservative leaning has continued under Chief Justice William Rehnquist (1986–present) appointed to the position by President Ronald Reagan.

The new advocates of the "law and order" philosophy (post–Warren Court) do not encourage police misconduct. They are in fact critical of past police misconduct. However, they maintain that the harsh realities of street crime do impact the manner in which law enforcement agencies fight crime and criminal elements to maintain a secure social environment in cities and the suburban areas of the nation. Although these modern advocates accept the basic premise that the police must uphold the law and apply justice on an equal footing, they caution that it is naive to believe that hard-core street criminals would respond positively to police officers who wish to meticulously abide by the book. A certain level of police toughness inculcating fear among criminal elements is required so that police can better deal with the tough inner city and its criminal elements, goes the argument. The graduates of police academies come face-to-face with these harsh realities of street crime and must be able to respond effectively, argue the advocates of law and order.[8] However, what is certain is that U.S. police can never go back to the pre–civil rights movement "law and order" style of policing.

During the tenures of Chief Justices Warren, Burger, and Rehnquist, the Supreme Court has made many landmark decisions concerning search and seizure activities. The following list shows the number of such decisions by topic, underscoring the importance with which the Court views the area of defendant rights.

- Confessions (twenty-nine cases, 1964–1994)
- Consent searches (five cases, 1974–1996)
- Entry into homes to arrest (five cases, 1967–1984)
- Exclusionary rule (six cases, 1964–1984)
- Expectation of privacy (six cases, 1967–1995)
- Investigation detention (eight cases, 1981–1993)
- Probable cause (five cases, 1959–1985)
- Search incident to custodial arrest (eighteen cases, 1969–1982)

- Search of motor vehicles (thirteen cases, 1965–1996)
- Search of persons (two cases, 1966–1985)
- Search of premises (six cases, 1986–1987)
- Stop and frisk (eleven cases, 1972–1997)[9]

In carrying out their search and seizure activities the police must abide by a set of legal procedures. These procedures have gradually evolved through the last four decades of the twentieth century and into the twenty-first. Incriminating evidence obtained by police officers who have either deliberately or inadvertently disregarded these procedures is subject to exclusionary rules. Simply put, incriminating evidence obtained through illegal means is excluded from a criminal trial.

The next question is whether a middle ground can be found between the two perspectives. Simply put, can the U.S. system of criminal prosecution be brought to a balanced position in which the following apply: (1) the constitutional rights of the accused are protected, while (2) the system is not pushed to extremes whereby a simple legal technicality can cause dismissal of a case? In other words, can we strike a balance in criminal trials between the rights of the defendants and those of the victims of crime?

Exclusionary Rules

One distinct feature of U.S. criminal prosecution is the manner in which incriminating evidence against a defendant is presented at trial. In all jurisdictions throughout the United States, it is the police detectives and investigators who investigate crime scenes to gather evidence. In addition, it is the police who conduct arrest, search, and seizure activities in relation to crime. Therefore, the overall integrity of a criminal case depends on the manner in which the police carry out their law enforcement activities. It is noteworthy that any evidence gathered by the police becomes incriminating only after the district attorney decides its evidentiary potential. Even at that stage, the evidence is subjected to cross-examination by the defense counsel.

The police are duty bound, among other things, not to violate citizens' Fourth Amendment rights. For example, as discussed in Chapter 1, police officers are not allowed to enter a citizen's home (or place of work) to search the premises without valid warrants. The police are not allowed to arrest or to interrogate suspects without probable cause. In carrying out these activities the police have to obtain warrants indicating the purpose of the police action against a suspect. There are exceptions that are discussed in Chapter 1.

Exclusionary rules mandate that any evidence illegally obtained by the police be barred from the criminal proceedings. In other words, these rules allow the defense attorney to ask the judge to exclude from the proceedings any evidence that has been obtained through illegal means. The same applies to evidence obtained through a warrant of arrest, search, or seizure obtained through perjury. For example, if a police officer gives false information to a judge in order to obtain a search warrant alleging that a crime is in progress, that officer has committed perjury. In the trial, if it could be shown by the defense attorney that incriminating evidence was obtained through such illegal means, the exclusionary rule applies. This would have dire legal consequences for the police officer implicated in perjury. Perjury is a felony and in most jurisdictions it is punished by a combination of penalties that include monetary fines, dismissal from one's job, or imprisonment.

As discussed in Chapter 1, these rights gradually emerged after the 1966 Supreme Court decision in *Miranda v. Arizona.* The case involved the interrogation of Ernesto Miranda by the Arizona state police while he was in police custody. Miranda was not informed of his constitutional right against self-incrimination prior to interrogation, which took place while Miranda was effectively cut off from the outside world. The confessions obtained by the police were admitted in Miranda's trial that subsequently led to his conviction. The case reached the U.S. Supreme Court, which overturned his conviction. The Court based its decision on the fact that the confession had been obtained from the suspect through violation of his Fifth Amendment right against self-incrimination. The *Miranda* decision has recognized a number of procedural rights that police have to observe in any interrogation (see Chapter 1 for details).

The *Miranda* decision has profoundly reshaped law enforcement activities in relation to arrest, search, and interrogation of suspects who are in police custody. If the defense lawyer can show that the defendant's *Miranda* rights were violated, the defense may ask the court to exclude evidence obtained as a result of the violation from the trial. However, if it can be shown that (1) the police gave the *Miranda* warnings to the defendant,

(2) he or she waived the right against self-incrimination despite the warnings, and (3) the wavier was voluntary, the incriminating evidence thus obtained is admissible in court.

This principle was reaffirmed in *Edwards v. Arizona* (1981).[10] While in police custody, Edwards was given the *Miranda* warnings. After acknowledging that he understood his rights, Edwards agreed to answer the questions that police asked about the case. Later he was informed that his accomplice had given corroborating evidence as to his guilt. At that point Edwards invoked his *Miranda* rights and demanded to consult with an attorney. The questioning stopped. Edwards was reinterrogated the next day without any defense lawyer present. The incriminating evidence thus obtained from Edwards in the absence of defense counsel was presented at the trial that led to his conviction. Edwards's appeal reached the Supreme Court, which ruled that the second interrogation was in violation of Edwards's *Miranda* rights. This was so because Edwards had already invoked his Sixth Amendment right to consult with a criminal defense lawyer but was not allowed to do so. Therefore, the evidence against Edwards obtained in the second interrogation was inadmissible.[11]

As mentioned above, critics of an expansive view of defendant rights argue that the exclusionary rules should be reformed. This reform is important because exclusionary rules restrict the efficacy of both the police and the prosecution in performing their duties. One critic of the exclusionary rule argues that *Miranda* warnings can be characterized as a tangible by-product of the exclusionary rules. The *Miranda* warnings undermine the efficacy of the U.S. criminal justice system. According to this critic, Justice John Harlan is on record that the 1966 ruling in *Miranda v. Arizona* is shameful because it seems as if criminal suspects are given "a right to conceal their crimes."[12] However, other scholars and practitioners disagree with this premise, to be discussed shortly.

Actual Guilt versus Legal Guilt

Another distinct feature of U.S. criminal prosecution is the manner in which the guilt of the accused is established. A meticulous procedure is followed by the system to distinguish between actual and legal guilt. The term *actual guilt* means recognition by those accused of the commission of the crime that they are indeed guilty as charged. However, the existence of actual guilt does not guarantee punishment.

In the Anglo-American legal tradition, punishment applies only when a defendant's legal guilt has been established through legal proceedings in a duly convened court of law. However, the Anglo-American tradition sets a high threshold for the establishment of legal guilt. This standard is known as guilt beyond a reasonable doubt. It could be argued that the "beyond a reasonable doubt" standard is a cornerstone of the Anglo-American notion of a fair trial embodied in the Sixth Amendment (see Chapter 1). The standard of guilt beyond a reasonable doubt, however, has been subjected to much criticism. One criticism relates to the jury's ability to decide a case not by following the law, but by following their own consciences. This ability is known as jury nullification. If the evidence pointing to the actual guilt of the defendant is strong and yet some trivial technicalities prevent the establishment of legal guilt, the jury may nullify the judge's directions and find the defendant guilty. Conversely, if the jury is sympathetic to a defendant because of the perception that he or she deserves mercy or that the law at issue is unfair, the jury may ignore the judge's instructions and acquit.[13]

The Adversarial Nature of Criminal Prosecution

Another distinct feature of U.S. criminal prosecution is the adversarial nature of the system. This feature is unique to the Anglo-American legal tradition, because in other legal traditions (Greco-Roman, Islamic, Socialist) the judge plays a significant role in fact finding. However, such is not the case in the Anglo-American legal tradition in which the main function of the judge is to interpret the law, not to find facts. (If the case is tried without a jury, the judge performs both functions.) It is the duty of the prosecuting attorney to prove guilt, and it is the duty of the defense attorney to mount a vigorous defense to refute the criminal charges leveled against the defendant. As discussed in Chapter 1, in a typical criminal prosecution there are two adversaries: the defense and the prosecution. The two sides present their contrasting views of the case as supported by evidence. Both parties try their best to win by persuading the jury that their view of the facts represents the truth. Here lies the gist of the problem, observe critics of the U.S. system of criminal prosecution.

The critics argue that the adversarial nature of criminal proceedings enables experienced defense lawyers to manipulate the justice system to confuse the facts that surround a case. Defense lawyers do this to create a gap between actual guilt and legal guilt. Some critics further argue that experienced defense lawyers hamper the efficacy of the criminal trial. They achieve this by using legal strategies that are borderline in terms of legality and morality. For example, one critic has observed that "too many lawyers are more committed to their own economic interests than to a sensible legal system."[14]

A group of researchers has proposed forty solutions to fix the U.S. legal system.[15] These researchers seem to imply that the U.S. system of justice is almost on the verge of breakdown. According to this study the breakdown is due to the following factors that have negatively impacted the U.S. criminal justice system:

- Laws are hard to find and even harder to understand.
- Lawyers' hourly fees run about ten times the average person's hourly wage.
- Court clerks and judges are generally hostile to self-help efforts; easy-to-use forms and procedures are rare.
- Many legal procedures, from transferring a house to probating an estate, are unnecessary and serve only to generate income for lawyers.
- Nonlawyers who try to compete with lawyers by providing high-quality, low-cost legal form preparation services are labeled criminals.[16]

Some of the more important reforms suggested by this legal research group include the following:

- Take simple actions out of court.
- Simplify legal paperwork.
- Regulate contingency fees.
- Add self-help court clerks.
- Provide legal help for the poor.
- Take lawyers out of house sales.
- Eliminate bias in the courts.

- Write laws in simple language.
- Make competent interpreters available.
- Help nonlawyers use law libraries.
- Expand small claims court limits.
- Do away with punitive damages.
- Reform the jury system.
- Abolish judicial elections.
- Discipline lawyers.
- Mediate neighborhood disputes.
- Require lawyer impact statements.[17]

Supporters of the status quo argue that the U.S. legal system is dynamic and self-regulating. They see no legal breakdown and believe that, in fact, the system operates with a good degree of efficiency despite occasional problems. In addition, the system's supporters argue that defense lawyers do not hamper the pursuit of justice. In fact, defense lawyers strengthen the legal system because they (1) protect our rights, (2) fight our legal battles, (3) contribute to the general well-being of the legal system, and (4) help keep society from falling into chaos, anarchy and even dictatorship.[18]

As to the charges of immorality of some defense lawyers, supporters of the status quo argue that the social cost of such immorality is compensated by the fact that, " [t]here is a great deal of good that lawyers do for our society."[19] Supporters of the system also point out that it is the legal responsibility of criminal defense lawyers to defend their clients vigorously, even if it means playing hard ball.[20] Ideally speaking, a vigorous defense should be based on the fair and moral use of all legal instruments that the U.S. system provides. However, it is a known fact that some overzealous defense lawyers engage in misconduct. But it is also a known fact that those defense lawyers involved in defense misconduct risk getting into serious trouble with law.[21]

Finally, the supporters of the system accept the fact that some defense lawyers misuse the legal system. However, they observe that there are competent prosecuting attorneys who similarly manipulate the system. The prosecuting attorneys manipulate the legal system based on their vast knowledge of how the legal system operates. Not only do they know how to interpret and apply criminal law and procedures, but having prosecuted many criminal cases, district attorneys are thoroughly familiar with the presiding judges in their jurisdictions.

Discretionary Powers of Prosecutors

Another distinct feature of U.S. criminal prosecution is the power the system gives to prosecuting attorneys. At the state level prosecuting attorneys are known as district attorneys, while at the federal level they are simply called U.S. attorneys. At each level, the prosecuting attorneys have discretionary power over a wide range of matters to resolve criminal cases. In the United States, a large number of street crimes take place every year that result in the arrest and prosecution of street offenders. Those who can't make bail are housed in local jails and detention centers waiting for their turn to be formally arraigned in a court of law. The detention of large numbers of offenders causes overcrowding in jails and on court dockets. In fact, some critics denounce this situation, arguing that the U.S. criminal justice system is on an "imprisonment binge."[22]

Facing the above realities, district attorneys (DAs) in many state jurisdictions are between a rock and a hard place. On the one hand, they are ethically obliged to prosecute those who have been charged with the commission of a crime. On the other hand, they must consider the actual cost of a criminal trial. In resolving this dilemma, the DAs have to make a number of important decisions. For example, at the very outset, a determination must be made as to whether a case is winnable by the prosecution. This is a very important decision because winning requires that many factors be brought together, including (1) solid evidence against the defendant, (2) a viable prosecution plan and strategy, and (3) meticulous legal and administrative work by the DA. All these efforts, however, do not guarantee that prosecution of the case will yield the desired result: a guilty verdict against the criminal defendant.

A carefully prepared criminal case may nevertheless go astray at any point during the course of the trial. For example, material witnesses may be ineffective on the witness stand. The forensic investigation of incriminating evidence may fail to produce the desired results. In fact, forensic evidence prepared by the prosecution may help, rather than hurt, the defense, as happened in the case of Marv Albert, the NBC sportscaster. Albert was accused of rape and sodomy of a woman in Arlington, Virginia, in 1997. However, he was exonerated when the DNA analysis of the semen sample showed that it did not belong to him as had been alleged by the plaintiff.[23] In some cases, the jury may not like the demeanor of the prosecuting attorney or simply may not be persuaded by the evidence.

As an alternative to formally trying a criminal case in court and in front of a jury, the prosecution has the option of offering a plea bargain to the defense. In return for a guilty plea by the defendant, the DA may agree (1) to lower the charges, (2) to put the defendant on probationary status, or (3) to seek monetary fines rather than incarceration as the prospective form of punishment. Once the two sides agree on the terms of the plea bargain, the presiding judge is informed of the decision. If the judge agrees with the terms of the plea bargain (which is usually the case), the plea bargain agreement is then recorded as the official disposition of the case. This document describes the terms of the plea agreement and is legally binding on both sides.

District attorneys are responsible for the prosecution of those they choose to charge with the commission of crime in state jurisdictions. A district attorney has a wide range of discretionary powers to use in discharging this duty. At the same time, both state and federal prosecutors enjoy almost absolute immunity as they carry out their legal duties. This immunity allows the prosecuting attorneys to vigorously enforce criminal law without any fear of repercussion. In effect, a criminal defendant is not allowed to sue a prosecuting attorney because of the prosecutorial options used against him or her. Therefore, the DA has much control over the fate of a defendant. If abused, the DA's power can endanger the life, health, property, and reputation of a defendant. At the same time, it could harm the integrity of the U.S. criminal prosecution system altogether.

Despite their sensitive nature, studies have shown instances of prosecutorial abuse.[24] Abusive practices may include improper use of the following practices:

- filing of multiple charges against a defendant;
- sentence bargaining (reducing sentences in exchange for a guilty plea, with the approval and knowledge of the presiding judge);
- charge bargaining (more serious charges are dropped for a less serious charge in return for a guilty plea);
- intimidating tactics (during plea bargaining the DA reminds the defendant of his or her immense prosecuto-

rial powers that could be utilized if the defendant does not cooperate or rejects the plea bargain);
- giving immunity from prosecution in return for helping the DA to go after bigger suspects.[25]

Based on these observations, it could be argued that the potential for miscarriage of justice becomes extreme, considering that as observed by one scholar, "Currently, approximately 90 percent of all local and state felony cases and 85 percent of federal charges are plea bargained (with sharp variations between jurisdictions)."[26]

Against those scholars and practitioners who argue that plea bargaining is an abusive practice that undermines justice, there are those who defend the practice. The supporters argue that plea bargaining is a legal necessity in the face of the realities of the U.S. crime scene.[27] The basis of this necessity is that there are too many criminal defendants to be processed in court and in front of juries. The supporters acknowledge the fact that plea bargaining is open to abuse. However, they believe that plea bargaining can be reformed. In the long run, the benefits of the plea bargain far outweigh its potential detriments, so this argument goes. Some legal scholars have cautioned against any attempts to abolish the plea bargain because, "Abolishing plea bargaining produces results quite irrelevant to our basic goal of reducing serious crime."[28] In fact, those states that have tried to abolish plea bargaining have not ended up reducing serious crime, some studies have concluded.[29]

"Beyond a Reasonable Doubt" Standard

Another distinct feature of U.S. criminal prosecution is that in convicting a criminal defendant, the finder of fact must be persuaded of his or her guilt "beyond a reasonable doubt. " Simply put, this standard mandates that in proceedings that take place in front of a jury, the members of the jury must not have any "reasonable" doubts as to the guilt of the defendant. If reasonable doubt exists in the mind of even one juror, then the criminal defendant is set free. But what is a reasonable doubt?

Reasonable doubt means any inconsistencies that a person of sound logic, judgment, and rationality may find among the facts that surround a case. The "facts" of a case are the legal and factual elements put together by the prosecution to demonstrate the guilt of a criminal defendant. These include elements such as the intent, ability, motive, opportunity, and mind set of the defendant at the time of the commission of the crime. Next to these, there is the bulk of the physical evidence that the police gather from the crime scene. The facts of a criminal case presented by the prosecution during the course of trial are subject to the reasonable doubt standard. As the case proceeds in front of the jury, the defense attorney is allowed to reexamine these facts and question their credibility, plausibility, and very existence as facts. In criminal cases, the jury must reach unanimity in pronouncing a guilty verdict. If unanimity is not reached, the jury must give a not guilty verdict. A hung jury is one in which at least one juror dissents from the judgment of guilt by the majority.

In colonial times in this country, it was much easier for the jurors to reach unanimity over the guilt of the accused. This was because colonial America was a much simpler society than the postindustrialized America of today. Today's U.S. society is dynamic, fast paced, and complex. In addition, the U.S. system of criminal prosecution is now equipped with what is known as the "science" of criminal investigation. This science includes a wide range of investigative techniques, tools, and methodologies.[30] For example such devices as DNA examination, forensic pathology reports, psychological profiling, examination of firearm residue, videotaping crime scenes, and polygraph tests are now standard tools of the science of criminal investigation.[31]

If properly utilized, the forensic tools help the police to conduct a relatively thorough search of the crime scene. At the same time, these tools allow experienced criminal defense lawyers to reexamine incriminating evidence. By such reexamination, criminal defense lawyers come up with different interpretations of the facts surrounding the case. In other words, they try to put incriminating evidence in its "proper context" to raise reasonable doubt in the minds of the jurors. Even the most diligently prepared criminal cases can be torn apart in the hands of experienced criminal defense lawyers.

To give an example, in 1994 the question as to what constitutes reasonable doubt was raised in the course of one of the most controversial murder trials of the twentieth century. The case involved O. J. Simpson, an ex-football hero who was indicted by a grand jury in California for the murder of his ex-wife, Nicole Brown Simpson, and her companion, Ronald Goldman.

Because of his celebrity status and considerable financial resources, Simpson was able to hire a team of highly competent criminal defense lawyers. The defense team utilized a wide range of legal means, defense strategies, and expert witnesses to defend Simpson. The lawyers methodically questioned the authenticity of much incriminating evidence that the prosecution brought against Simpson. The defense team succeeded in its strategy and raised reasonable doubt in the minds of the jury.

The Simpson defense team argued that the prosecution's evidence did not stand up to the scrutiny of the scientific method. The defense team also argued that Simpson was the victim of a "conspiracy" hatched against him by a number of "racist" police officers in the Los Angeles Police Department (LAPD). The last argument was quite powerful because the LAPD had a rather dubious reputation in its treatment of African Americans and other racial minority suspects. Simpson was acquitted of all criminal charges and released.

Later, in 1997, Simpson was found liable for the wrongful death of his wife and her companion in a civil suit brought against him by the Goldman family. This time, the jury had to decide Simpson's liability, or lack thereof, in a civil trial. A civil trial operates differently from a criminal trial. In civil trials the liability of the defendant is determined based on the "preponderance of evidence" standard. This standard of proof is less strict than the "beyond a reasonable doubt" criterion used in criminal trials. In a civil trial, the jury does not have to be unanimous in its decision. However, a majority of the jurors must reach an agreement on the fate of the defendant. Being found liable, Simpson was ordered by a California court to pay $33 million to the Goldman family to compensate for its pain and suffering due to Simpson's actions.[32]

The O. J. Simpson case in its criminal phase, however, proved that experienced defense lawyers can effectively manipulate the "reasonable doubt" standard in order to create doubt in the minds of the jurors. This can be done, as the Simpson case proved, to even the most iron-clad set of incriminating clues that the prosecution may put together against a criminal defendant.

This said, it is noteworthy that of the large number of criminal defendants prosecuted in the United States every year, very few are capable of retaining the services of highly competent defense lawyers. Nor can many retain the services of expert witnesses to benefit from forensic evidentiary tools for defense purposes. There are those scholars who argue that a verdict of innocence in the U.S. criminal justice system has become a commercial product. The verdict of innocence, like any other commercial product, can be purchased by those who can afford to pay its prevailing market price.[33] Criminal defendants with financial resources are in a much better position to buy a verdict of innocence than those who are not in a financially viable position.[34]

Burden of Proof

In the U.S. system of criminal justice the burden of proof falls upon the prosecution to show that the defendant has committed the criminal act. If the burden of proof is not met, the defendant is legally absolved of all criminal charges.

Some scholars argue the legal process is not concerned with establishing the truth but has turned into what these scholars characterize as "trial advocacy."[35] The argument is that despite a widely held belief that a trial is an attempt to determine the truth as to what has taken place and who the culprit is, in reality, however, " [a] trial presents selected witnesses who recite selected portions of their respective memories, concerning selected observation of the disputed event."[36] In other words, the proof is established through a selective process. Each stage of the process is encumbered by the previous one because in each stage various details pertaining to the facts of the case are arbitrarily eliminated from the larger process, observe trial advocacy scholars.

On the other end of the spectrum, many scholars argue that this filtering process is inevitable because the evidentiary process can't go on indefinitely. The appeal has been established in order to reconsider and correct some of the inevitable procedural mistakes that occur during the trial proceedings. Making a comparison between the Anglo-American criminal system and other legal systems, these scholars observe that the Anglo-American trial system has a wide range of truth-seeking steps that allow it to establish a relatively accurate picture of the truth without undermining the integrity of the system.[37]

Defendant Rights versus Victim Rights

So far, we have concentrated on the procedural rights that criminal defendants enjoy in the U.S. system of criminal prosecution. The question has been raised as to whether the victims of crime have rights, too. In the 1970s, it was women's rights advocates who first raised this issue, noting that the police, courts, and corrections departments did not properly handle the cases of female victims of rape or domestic violence.

The notion of victims' rights owes its rationale to the manner in which the U.S. public and criminal justice systems have reacted to the female victims of rape and domestic violence until very recent times. Historically speaking, both adult and young females have been subjected to crimes of domestic violence comprised of assault and battery, conjugal rape, and incest, as well as various forms of exploitation, threats, and humiliation. The literature shows that until very recent times, most victims of this category of crime remained reluctant to report incidents to the police because of (1) fear of adverse reactions at home, and (2) apprehension about the manner in which they would be treated by the police, the courts, and the medical institutions involved in the investigation of such criminal incidents.

Prior to the rise of the victims' rights movement, authorities who investigated rape committed against women were largely insensitive to the devastating and traumatic impact of the crime on victims. The same attitude applied in relation to the female victims of domestic violence and/or violent crime (e.g., aggravated rape by a stranger). Instead, the authorities treated the female victims as evidentiary sources, particularly of physical traces such as the pubic hair, semen, and/or blood of the perpetrator. If expeditiously extracted from the victim, these elements can help the police to identify the criminal. Such evidence can also help exonerate those who may have been wrongly accused of the commission of such crimes.

The problem is that most victims of forcible rape (usually committed under threat of bodily harm) go through a posttraumatic experience with long-lasting and devastating effects. Initially, victims may ignore the evidentiary potential of the evidence that they carry on their bodies and frantically attempt to cleanse themselves and expunge the fact of the crime against them by taking showers or cleaning the premises in which the crime took place. Unfortunately, by doing so, the victims also destroy much incriminating evidence that the authorities would want to access to better investigate the crime.

Rape is a heinous and violent crime that devastates the victim. It has nothing to do with sexual desire. Thanks to the women's rights movement, rape is now recognized as what it is: a crime of violence. The change in the perception of rape from a crime of passion to a crime of violence has profoundly changed the legal ramifications for both the victims and the defendants of the crime of rape.

In the past, the defendant accused of rape would be portrayed as a sexually frustrated male whose primary motivation was to satisfy his sexual desires and fantasies. The defense would also try to blame the victim by portraying her as partially responsible for the assault. For example, the defense would argue that the victim enticed the defendant by her sexually provocative acts, flirtatious behavior, and the manner of her dress and appearance. In addition, the defense would also try to besmirch the reputation of the victim by prying into her sexual activities to imply that she had a sexually active past and was not all that "innocent " after all. In short, the victim would be subjected to a series of public humiliations and embarrassments to the effect that most rape victims will not report the crime to the police and will not bring charges against the perpetrator of the crime.

From the 1970s on, women's rights supporters have lobbied the U.S. Congress and state legislatures to pass laws to prevent victims of rape or domestic violence from revictimization at the institutional level. Congress passed the so-called rape shield laws to put a decisive end to such abusive defense strategies. The new laws prohibit any prying into the past sexual activities of the victims for evidentiary purposes except when the victim of the alleged rape has had sexual liaisons with the defendant in the past.

In 1994, Congress passed the Violence Against Women Act. Its purpose is to protect women against different forms of violence perpetrated at home or in public. The act provides for state-funded victim centers in addition to legal assistance for victims of domestic violence. The act has codified different forms of protection orders aimed at protecting battered women and children from their abusers.

In short, it can be argued that concerns over the scope of defendant rights in conjunction with the perception that the U.S. justice system has been unresponsive to the plight of victims has gradually led to the development of a countermovement known as the victims' rights movement.

Advocates of victims' rights argue that the U.S. criminal justice system has to address the justice needs of the victims of crime as well as those of the criminal defendants.[38] They observe that the system is almost blind to the amount of hurt and resentment inflicted on the survivors of a crime when justice is not served. This is especially true when a case is dismissed because police have not followed a certain legal procedure. This is quite problematic because criminal defendants seem to have innumerable rights that they enjoy while in police custody, as discussed in Chapter 1. Once it is exposed that one of these rights has been violated, the case can be dismissed.

Another concern of victims' rights advocates regards the punishment phase. These advocates argue that the imposition of inappropriate punishments inflicts much agony and hurt on the victims. These improper punishments include the following:

- lenient sentences
- plea bargaining
- imposition of fines instead of imprisonment
- suspended sentences
- early parole

This hurt over improper punishment is compounded when lenient sentences are given to repeat or habitual offenders, or when such offenders are paroled. That is why some argue that U.S. criminal prosecution is in need of a mechanism through which the voice of the victim is heard. This hearing should be held during both the sentencing and postconviction phases. As observed by one scholar of the subject, "Victims have no rights at all—merely privileges to be granted or withheld at the whim of criminal justice insiders."[39] One remedy is to allow the victims, or their survivors, to be heard during sentencing or parole hearings of the convicted criminals. This is done through what is known as victim impact statements.

Victim impact statements are testimonies of the victims, or of their close relatives, given to a court of law before a judge imposes punishment on a defendant who has been found guilty by the jury. Such impact testimonies can also be given to state or federal boards of parole in relation to cases that have been scheduled for parole hearings. Parole is early release of a prisoner because of good conduct. The purpose of victims' impact testimonies is to inform the legal authorities as to what extent the survivors of a crime have been impacted by the criminal act of the defendant. The impact can be emotional, psychological, physical, financial, or a combination of these factors. There are cases that have shown that victim impact statements may affect the severity of the punishment imposed on criminal defendants. For example, in 1987, Pervis Tyrone Payne was tried for the murder of a mother and her baby daughter in Millington, Tennessee. Payne's extremely violent criminal acts, which included multiple stabbings of his victims, took place in front of the victim's three-year-old son. The little boy also suffered wounds, but survived. During the sentencing phase, the boy's grandmother gave a victim impact statement to the court. She testified that, "the boy cried out for his mother and baby sister at night and did not understand why they did not come home."[40] Payne was subsequently found guilty and sentenced to death.

The *Payne* trial has been considered a triumph for the victims' rights movement. The victim impact statement provided by the grandmother contributed to the jury's decision to impose the death penalty on Payne. The sentence was appealed and the case reached the Supreme Court. In *Payne v. Tennessee* (1991), the Court rejected the appellant's argument that it was unconstitutional to consider the victim impact statements at the sentencing phase of a capital crime. In fact, the high Court, through the Payne decision, overruled two precedents, *Booth v. Maryland* (1987) and *South Carolina v. Gathers* (1989). In both of these decisions the Supreme Court had ruled it unconstitutional to allow the victim's impact testimony to be heard during the sentencing phase of capital crimes.[41] The *Payne* decision reversed the situation, allowing for the inclusion of such statements during the sentencing phase.

In 1984, the U.S. Congress passed another important piece of legislation entitled "The Victims of Crime Act." Its purpose was to prevent the victimization of the survivors of serious crimes. It also aimed to provide compensation for such victims through the forfeiture of financial assets belonging to convicted criminals. The act, through its "Son of Sam" provision, also prevents convicted criminals from profiting from their crimes. This provision owes its name to the outcome of the trial of David R. Berkowitz, who was convicted of a number of extremely violent murders that took place between October 1976 and August 1977 in New York City and became known as the "Son of Sam" case. Berkowitz's bizarre case (including his belief that his neighbor's dog was a demon enticing him to commit the murders) was devoured by the media and led to numerous lucrative offers from publishers and the entertainment industry to tell his story. The "Son of Sam" provision puts any monetary profits derived from such activities in an escrow account to compensate the victims of the convicted criminal rather than allowing the criminal to profit. In 1999, Senators Dianne Feinstein and Jon Kyle proposed that it was time to give victims' rights constitutionally protected status. The two senators put their proposal in the form of a Senate joint resolution.[42]

The resolution called for a constitutional amendment giving the victims of crime the rights:

- to reasonable notice of, and not to be excluded from, any public proceedings relating to the crime;
- to be heard, if present, and to submit a statement at all such proceedings to determine a conditional release from custody, an acceptance of a negotiated plea, or a sentence;
- to the foregoing rights at a parole proceeding that is not public, to the extent those rights are afforded to the convicted offender;
- to reasonable notice of a release or escape from custody relating to the crime;
- to consideration of the interests of the victim that any trial be free from unreasonable delay;
- to an order of restitution from the convicted offender;
- to consideration for the safety of the victim in determining any conditional release from custody relating to the crime; and
- to reasonable notice of the rights established by this article.[43]

However, to date the proposal has not gained enough support for further action and has been shelved.

Opponents of the victims' rights movement argue that defendant rights are protected by the Constitution but that victims' rights are not.[44] One opponent has observed that, "The use of victim impact evidence . . . advances victims' interests only at a serious cost to capital defendants' Eighth Amendment rights."[45] The Eighth Amendment, as discussed in Chapter 1, prohibits the use of cruel and unusual punishment. Allowing the inclusion of victim impact statements in the justice process, argue opponents, may tip the balance against the defendant in the punishment phase, as occurred in the *Payne* case cited above.

Opponents also argue that the inclusion of victims' rights in the justice process is an intrusion into the constitutionality of defendant rights and that in the long run such intrusions could undermine the integrity of U.S. criminal prosecution. This is because victims' rights are considered extra-legal matters not relevant to the application of the justice process, argue the opponents.

Some legal scholars and practitioners argue that victims' rights have been gained at the expense of the suspects and criminal defendants.[46] However, there are those who argue otherwise, noting that: (1) few victims are notified of their rights during the criminal proceedings or during the pre- and postsentencing phases; (2) the concept of victims' rights has yet to be embraced by the police, prosecuting attorneys, judges, and parole and probation boards throughout the country; and (3) there are many in the criminal justice system who have found the practice time-consuming and cumbersome. Therefore, those in the position of legal authority often ignore the procedural requirements of the victims' rights altogether.[47]

Defendant Rights and the USAPATRIOT Act

The "Uniting and Strengthening America by Providing Appropriate Tools Required to Intercept and Obstruct Terrorism" (USAPATRIOT) Act was passed by the Congress of the United States on 24 October 2001. Its main purposes are, "To deter and punish terrorist acts in the United States and around the world, to enhance law enforcement investigatory tools, and for other purposes."[48]

The USAPATRIOT Act is one of the most complex and detailed legal measures that the U.S. Congress has passed in its two centuries of legislative history. The act is composed of ten titles divided into sections detailing how each is to be implemented and what legal responsibilities each entails. The titles of the USAPATRIOT Act are as follows:

- Title I: Enhancing Domestic Security against Terrorism (six articles).
- Title II: Enhanced Surveillance Procedures (twenty-five sections).

- Title III: International Money Laundering and Related Measures (forty-six sections and subsections).
- Title IV: Protecting the Border (twenty-one subsections).
- Title V: Removing Obstacles to Investigating Terrorism (eight sections).
- Title VI: Providing for Victims of Terrorism, Public Safety Officers, and Other Families (eight sections).
- Title VII: Increased Information Sharing for Critical Infrastructure Protection (one section).
- Title VIII: Strengthening the Criminal Law against Terrorism (seventeen sections).
- Title IX: Improved Intelligence (eight sections).
- Title X: Miscellaneous (fifteen sections).

The passage of the USAPATRIOT Act has been praised as an important legal measure in the U.S. war against international terrorism. Title II of the act is to enhance U.S. state and federal law enforcement agencies' surveillance procedures. It gives the police legal authority "to intercept wire, oral, and electronic communications relating to terrorism."[49] The same surveillance power is also granted to police to monitor computer-based activities that the police may deem "abusive." Evidence seized pursuant to these provisions can be used in the prosecution of both terrorist and nonterrorist criminal activities.

Title III of the act is to curtail financing of international terrorism by preventing terrorist organizations from using banks and other financial institutions for money laundering and funds transfer.

Title IV of the act is to secure the borders of the nation against terrorist infiltration. To this end, Title IV aims to gradually reshape the structural security of the borders, which requires new immigration and naturalization policies in relation to how legal aliens are allowed to enter the country. In addition, a new system to better keep track of the movement, activities, and associations of aliens is required, as advised by this title.

Title V of the act is to facilitate investigation of terrorism by removing obstacles that this title has identified. One obstacle is lack of coordination among different agencies that investigate the crime of terrorism. In the past, the Federal Bureau of Investigation (FBI) was responsible for the prevention of domestic acts of terrorism. Other agencies such as the Bureau of Alcohol, Tobacco and Firearms (ATF), the state police, and the Border

Patrol helped the FBI in its antiterrorism investigations. After the events of 11 September 2001, the FBI could no longer carry this heavy burden. Thus, Title V of the USAPATRIOT Act aims to establish a coordinated effort among different law enforcement agencies to combat both domestic and international terrorism at home and abroad.

Title VI of the act aims to compensate the family members of public safety and law enforcement officers who have fallen as victims of terrorism. Besides benefit packages and financial considerations, Title VI also includes amendments to the Victims of Crime Act of 1984.

Title VII of the act aims to organizationally enhance intelligence gathering and sharing between federal, state, and local law enforcement agencies in order to prevent terrorist organizations from carrying out their schemes throughout the nation.

Title VIII of the act aims to strengthen criminal laws against terrorism. Because of its strategic relation to criminal defense and prosecution, I will discuss this title in some detail shortly.

Title IX of the act aims to strengthen intelligence gathering by the Central Intelligence Agency (CIA) under the Foreign Intelligence Surveillance Act of 1978. What is significant about this title is the fact that it allows the CIA to collect intelligence both at home and abroad on international terrorist activities.

Title X of the act is about miscellaneous factors in relation to the whole act.

Title VIII of the USAPATRIOT Act is of special significance for defendant rights. It seeks to enhance criminal law against those defendants who are either suspected of, or charged with, the crime of terrorism. It has seventeen sections, which define the following subjects related to criminal prosecution of terrorism:

- Sec. 801: Terrorist attacks and other acts of violence against mass transportation systems.
- Sec. 802: Prohibition against harboring terrorists.
- Sec. 803: Jurisdiction over crimes committed at U.S. facilities abroad.
- Sec. 806: Assets of [members of] terrorist organizations.
- Sec. 807: Technical clarification relating to provision of material support to terrorism.
- Sec. 807: Definition of Federal crime of terrorism.
- Sec. 808: No statute of limitation for certain terrorism offenses.

- Sec. 809: Alternate maximum penalties for terrorism offenses.
- Sec. 810: Penalties for terrorist conspiracies.
- Sec. 811: Post-release supervision of terrorists.
- Sec. 812: Inclusion of acts of terrorism as racketeering activity.
- Sec. 813: Deterrence and prevention of cyberterrorism.
- Sec. 814: Additional defense to civil actions relating to preserving records in response to Government requests.
- Sec. 816: Development and support of cybersecurity forensic capabilities.
- Sec. 817: Expansion of the biological weapons statute.[50]

The above sections, if implemented successfully, would drastically impact the U.S. criminal defense and prosecution system in several ways.

First, the USAPATRIOT Act has been praised as America's toughening on international terrorism after the tragic events of 11 September 2001 that shook this country to its foundations. President George W. Bush has pledged to hunt down the perpetrators of the 9/11 events to bring them to justice. At the same time, there has emerged a new sense of urgency to secure the borders of the nation. These tragic events showed the vulnerability of U.S. society to a new class of international terrorists who had not infiltrated clandestinely into the country, but quite legally by holding valid visas and work permits as foreign students studying in U.S. colleges and universities. Although a majority of legal aliens are law-abiding, honest, and hard-working individuals, there were some aliens who turned out to be sleeper cells of an enemy who has declared total war on this country. Therefore, it is quite logical to argue that such enemy cells must be hunted down and legally neutralized before they can inflict more terrorism on U.S. society. To this end, the USAPATRIOT Act can be looked upon as a comprehensive piece of legislation that intends to combat terrorism at home and abroad. Because of this aim of the act, those charged with the crime of terrorism would not be accorded the same procedural rights that ordinary criminal defendants are entitled to as they go through the justice process.

Second, according to the text of the USAPATRIOT Act, acts of international terrorism:

(A) involve violent acts dangerous to human life that are a violation of the criminal laws of the United States or of any State, or that would be a criminal violation if committed within the jurisdiction of the United States or of any State;

(B) appear to be intended—

(i) to intimidate or coerce a civilian population;

(ii) to influence the policy of a government by intimidation or coercion; or

(iii) to effect the conduct of a government by mass destruction, assassination, or kidnapping; and

(C) occur primarily outside the territorial jurisdiction of the United States, or transcend national boundaries in terms of the means by which they are accomplished, the persons they appear intended to intimidate or coerce, or the locale in which their perpetrators operate or seek asylum.[51]

Since the act's passage, U.S. law enforcement agencies have cooperated at home and internationally to hunt down, apprehend, or neutralize a good number of Al Qaeda members and sympathizers. A large number of countries have pledged support to, and have cooperated with, the United States in its efforts to dismantle terrorist networks and sleeper cells throughout the world. This cooperation has taken place on every level and ranges from intelligence gathering and sharing to actual investigation of the terrorism suspect to bring him or her to justice.

Despite its successes, civil libertarians, social critics, and legal scholars have raised concerns about the multifaceted intrusive nature of the USAPATRIOT Act, as well as its curtailing the rights of those who are accused of the crime of terrorism. For example, based on the above general definition of international terrorism, anyone who is involved in any type of politically motivated violent act against any government in any part of the world can be portrayed as an international terrorist. In addition, whoever harbors or gives material help to such a person is an accomplice subject to prosecution. It also does not matter as to the nature of the government against which such political violence is perpetrated.

For example, based on the above definition, many third-world political organizations that use politically motivated violence in fighting against oppressive and totalitarian regimes to replace them with pluralistic and parliamentarian forms of governance are as much terrorist entities as those who perpetrated the terrorism of 9/11 in this country. Based on this definition, there is no difference between terrorism perpetrated against innocent civilians in resort areas and legitimate resistance against oppressive, corrupt, and dictatorial regimes in Asia, Africa, Latin America, and in the Middle East. In fact, based on this definition, all American Founding Fathers who fought against the British monarch, King George, and all those American patriots who participated in the Boston Tea Party revolt would become international terrorists.

Another problem of the USAPATRIOT Act is over the question of content. According to the act, anyone who commits acts that are defined as criminal by U.S. criminal codes (be they federal or state) in any part of the world has committed acts of international terrorism. By extension, such a suspect should be extradited to the United States to stand trial. The problem is that many countries do not agree with the U.S. definition of terrorism, nor do they feel any obligation to accept the rhetorical argument of President Bush's famous formula that countries are either with the United States or with the terrorists. For example, there are European, Asian, and Middle Eastern governments, intellectuals, political activists, and human rights organizations that do not agree with U.S. policies concerning the Palestinian-Israeli conflict. There are those who consider Palestinian groups, such as Hamas, Islamic Jihad, Hezbollah, and al-Fatah as political groups who are fighting Israel over the issue of Palestinian statehood. When these organizations use terrorism against innocent Israeli civilians, such acts are condemned. However, the whole movement and its aspirations cannot be characterized as terrorism per se. Countries such as Egypt, Sudan, Syria, Jordan, Lebanon, Saudi Arabia, a number of Persian Gulf sheikhdoms, Pakistan, Malaysia, Singapore, and Indonesia are on record that they do not agree with the U.S. view that these organizations should be treated as terrorist entities. In fact, there are a good number of these Islamic countries that are giving financial and moral support to these groups.

It may sound cliché to say that one man's terrorist is another man's freedom fighter. However, in the 1980s, President Ronald Reagan gave financial and moral support to the Contra guerrillas who were fighting against the Marxist revolutionary regime of the Sandinistas in Nicaragua. The people of this small Central American country had just revolted against the corrupt and dictatorial regime of General Batista who had ruled Nicaragua with an iron fist for two decades. The Contras were a ramshackle force composed of the remnants of the despised Batista's secret service personnel who fought the Sandinista regime tooth and nail and used a lot of violence against civilian populations in the process. However, because it was friendly to the United States and because it was fighting a Marxist regime, Reagan likened the Contras to the American Founding Fathers and praised them as freedom fighters.

The point is how to differentiate between the crime of terrorism and political struggle against third-world dictatorships that inflict violence on their opponents to stay in power. If one is to argue that any form of political violence is equal to terrorism, as the USAPATRIOT Act implies, no place is left for legitimate political violence against corrupt and dictatorial regimes in Asia, Africa, South America, the Middle East, and other places. In fact, these odious regimes would welcome such a definition of terrorism because it would allow them to depict their opponents as terrorists, despite the fact that some of these regimes are known sponsors of state terrorism at home and abroad. For example, the U.S. State Department has identified the Islamic Republic of Iran as the most active sponsor of international terrorism because it gives moral, military, and financial support to a number of Palestinian groups such as Hezbollah, the Islamic Jihad, and Hamas.[52] At the same time the State Department has identified the largest Iranian armed group, the People's Mojahedin Organization of Iran (known as PMOI) as an international terrorist organization whose declared policy is to topple the Islamic Republic in order to replace it with a democratic, parliamentarian, and secular form of governance. This designation is ironic, to say the least, considering that President George W. Bush has declared Iran to be one member of the "axis of evil."

Another problem with the USAPATRIOT Act is over the issue of jurisdiction. The act's definition of terrorism is so vague that any violent act committed in any part of the world can be defined as an act of terrorism. In addition, it is the U.S. federal and state criminal codes that the act adopts as the basis of prosecution, be it from the standpoint of content or procedure. However, many countries have not agreed with the act's definition of terrorism, as previously mentioned. There are many countries that have abolished the death penalty, as well as those that do not have extradition treaties with the United States concerning the crime of terrorism. By the same token, the United States is not a signatory to some of the international treaties whose aim is to serve the cause of justice on an international basis as, for example, the International Court of Justice in the Hague.

The next question is whether the USAPATRIOT Act is riddled with legal inconsistencies over the treatment of those charged with the crime of international terrorism and those who are considered illegal combatants. One big area of concern is whether defendants charged with terrorism are entitled to procedural rights. Legal scholars, civil rights activists, criminal defense lawyers, and criminal justice practitioners have already started expressing concerns over the negative impacts of the USAPATRIOT Act on the U.S. system of criminal defense and prosecution. The largest concern is that the USAPATRIOT Act seems to have made a distinction between the procedural rights that apply to those who have been charged with "traditional"crimes and those charged with acts that the USAPATRIOT Act considers terrorism. Whereas the former enjoy the procedural rights of the Fourth, Fifth, Six, Eighth, and Fourteenth Amendments, those charged with terrorism are not entitled to the full protection of these rights, or at least much confusion exists about the extent to which such rights apply to those charged with terrorism.

To give an example, Title VIII of the USAPATRIOT Act aims to strengthen the criminal laws against terrorism, as discussed above. Besides defining terrorism, the act aims to strengthen U.S. police in their ability to gather incriminating evidence against those suspected of being involved in terrorism. That is why the USAPATRIOT Act has authorized the police to enhance surveillance procedures as expressed in Title II, which has twenty-five sections. The first four sections are of most relevance to our discussion here. These four sections are as follows:

- Section 201. Authority to intercept wire, oral, and electronic communications relating to terrorism.
- Section 202. Authority to intercept wire, oral, and electronic communications relating to computer fraud and abuse offenses.
- Section 203 Authority to share criminal investigation information.
- Section 204. Clarification of intelligence exceptions from limitations on interception and disclosure of wire, oral, and electronic communications.[53]

According to Section 201, the police are authorized to intercept three major routes of communication (wire, oral, and electronic) in relation to terrorism. This includes communications via computer, provided the usage is of a "fraudulent" and "abusive" nature. What does this mean? How can police investigators determine if somebody is using a computer in a fraudulent or abusive manner without actual surveillance of the suspect's computer usage at home, work, or at public venues that provide commercial Internet services?

Naturally, the police must first establish probable cause in order to get a warrant for such intrusive surveillance in relation to one's computer usage. That is why Section 206 authorizes "Roving surveillance authority under the Foreign Intelligence Surveillance Act of 1978."[54] This act was passed by Congress to safeguard U.S. national secrets against espionage. It allowed U.S. intelligence and counterintelligence agencies such as the FBI and CIA to monitor activities of those suspected to be spying for foreign governments. However, the Foreign Intelligence Surveillance Act (FISA) made a distinction between criminal surveillance and intelligence surveillance. Criminal surveillance is conducted when a person is suspected of criminal activities. The authority for such surveillance is established through a warrant obtained from a court. Prior to the passage of the USAPATRIOT Act, incriminating evidence gathered through criminal surveillance could only be used in criminal prosecution of the suspect. The police investigators were not legally allowed to share information obtained through criminal surveillance with the FBI or CIA agents involved in intelligence surveillance. This is no longer the case. Under Section 201 of the USAPATRIOT Act, that distinction between criminal and intelligence surveillance does not apply any more. The fruits of criminal surveillance and investigation are allowed to be utilized in terrorism investigations of the same suspect. Because of this interconnection between the two, local and state police departments are gradually drawn into the war on terrorism. By the same token, intelligence-gathering agencies are in the forefront of America's war on international terrorism.

This cooperation between police and intelligence agencies is capable of enhancing America's ability to counter international terrorism. However, there are those who are rightfully concerned about the social cost of such enhancement. For example, the American Bar Association has asked Congress to conduct oversight on FISA because it appears that intelligence-gathering agencies have already started violating the civil liberties of average citizens in their application of different clauses of the USAPATRIOT Act. At least one FBI memorandum has surfaced revealing illegal surveillance conducted by the agency, including illegal interception of electronic mail, recording of the wrong telephone conversations, and similar acts.[55]

The American Civil Liberties Union and others have petitioned the United States Intelligence Surveillance Court of Review to reconsider the issue of the constitutionality of the restrictions imposed by FISA. The reason for the appeal can be summarized in the following paragraph from the petition:

> Law enforcement officials shall not make recommendations to intelligence officials concerning the initiation, operation, continuation or expansion of FISA searches or surveillance. Additionally, the FBI and the Criminal Division [of the Department of Justice] shall ensure that law enforcement officials do not direct or control the use of FISA procedures to enhance criminal prosecution, and that advice intended to preserve the operation of a criminal prosecution does not inadvertently result in the Criminal Division's directing or controlling the investigation using FISA searches and surveillance toward law enforcement objectives.[56]

In lay person's language, the concern expressed by the petition is that overzealous agents may disregard procedural safeguards of the Constitution and the Bill of Rights in the name of the war on terrorism. Most Americans don't want to give a free reign to intelligence agencies at the expense of our civil liberties that make this country unique among postmodern democratic societies of the world. That is why the FISA Court, reports the Electronic Privacy Information Center, has "chastised" the Department of Justice (DOJ) and the FBI "for providing the tribunal misleading information in 75 cases."[57]

This is not to mention the fact that there are many ways in which one can abuse the public or private computer networks of the country without having anything to do with terrorism. Use of computers for viewing pornographic material is an example of such abuse. However, some civil libertarians would argue that viewing pornographic material on the Internet is hardly an abusive practice, but is a constitutionally protected form of expression. Is this an abuse of a computer network? In some quarters it may be so, but how is such usage a form of terrorism? Section 202 does not seem to go so far as to imply that it is, but police are given the authority to snoop into the computer usage of anyone who is a suspect of the vague crime of international terrorism. Although legal authority for such sweeping surveillance is to be issued by the court, the problem is the arbitrary and vague definition of terrorism that the USAPATRIOT Act has utilized and the fact that the purpose of the act is not only to fight terrorism in the United States, but all over the world as well.

In short, the above are among some of the problems that the post–11 September 2001 war on terrorism initiated by the USAPATRIOT Act faces. The resolution of these problems would require international cooperation and depoliticization of the legislation that aims to define and fight international terrorism in this country and elsewhere.

Conclusion

Criminal defendants enjoy many procedural rights in the U.S. system of criminal prosecution. These rights have been inserted in several amendments in the Bill of Rights section of the U.S. Constitution and have been widened through case law. As observed by one scholar, the list of defendant rights in U.S. criminal prosecution is a long one as follows:

- A right to be assumed innocent until proven guilty
- A right against unreasonable search of person and place of residence
- A right against arrest without probable cause
- A right against unreasonable seizure of personal property
- A right against self-incrimination
- A right to fair questioning by the police
- A right to protection from physical harm throughout the justice process
- A right to an attorney
- A right to trial by jury
- A right to know the charges
- A right to cross-examine prosecution witnesses
- A right to speak and present witnesses

- A right not to be tried twice for the same crime
- A right against cruel or unusual punishment
- A right to due process
- A right to a speedy trial
- A right against excessive bail
- A right against excessive fines
- A right to be treated the same as others, regardless of sex, religious preference, and other personal attributes.[58]

Many scholars of the U.S. system of criminal prosecution argue that each and every one of these procedural rights are important for a system of justice that values human dignity and follows the rule of law in the application of the justice process. These scholars remind us that due process is the basis of the U.S. notion of fairness in dealing with those accused of criminality. To remain faithful to that ideal, the U.S. system of criminal prosecution has to be vigilant against any negative intrusion into the procedural rights of defendants, be it in state or federal forums.

Critics of the U.S. system of criminal prosecution argue that there are too many procedural rights that allow criminal defendants to either get lenient sentences (e.g., through plea bargains) or to go free. The reason for this has a lot to do with the large number of procedural rights that the system has recognized. The longer the list, the more likely that some unintended violation of these procedures may occur. In addition, these rights add to the overall complexity of the U.S. criminal prosecution process. Also, depending on their overall social status, a good number of criminal defendants get punishments that simply do not fit the crime. As discussed in Chapter 1 and above, during the pretrial phase, defendants who can afford bail are not detained in jail waiting for the trial to commence. It is a known fact that pretrial detention adversely impacts a defendant's ability to mount a successful defense during criminal proceedings.

Those criminal defendants represented by competent and experienced criminal defense lawyers are also in a better position to negotiate with the prosecution. It is these defendants who, by and large, get the best plea-bargain agreement with the minimum amount of jail or prison time. At trial, these competent defense lawyers defend their clients in the most vigorous and effective way possible. If their clients are convicted, these defense lawyers are well versed in appealing the trial court's decision to the appellate court. At the appellate level, the defense tries to show that the trial court has erred in the application, or omission, of one or a multitude of procedures. Naturally, the more procedural rights there are, the higher is the probability of the trial court erring in its procedures.

It is because of these endemic problems that the U.S. legal scene is now witnessing the rise of the victims' rights movement, whose battle cry is striking a balance between the rights of the criminal defendant and those of the victims of crime. It is my educated guess that this movement will not dissipate and will assume an important role in setting the agenda for the U.S. system of criminal prosecution in the coming decades. However, it is also possible that this movement will engender its backlash as the prison population rises in response to mandatory sentencing laws and "three strikes and you're out" type legislation. The U.S. has the highest proportional prison population in the world. Huge numbers of nonviolent offenders languish in jail because of minor drug offenses or major addictions for which they do not receive treatment. Even many judges rail against the deprivation of their discretion to make the punishment fit the crime. Because of mandatory sentencing rules, they feel they are mere rubber stamps and dispensible.

Notes

1. David Luban, "The Rights of the Accused Must Be Zealously Protected," in Michael D. Biskup, ed., *Criminal Justice: Opposing Viewpoints* (San Diego, CA: Greenhaven, 1990), p. 63.

2. Gordon Crovitz, "Zealous Protection of the Rights of the Accused Undermines Justice," in Biskup, p. 69.

3. Dean J. Champion, *Police Misconduct in America: A Reference Handbook* (Santa Barbara, CA: ABC-CLIO, 2001), p.2.

4. *Ibid.*, pp. 3–4.

5. Larry K. Gaines and Victor A. Kappeler, *Policing in America,* 4th ed. (Cincinnati, OH: Anderson, 2003), pp. 390–394.

6. John Van Maanen, "The Asshole," in Steven G. Brandl and David E. Barlow, eds., *Classics in Policing* (Cincinnati, OH: Anderson, 1996) pp. 161–180.

7. *Ibid.*, pp. 169–176.

8. Angelo DeLeon and Gary H. Weddle, *A Summary of U.S. Supreme Court Decisions for the Criminal Justice Community* (Flushing, NY: Looseleaf Law, 1998), pp. i–vi.

9. Rolando V. del Carmen and Jeffery T. Walker, *Briefs of Leading Cases in Law Enforcement*, 4th ed. (Cincinnati, OH: Anderson, 2000), p. 176.

10. "*Edwards v. Arizona*," in del Carmen and Walker, pp. 181–183.

11. *Ibid.*, p. 182.

12. Paul Savoy, "The Miranda Rule Undermines the Criminal Justice System," in Biskup, p. 74.

13. Gary Rabe and Dean J. Champion, *Criminal Courts: Structure, Process, and Issues* (Upper Saddle River, NJ: Prentice Hall, 2002), pp. 156–183.

14. Robert J. Samuelson, "Lawyers Hamper the Legal System," in Biskup, p. 152.

15. Stephen Elias, Mary Randolph, Barbara Kate Repa, and Ralph Warner, *Legal Breakdown: 40 Ways to Fix Our Legal System* (Berkeley, CA: Nolo Press, 1991).

16. *Ibid.*, p. 7.

17. *Ibid.*, contents page.

18. Peter Hay, "Lawyers Strengthen the Legal System," in Biskup, pp. 147–151.

19. *Ibid.*, p. 147.

20. Stephanie B. Goldberg, "Playing Hardball," in Richard C. Monk, ed., *Taking Sides: Changing Views on Controversial Issues in Crime and Criminology* 3rd ed. (Guilford, CT: Dushkin Group, 1989), pp. 194–199.

21. Rabe and Champion, *Criminal Courts*, pp. 78–82.

22. James Austin and John Irwin, *It's about Time: America's Imprisonment Binge*, 3rd ed. (Belmont, CA: Wadsworth, 2001), pp. 1–15.

23. Rabe and Champion, p. 80.

24. See, for example, Bennett L. Gershman, "Prosecuting Attorneys Abuse Their Power," in Biskup, pp. 156–162.

25. See, for example, Samuel Walker, "Should Plea Bargaining Continue to Be an Accepted Practice?" in Monk, pp. 132–142.

26. *Ibid.*, p. 132.

27. See, for example, Samuel Walker, *Sense and Nonsense about Crime: A Policy Guide*, 2nd ed. (Pacific Grove, CA: Brooks/Cole, 1989). See also A.W. Alschuler, "The Changing Plea Bargaining Debate," *California Law Review* 69 (1981).

28. Samuel Walker, "Close the Loopholes," in Monk, pp. 134–138.

29. *Ibid.*, p. 136.

30. See, for example, John P. Kenny and Harry W. More, *Principles of Investigation,* 2nd ed. (St. Paul, MN: West, 1994).

31. *Ibid.,* p. 219.

32. See Frank Schmalleger, *Criminal Justice Today: An Introductory Text for the Twenty-First Century,* 6th ed. (Upper Saddle River, NJ: Prentice Hall, 2001) p. 8–9, 61, 141, 154, 155, 297, 334, 343.

33. See Jeffry Reiman, *The Rich Get Richer and the Poor Get Prison: Ideology, Class and Criminal Justice,* 5th ed. (Needham Heights, MA: Allen and Bacon, 1998).

34. See, for example, Samuel Walker, Cassia Spohn, and Miriam DeLone, *The Color of Justice: Race, Ethnicity, and Crime in America,* 2nd ed. (Belmont, CA: Wadsworth, 2000).

35. Richard Markus, "A Theory of Trial Advocacy," *Tulane Law Review* 56 (1981): 95, 97–99, cited in Sanford H. Kadish and Stephen J. Schulhofer, eds., *Criminal Law and Its Processes: Cases and Materials,* 5th ed. (Toronto, Canada: Little, Brown, 1989), pp. 15–16.

36. *Ibid.,* p. 15.

37. See, for example, L. Gordon Crovitz, "Zealous Protection of the Rights of the Accused Undermines Justice," in Biskup, pp. 68–71; Marion S. Rosen, "A Case for Not Defending the Guilty," in Biskup, pp. 143–146; Paul Savoy, "The Miranda Rule Undermines the Criminal Justice System," in Biskup, pp. 72–76.

38. Deborah Kelly, "Victims' Rights Must Be Extended," in Biskup, p. 103.

39. *Ibid.,* p. 102.

40. *Ibid.,* p. 106.

41. Schmalleger, p. 383.

42. *Ibid.*

43. Catherine Bendor, "Victims' Rights Threaten Defendant's Rights," in Biskup, pp. 119–125.

44. *Ibid.,* p. 119.

45. Andrew Karman, *Introduction to Victimology.*

46. Kelly, pp., 104–105.

47. USA PATRIOT Act (H.R. 3162) at http://www.epic.org/privacy/terrorism/hr3162.html.

48. *Ibid.,* p. 2.

49. *Ibid.,* pp. 7–8.

50. Section 2331 definitions at http://www.findlaw.com.

51. See U.S. State Department, "Overview of State-Sponsored Terrorism," from *Patterns of Global Terrorism, 2000,* available at http://usinfo.state.gov/products/pubs/terrornet

52. See USAPATRIOT Act Section 206.

53. See Electronic Privacy Information Center website, "Memo Reveals FBI Wiretap Violations," available at: http://www.epic.org/privact/terrorism/fisa.

54. *Ibid.*, p. 2.

55. Foreign Intelligence Surveillance Court of Review Opinion website, available at: http://www.fas.org/irp/agency/doj/fisa, p. 2.

56. *Ibid.*, p.2.

3

Chronology

This chapter provides a timeline of the most important legal developments in the area of defendant rights in the Anglo-American tradition. Because of the complex nature of the subject, first a number of significant eras are presented, followed by a timeline tracing the origination and application of the relevant legal rights.

Dooms Law Era (560–975)

The dooms law era refers to a relatively long period of time during which the Anglo-Saxon kings of England enacted legal codes, known as dooms, that defined crimes and specified punishments, as well as established criminal defense procedures—though in a very rudimentary format. The era started with the enactment of the dooms of Aethelberht, the king of Kent (560–616), and continued with the dooms of succeeding Anglo-Saxon kings: Hlothhaere and Eadric, (673–686), Wihtraed, (690–725), Alfred (871–901), Edward the Elder (901–942), Athelstan, (924–939), Edmund I, (939–946) and Edgar (959–975).[1] By and large, the pagan dooms law era represents a period during which a secular notion of crime was formed and a rudimentary criminal defense procedure instituted.

Christian Dooms Law Era (975–1215)

By the ninth century, the pagan-secular dooms laws went through important changes the sum total of which initiated a new era that can be characterized as Christianization of the dooms law era; this was a complex development that owed its rationale to a whole-sale conversion from paganism to Christianity. This conversion took place among the Germanic tribes (e.g., Franks, Lombards, Visigoths, Anglo-Saxons, etc.) who, as the "barbarian" conquerors of the western Roman Empire, had established a number of pagan kingdoms in its place. The newly converted Christian kings, under the impression that it was their religious duty to serve God's law, started inserting biblical criminal defense procedures into the once pagan-secular dooms of their predecessors. The shift from a pagan notion of law to a Christian one is noticeable in the dooms of Kings Alfred, Guthrum, and Edward the Elder.

In the introductory section of their respective dooms, each king gives homage to the Christian notion of one God, renounces paganism, and proclaims that the mere existence of a legal code is not enough to prevent common people from committing crime, but that it is the possession of earnest Christian faith in, and the fear of, God that protects the faithful against the lure of criminality.[2]

Inquisition Era (900–1215)

The shift from a pagan-secular dooms to a Christian notion of law led to two developments that had dire consequences for the rudimentary criminal defense procedures that had developed during the pagan era. One was the development of the system of inquisition, the other was the development of so-called diabolical crimes as the wholesale conversion to Christianity gained momentum in the ninth century. The new Christian dooms criminalized pagan rituals by characterizing them as diabolical crimes. (Most of these rituals celebrated aspects of nature and natural forces harking back to the tribal origins of the pagan dooms law era.) As a consequence, the burden of proof shifted from the shoulders of the accuser to those of the accused. Diabolical crimes in turn reinvigorated trial by ordeal under the jurisdictional authority of the Catholic Church, which relied on inquisition to investigate charges of criminality.

Under the inquisition system, one could be accused of having committed diabolical crimes based on what is known as hearsay evidence. Simply put, suspects would be summoned before church authorities to be questioned about their beliefs, lifestyles, or the sincerity of their faith to discover whether the suspects had any associations with evil forces. The proof of innocence (e.g., nonpossession of such powers and noninvolvement in Satanic rites) rested on denial of the charges coupled with acts of repentance—throwing oneself on the mercy of the church, seeking clemency through repentance; if all else failed, submission to the rites of exorcism to escape demonic possession or to trial by ordeal.

Because trial by ordeal involved undertaking tasks entailing excruciating physical pain, many accused of diabolical crimes would simply confess to the charges in order to avoid the ordeal. Thus, the very charge of diabolical crimes would usually seal the fate of the accused as guilty, unless he or she could endure the ordeal unscathed, a very unlikely event. Simply put, diabolical crimes introduced an element of arbitrariness into both prosecution and defense. The fear of trial by ordeal continued until the convention of the Lateran Council of 1215, which prohibited trial by ordeal, among other things, thus taking a big step in the reformulation of defense in criminal trials.

Magna Carta Era (1215–1225)

The term *Magna Carta* means "Great Charter." Scholars have commonly observed that the charter was imposed on the sovereign, King John, by the British nobility in 1215. King John, goes the story, was involved in a dispute with a powerful and external adversary, Pope Innocent III. The king needed the backing of the powerful British nobility at home to prevail against the pope. Because he was not in a position to fight two powerful adversaries at the same time, the king accepted the Magna Carta and signed it as the law of the land. The charter, among other things, restricted the arbitrary powers of the king and of his functionaries in relation to the arrest of persons accused of criminality. Prior to the imposition of the charter, just being charged with a crime could result in confiscation of property. The kings who succeeded John confirmed these changes, despite the fact that the document itself went through some changes in 1216, 1217, and 1225.[3]

The Magna Carta era (1215–1225) changed some of the crime and punishment categories that had been established during the Anglo-Saxon dooms law era. These changes, in turn, led to procedural changes in the defense and prosecution of criminal cases. For example, prior to the enactment of the Magna Carta, the functionaries of the king (e.g., sheriffs, bailiffs, and constables) conducted arrest, search, and seizure activities in an arbitrary manner. In the Magna Carta, legal measures were inserted to curtail abuses arising from such arbitrariness. One such measure was the requirement for a written summons that had to be issued specifying the charges and thus the reason for arrest. To be valid, the summons for arrest had to actually be served on the accused.

Post–Magna Carta Era (1225–1613)

The Magna Carta is considered the first comprehensive legal document to give British citizens charged with crimes a set of legal rights safeguarding their reputations, lives, liberty, and property in a duly convened court of law. However, it was only in the seventeenth century that the legal protections that the charter had provided were officially recognized as applicable to all common British citizens. In 1613, "Sir Edward Coke, Chief Justice under James I," writes one scholar, "held that the Magna Carta guaranteed basic liberties for all British citizens and ruled that any acts of Parliament which contravened common law would be void."[4] In other words, the Magna Carta became a guiding instrument in the hands of British criminal defense lawyers to defend ordinary British citizens charged with having committed a crime in a court of law.

Colonial Era (1613–1776)

With the establishment of the British colonies along the Atlantic shores of the New World, the British ideals of law and justice found their foothold in North America. These ideals, as already discussed in Chapter 1, had their origins in the Magna Carta and were further developed during the post–Magna Carta era. Several of these fine-tuned clauses of the charter found their way into colonial America. In the aftermath of the American Revolution (1776) when the thirteen original colonies united to form the United States of America, these clauses were adapted to the Bill of Rights section of the U.S. Constitution. It is these clauses (variously encoded in Amendments Four, Five, Six, and Eight of the Bill of Rights) that historically provided the genesis of defendant rights in the United States and institutionalized the most comprehensive system of criminal prosecution and defense in the world.

Constitutional Era (1776–1950)

The U.S. Constitution is rightly considered the blueprint for a system of conflict resolution in which defense against charges of criminality is situated. The Bill of Rights has played a significant role in the American style of conflict resolution based on law, justice, and equity. Inspired by the Magna Carta and composed of ten amendments to the Constitution, the Bill of Rights, ratified by the U.S. Congress in 1791, protects basic civil liberties and through its justice amendments (Four, Five, Six, Eight, and Fourteen) facilitates operation of the components of the U.S. criminal justice system including criminal defense and prosecution. These amendments are discussed in some detail in Chapters 1 and 2.

Civil Rights Era (1950–1980)

The civil rights era started in the 1950s and continued until the rise of the new conservative era in the early 1980s. It changed the U.S. criminal defense and prosecution system by subjecting it to the checks and balances of the justice amendments of the Bill of Rights section of the Constitution. This was achieved through a number of landmark decisions that the U.S. Supreme Court made in relation to different aspects of the criminal justice system, including the right to a fair trial. These developments took place during three decades that covered the Warren and Burger Courts, as previously discussed.

New Conservative Era (1980–2001)

In the 1980s, the United States entered a new era that a number of legal scholars have characterized as an era of neo-conservatism. With the appointment of William Rehnquist as chief justice of the Supreme Court, the Court has actively sought to apply the conservative philosophy of crime control through a number of landmark decisions in which exceptions to aspects of due process have been recognized. These exceptions are discussed in Chapters 1 and 2.

Post–11 September 2001 Era

On 11 September 2001, the twin towers of the World Trade Center in New York City became the target of terrorist elements affiliated with Osama Bin Laden's Al Qaeda organization, headquartered in Afghanistan under the protection of the Taliban, who had established an Islamic fundamentalist form of governance there. On the same day, the Al Qaeda terrorists carried out similar attacks in Pennsylvania and Washington, D.C. These tragic events drastically changed U.S. views of security and led to the enactment of the USAPATRIOT Act by Congress. The USAPATRIOT Act has not been fully implemented as of 2004, and some of its sections are set to expire under sunset provisions in 2005 unless extended by Congress. However, the act has raised many concerns in relation to its impacts on civil liberties and prosecution of those accused of the crime of terrorism.

Defendant Rights Timeline

560–
616
A.D.
Aethelberht, the king of Kent, enacts a legal code named dooms that initiates an era of lawmaking in which crime and punishment categories are specified and criminal defense procedures are established in a rudimentary format.[5]

690–
715
King Wihtraed enacts additional clauses to the dooms laws of his predecessors and makes some changes in criminal defense and prosecution procedures. It is decreed that the word of a king or bishop is incontrovertible. Therefore neither is required to take an oath of affirmation in a court of law.

871–
901
King Alfred enacts one of the most comprehensive dooms codes, detailing criminal defense procedures in relation to oath of affirmation and the range of the clemency powers of both the Catholic church and those of the Christian sovereigns.

901–
924

Edward the Elder follows suit. His dooms cover both criminal defense and prosecution in relation to commercial transactions, theft, perjury, or those officials of the state who deny justice to their fellow men.

924–
939

King Athelstan promulgates his dooms laws, which cover crime and punishment categories. It is in Atehlstan's dooms that trial by ordeal is instituted as a distinct form of defense against charges of criminality.

939–
946

With the help of religious authorities, King Edmund I enacts dooms to regulate ecclesiastical and secular approaches to crime and prosecution within the context of the rudimentary defense procedures already established.

1066

The Normans, led by William the Conqueror, take control of the British Isles, initiating significant advances in the development of British common law, which has produced one of the most complex systems of criminal defense and prosecution in history.

1116

Henry I, the son of William the Conqueror, promulgates a legal code that divides crimes into felonies and misdemeanors, establishes judicial districts, and authorizes the office of *shire reeve* (sheriff) to pursue criminals.

1215

Pope Innocent III calls into session the Fourth Lateran Council in Rome to discuss important matters concerning law, justice, and criminal prosecution and defense.

King John of England signs the Magna Carta as the law of the land. Some of the law and justice clauses of the Magna Carta are complementary to some of the canons of the Fourth Lateran Council.

1368

King Edward III (r. 1327–1377) makes a number of decrees enhancing defendant rights in criminal prosecution.[6] He decrees that (1) the clauses of the Magna Carta carry the force of law, (2) no law supersedes the clauses of the Magna Carta, and (3) the text of the law is to be made accessible to the general public for easy reference.[7] The public's knowledge of its legal rights and responsibilities

1368 makes the enforcement of the Magna Carta's provisions
cont. much easier. In due time, the idea that a criminal defendant is entitled to procedural rights becomes an accepted norm in the Anglo-American legal tradition.

1613 Sir Edward Coke, chief justice of England, declares that the "original intent" of the Magna Carta was that all British citizens were entitled to defend their good names, life, limbs, and properties in a court of law, regardless of their social status. This declaration plays an important role in the development of defendant rights in the Anglo-American system.

1628 Sir Edward Coke presents to the House of Commons a document known as the Petition of Right. It enhances civil liberties in Britain by demanding that "no British subject shall be imprisoned without cause."[8]

1637 In the absence of legal counsel, Anne Hutchinson, accused of the crime of heresy, is tried in the Massachusetts Bay Colony, found guilty, and banished from the colony.

1656 Judith Catchpole, a resident of Maryland Colony accused of the crimes of infanticide and witchcraft, is tried before an all-female jury who dismiss all charges against her. This trial sets a precedent for the use of all-female juries in cases involving women's issues.

1689 The British Parliament passes a measure known as the English Bill of Rights whose purpose is to limit the centuries-old doctrine of the "divine right of the king." This doctrine gave absolute power to British monarchs to do whatever they thought expedient. By restricting the sovereign's powers, the English Bill of Rights inadvertently enhances defendant rights in the British system of criminal prosecution. Later, the U.S. legal tradition follows the British Bill of Rights in its version of the U.S. Bill of Rights.

1692 Prosecution of 200 defendants accused of diabolical crimes commences in Salem, Massachusetts. Because most of the defendants are women accused of witchcraft, these trials become known as the Salem Witchcraft Trials. The trials take place in the absence of legal counsel, and twenty-nine are found guilty, of whom nineteen get the sentence of death by hanging, and the rest get lesser sentences and are released upon completion of their terms. Perhaps the unjust and horrendous nature of the Salem Witchcraft Trials influenced the next generation of revolutionaries into humanizing the colonial American legal tradition. As the framers drafted the U.S. Constitution and the Bill of Rights, they emphasized the notion of a fair trial and a penology devoid of cruel and unusual punishment, such as burning at the stake. It is no wonder that in modern U.S. legal thinking, unjust prosecutions are compared to "witch hunts," implying that the accused is being deprived of his or her right to a viable defense.

1761   In what is known as the Writs of Assistance Trial, the extent of British legal authority over search and seizure activities in American colonies is contested. The trial later influences the formation of the protective clauses of the Fourth Amendment.

1765   Sir William Blackstone, a prominent British jurist, judge, and lecturer, publishes his *Commentaries on Laws of England.* His four-volume monumental treatise gives to both the British public and the American colonies a text of the laws of England that is easy to read and to understand its legal procedures and arguments.

1770   The Boston Massacre Trials held in Boston, Massachusetts, uphold the right of self-defense in the colonial American system of criminal defense and prosecution. These trials are remarkable because, despite the charged atmosphere of revolutionary turmoil, they result in the acquittal of a British officer and his soldiers on charges of murder and accessory to murder of American patriots.

1787   The U.S. Constitution is ratified. It is a remarkable legal document that will have a profound influence on the development of defendant rights in the U.S. system of criminal prosecution. One essential feature of the U.S. Constitution is its stress on human dignity. The intellectual thrust of the Constitution is that human dignity can

1787   only be preserved when liberty, rule of law, justice, and
cont.   tolerance of others are respected.

1789   Congress passes the Judiciary Act of 1789, which will play
            an important role in the creation of the U.S. federal court
            structure, as well as in the procedural development of the
            federal system of criminal prosecution and defense.

1791   The U.S. Congress ratifies the four Justice Amendments
            (Fourth, Fifth, Sixth, and Eighth). These amendments
            regularize various aspects of criminal trial and defense
            procedures in the U.S. legal tradition.

1801   The regulatory aspects of the Judiciary Act of 1789 are
            fine tuned. (They will be followed by other judiciary acts
            in 1802, 1817, 1837, 1863, 1867, 1869, and 1925.) These acts
            gradually enhance the manner in which the U.S. criminal
            justice system deals with those accused of federal crimes.

1863   President Lincoln makes the Emancipation Proclama-
            tion, taking the first step toward putting an end to the
            arbitrary nature of the treatment of ex-slaves accused of
            criminality. Although it would be another century until
            African Americans began to approach full and equal
            rights with whites in courts of law, this was a first step in
            recognizing African Americans as citizens governed by
            the U.S. Constitution and Bill of Rights.

1866   The Civil Rights Act passed by Congress recognizes the
            civil rights of Americans regardless of race.

1868   Congress ratifies the Fourteenth Amendment to the U.S.
            Constitution, guaranteeing due process and equal pro-
            tection of the law to all U.S. citizens (whether born in this
            country or naturalized).

1878   The American Bar Association is established in Saratoga
            Springs, New York. It will play a significant role in artic-
            ulating the goals and the professional standards of the
            legal profession, including the rationale for the defense
            of indigent criminal defendants in court.

1891   Congress passes the Circuit Court of Appeal Act. The act will play an important role in bringing order to the federal appeal procedure.

1911   The National Legal Aid and Defender Association is founded. It will become the largest nonprofit organization dedicated to advocacy of equal justice for all Americans who can't afford the cost of legal services in both criminal and civil matters.

1914   Congress passes the Harrison Act criminalizing different aspects of narcotics usage and sale in the United States. The act opens the floodgates for drugs laws and prosecutions with dire repercussions for civil liberties.

1920   The American Civil Liberties Union is founded by civil libertarian activists dedicated to the preservation of the basic civil liberties that the U.S. Constitution and the Bill of Rights have recognized, including for criminal defendants.

1925   Congress passes the Judiciary Act of 1925, which enhances the development of procedural rights for defendants in federal cases.

1937   President Franklin D. Roosevelt presents his Court Reform Proposal to Congress. The proposal aims at reforming the federal court system, but is rejected by the Senate on the ground that it allows the president free reign to fill vacant federal judgeships based on political considerations rather than judicial merits.

    The National Lawyers Guild is founded in New York City. It is a nonprofit, progressive association of lawyers dedicated to the American ideal of justice for all regardless of race, gender, religion, or economic status. The association believes that justice is inherently linked to the social and economic structure of U.S. society and therefore promotes the civil rights of the working men and women of this country.

1946   The International Association of Democratic Lawyers (IADL) is created in Paris, France, to achieve the aims articulated in the Charter of the United Nations. It will continuously urge the United Nations to pass internationally binding legislation against the violation of human rights throughout the world and particularly encourage the formation of independent judiciaries adhering to the rule of law in developing countries.

1948   The General Assembly of the United Nations passes a resolution expressing the need for an International Criminal Court (ICC) to prosecute crimes whose commission impacts the whole of humanity.

1950   Congress passes the Subversive Activities Control Act allowing U.S. secret services to obtain a court's permission to clandestinely monitor those suspected of carrying out subversive activities in the United States. It leads to the abuse of civil liberties of political activists and parties who embrace unpopular views and ideologies.

1953   President Dwight D. Eisenhower nominates Earl Warren as chief justice of the Supreme Court. The Warren Court plays a significant role in steering the U.S. criminal justice system in the direction of due process.

1956   The U.S. Supreme Court decides *Ullmann v. United States,* sustaining the Immunity Act of 1950 in relation to self-incrimination, ruling that a witness who has been given immunity from prosecution may not use his or her Fifth Amendment privilege against self-incrimination.

1957   In *Mallory v. United States,* the Supreme Court reverses the conviction of Mallory because his due process rights had been violated by the police. The police are faulted for interrogating Mallory without informing him of his constitutional rights and for detaining him for a long period of time between arrest and arraignment.

1958   In *Trop v. Dulles,* the Supreme Court rules that the Eighth Amendment's prohibition of cruel and unusual punishment applies to those who desert the ranks of the U.S. armed forces during time of war.

The National Association of Criminal Defense Lawyers is founded as a permanent organization whose primary purpose is to facilitate the representation of those accused of crime.

1960   In *Elkins v. United States*, the Supreme Court abandons the so-called silver platter doctrine that allowed the federal courts to utilize evidence illegally gathered by state authorities.

1961   The Supreme Court decides in *Mapp v. Ohio* that evidence obtained through illegal search and seizure activities cannot be admitted into criminal trials in state courts.

In *Hoyt v. Florida*, the Supreme Court affirms a Florida law excluding women from jury duty on the grounds that it distracted women from their motherhood and home-making responsibilities. The Court rejects the plaintiff's argument that such an exclusion violates the equal protection guarantee of the Fourteenth Amendment.

1962   In *Robinson v. California*, the Supreme Court rules that the state of California violated the Eighth Amendment's ban on cruel and unusual punishment by making addiction to narcotics a criminal offense.

1963   In the landmark case of *Gideon v. Wainwright*, the Supreme Court rules that the due process clause of the Fourteenth Amendment applies to both state and federal criminal defendants.

The Supreme Court decides in *Kerr v. California* that in both state and federal search and seizure activities the legal standard is the same as that stipulated by the Fourth Amendment.

1964   The Supreme Court decides *Escobedo v. Illinois*, ruling that the Sixth Amendment right to counsel applies to

1964   criminal defendants interrogated by the police, and that
cont.   the police must inform suspects of that right. The Court
further rules that confessions obtained by the police
without a suspect's knowledge of that right may not be
used in trial proceedings.

1965   The President's Commission on Law Enforcement and
Administration of Justice is formed to study crime and
justice in America.

In *Pointer v. Texas,* the Supreme Court rules that the right
to confront and cross-examine witnesses, as stipulated
by the Sixth Amendment, applies to defendants prosecuted in state court because the due process clause of the
Fourteenth Amendment applies to the states.

The Supreme Court issues its ruling in *Griffin v. California*
that a criminal defendant's Fifth Amendment right
against self-incrimination is violated when a presiding
judge or prosecuting attorney suggests that the defendant's failure to testify in his or her own behalf is evidence of guilt.

1966   In the landmark case of *Miranda v. Arizona,* the Supreme
Court rules that suspects in police custody must be
informed of their constitutionally protected rights
against self-incrimination.

1967   The Supreme Court decides in *Klopfer v. North Carolina*
that a criminal defendant's right to a speedy trial as stipulated by the Sixth Amendment applies to state as well
as federal prosecutions.

President Lyndon B. Johnson appoints Thurgood Marshall to the Supreme Court as the first African American
on the nation's highest bench. He played a central role in
the Civil Rights movement and will be considered one of
the most important advocates of civil liberties and due
process during his long tenure as an associate justice
(1967–1981).

Congress passes the Omnibus Crime Control and Safe Street Acts, which leads to the establishment of the Law Enforcement Assistance Administration that initiates much research into the operational dynamics of the U.S. criminal justice system, including criminal prosecution and defense.

In *Katz v. United States,* the Supreme Court rules that any form of electronic surveillance of a criminal defendant is part of the search and seizure activities subject to the requirements of the Fourth Amendment.

Addressing the issue of the right to counsel in police lineups for identification purposes, the Supreme Court in *United States v. Wade* rules that a criminal defendant is constitutionally entitled to the presence of an attorney at a lineup in which the accused is ordered to participate.

The President's Commission on Law Enforcement and Administration of Justice issues its report entitled "The Challenge of Crime in a Free Society," which points to the structural and procedural weaknesses of the U.S. criminal justice system in effectively fighting crime and applying justice. The report leads to many reform initiatives for the criminal justice system in this country.

1968   The Supreme Court decides *Duncan v. Louisiana,* ruling that a defendant facing charges of serious crime in a state court has the constitutional right to a jury trial as stipulated by the Sixth and Fourteenth Amendments.

In *Terry v. Ohio,* the Supreme Court sets a new legal standard as to what constitutes "reasonableness" in police search and seizure activities, ruling that it is legal for police to "frisk" a suspect if the officer believes a crime is being committed. The Court further rules that frisking under these circumstances does not violate a suspect's Fourth Amendment protections.

The Mexican American Legal Defense and Education Fund is created as a national organization dedicated to promoting and safeguarding the legal and educational

1968
cont.

needs of Mexican Americans. It will provide valuable legal help to indigent Mexican American defendants entangled with gang and illicit drug-related activities.

1969

The Law Enforcement Assistance Administration (LEAA) is formed to help U.S. law enforcement agencies acquire the latest technologies and strategies for effective law enforcement. Inadvertently, the LEAA changes criminal defense procedures by introducing a wide range of evidence-gathering techniques and procedures.

President Richard Nixon appoints Warren E. Burger as chief justice of the Supreme Court. Under Burger, although the Court does not ignore the importance of due process, it nevertheless applies a more conservative view in regard to the extent of due process.

The Supreme Court decides *Benton v. Maryland,* ruling that the Fifth Amendment's protection against double jeopardy applies to the states through the due process clause of the Fourteenth Amendment.

In *Chimel v. California,* the Supreme Court rules that if a search is incidental to the arrest of a suspect, the police are allowed to conduct a warrantless search of the suspect's immediate surroundings. However, the high Court also rules that there is a limit to what is legally permissible in such warrantless searches.

1973

The Law Enforcement Assistance Administration establishes the Exemplary Projects to help law enforcement agencies better fight urban crime and gather incontrovertible evidence to expedite criminal defense and prosecution procedures. These include undercover crime units of police departments, hidden camera projects in large cities, and silent witness projects.

1974

President Nixon appoints Harry Blackmun to the Supreme Court. Blackmun will play an important role in the enhancement of civil liberties and due process rights, despite the fact that he was appointed as a legal conservative.

1978   The National Archive of Criminal Justice Data is created as a crime and justice clearinghouse under the supervision of the Bureau of Justice Statistics, an agency of the U.S. Department of Justice. The archive provides a wealth of information about crime and justice in this country including data on various aspects of criminal defense.

1984   President Ronald Reagan appoints Justice William Rehnquist to be chief justice of the U.S. Supreme Court. Under Chief Justice Rehnquist, the high Court starts chipping away at some of the more liberal and controversial aspects of due process.

The Supreme Court decides *Nix v. Williams,* applying a much more restricted standard for the exclusionary rule to keep incriminating evidence gathered by the police through questionable methods out of court.

The Supreme Court decides *United States v. Leon,* applying the so-called good-faith exception to the exclusionary rule to hold that if it can be established that police acted in good faith, illegally obtained evidence can be used in a criminal prosecution.

1989   The Association of Federal Defense Attorneys is established to represent the professional interests of those involved in the defense of those charged with federal crimes.

The International Criminal Court is officially inaugurated by the United Nations. Its legal jurisdiction covers the so-called core crimes. These include genocide, crimes against humanity, and war crimes.

1993   Equal Justice America is established as a nonprofit corporation to enhance legal representation of low-income and indigent defendants in both civil and criminal cases.

1997   The Innocence Project Northwest is initiated at the University of Washington Law School. It is a nonprofit project developed by a group of lawyers and forensic patholo-

1997
cont. gists to help promote more scientifically accurate determinations of the guilt or innocence of criminal defendants.

2001 Congress passes the USAPATRIOT Act. It is praised as an important legal measure in the U.S.-led war against international terrorism. However, civil libertarians, social critics, and legal scholars raise concerns about the intrusive nature of the act, as well as its curtailing the rights of those accused of terrorism.

2002 The Foundation for Criminal Justice is established as a nonprofit affiliate of the National Association of Criminal Defense Lawyers. It aspires to expedite the organizational support of basic fairness in the U.S. criminal justice system.

Notes

1. Paul Halsall, *Medieval Source Book: The Anglo-Saxon Dooms, 560–975* available at http://www.fordam.edu/halsall/source/560–975dooms/html, 1998, pp. 1–34.
2. "The Laws of Alfred, Guthrum, and Edward the Elder" in Halsall, pp. 12–16.
3. Dick A. E. Howard, *Magna Carta: Text and Commentary*, rev. ed. (Charlottesville: University Press of Virginia, 1998), p. 24.
4. Shmalleger, Frank, *Criminal Justice Today: An Introductory Text for the 21st Century*, 6th ed. (Upper Saddle River, NJ: Prentice Hall, 2001), p. 121.
5. Halsall, pp. 1–34.
6. Howard, pp. 24–25.
7. *Ibid.*
8. "Petition of Right," in the *Columbia Electronic Encyclopedia*, available at http://www.bartleby.com.

4

A World Perspective

This chapter provides a brief sketch of the historical development of defendant rights in four legal systems from antiquity to the present. These are the ancient Middle Eastern legal traditions; the Greco-Roman legal tradition; the British common law tradition; and the Islamic legal tradition.

This outline includes each legal system's notion of defense in criminal prosecution. Next to the Anglo-American system, Islam's legal tradition is discussed in the most detail. This is important because at the present time a certain radical view of Islam has assumed a prominent place in the world. There are scholars who argue that radical Islam is antagonistic to Western values, especially to Western secular laws. On the contrary, I argue that these four legal traditions are generically linked to one another. This means that all traditions share similar views, legal doctrines, and procedures. However, despite these commonalities, there are important differences between them that I also discuss in this chapter. Because the Anglo-American legal tradition has produced the most comprehensive list of the rights of criminal defendants, as well as an elaborate system of criminal prosecution, it is this tradition that I treat as the model and yardstick for comparison. Many developing countries in Asia, Latin America, the Middle East, and the ex-Soviet republics of Eastern Europe are emulating the Anglo-American legal tradition as the twenty-first century begins.[1]

Ancient Middle Eastern Legal Tradition

It is a known historical fact that in both the ancient and medieval empires that formed in the Old World there were court systems that attended to the business of crime and punishment. These systems allowed those accused of crime to defend themselves. Written documents from the past show that in the ancient empires of the Middle East, North Africa, the Mediterranean basin, and East Asia different legal systems existed. One legal scholar has produced "the timetable of world legal history,"[2] which includes the following timeline:

- 2350 B.C.: Urukagina's Code
- 2050 B.C.: Ur Nammu's Code
- 1850 B.C.: The Earliest Known Legal Decision
- 1700 B.C.: Hammurabi Code
- 1300 B.C.: The Ten Commandments
- 1280 B.C.: The Laws of Manu
- 621 B.C. Draco's Law
- 600 B.C.: Lycergu's Law
- 550 B.C.: Solon's Law
- 536 B.C.: The Book of Punishments
- 450 B.C.: The Twelve Tablets[3]

In the next sections, synopses of some of the more important ancient legal codes are presented. The purpose of this part of the chapter is to establish that from very early on, even the primitive ancient legal systems recognized the procedural importance of defense against charges of criminality. The difference between ancient or premodern legal systems and modern ones is in the scope of defendant rights that they have recognized. Modern legal traditions have recognized a wide range of procedural rights and have practiced them in criminal prosecutions.

Ancient Egypt

Egypt, located in the northeastern corner of North Africa, constitutes one of the oldest known human civilizations. Its long history can be divided into two distinct periods known as the pharaonic and the Islamic periods. The term *pharaonic* signifies the historical period when local kings, known as the pharaohs, ruled Egypt. This period extends as far back as the fourth millennium B.C., during which time Egyptian pharaohs created large empires as, for example, under Ramses II (c. 1300–1234 B.C.), conquering other societies in the Middle East and North Africa. These conquests brought wealth and pride to Egypt. However, with the passage of time, Egypt started to decline and was conquered by rival powers such as the Assyrians, the Babylonians, the Persians, and the Greco-Romans. With the conquest of Egypt by Muslim Arabs in 641 A.D., Egypt went through a complex Islamization process and was transformed into one of the most important Arab-Islamic countries in the Middle East region.

Egyptians believed that their reigning pharaohs were divine entities and therefore they wholeheartedly obeyed their wishes and considered their words the law of the land. As observed by one scholar of the subject, "Since Egypt was blessed with having on earth a god as a king, law proceeded from his mouth, always vitally renewed, and no codification was necessary or even proper."[4]

Despite the many written documents that have reached us showing different aspects of Egyptian life under the pharaohs, no complete document depicting the criminal procedures followed under the pharaonic legal system is among them. There are reasons, however, to believe that the pharaohs allowed criminal defendants to appeal to their presumed "divine" sense of justice and ask for reconsideration of the verdict, or for clemency. This was contingent on whether such defendants enjoyed the social status of free men as against being slaves. The lives and limbs of the slaves were at the mercy of their masters, who could inflict any type of punishment on them, including death.

Egyptian legal thinking was based on what a scholar of the subject has characterized as, "a commonsense view of right and wrong, following the codes based on the concept of Ma'at."[5] Ma'at, according to the Egyptian belief system, was the base of four elements that comprised "truth, order, balance and justice in the universe."[6]

In Egyptian legal thinking, crime was considered a disruptive element. Crime was believed capable of disturbing the ideal balance that the Egyptians believed held the universe together. Thus, it was the pharaohs who were deemed responsible for maintaining the universal balance through their just reign. Therefore, all Egyptians of free status were legally bound to obey the pharaohs so that an ideal social and legal balance could be achieved in Egypt, the center of the universe.

Under the pharaohs, all free Egyptians were considered equal before the law. Minor cases were decided by local councils of elders, whereas capital ones were referred to "Mansions," somewhat equivalent to our modern magistrates.[7]

Because the pharaohs were considered divine entities, they were also the ultimate judges in the realm. From the remnants of documents that have reached us, it seems that anyone found guilty of a capital crime could appeal to the pharaoh's sense of justice and eternal wisdom. If the pharaoh decided that the person was innocent, he could exonerate the accused of all charges and set him or her free. However, if the pharaoh concurred with the guilt of the accused, as determined by the lower court (e.g., the Mansions), the verdict would be carried out against the convict.

In capital cases, punishments were severe and of a collective nature. This means that punishment applied not only to the culprit, but to his or her entire family as well. From the available remnants, we know that criminal law under the pharaohs sanctioned the following categories of crimes and punishments:

- tomb robbery: death penalty
- homicide: various forms of death penalty, banishment, and exile
- stealing or embezzling of goods: monetary restitution, fine, or corporal punishment
- indebtedness: imprisonment.[8]

Egypt was conquered by Alexander the Great in 332 B.C. Under Alexander's general, Ptolemy, the Egyptian elite started adopting some aspects of Greek culture and institutions, which included a new philosophy of law and justice more in line with Greco-Roman ideals. As a result, a more systematic procedural defense against charges of criminality developed. Later, under the Romans, Egyptian legal thinking went through further adaptations of the Greco-Roman tradition. With the Muslim conquest, Egypt went through a wholesale Islamization process whereby the Greco-Roman legal system was replaced by an Islamic one that continued until the early decades of the twentieth century, to be replaced by modern secular codes and procedures.

Ancient Babylonia: The Hammurabi Code

Unlike the Egyptian pharaohs, the rulers who rose to power in various kingdoms in Mesopotamia (the fertile land between the Euphrates and Tigris rivers in modern Iraq) were all considered mortal beings. These sovereigns, nevertheless, were quite powerful because they were portrayed as the earthly representatives of deities. Thus Babylonian kings had the authority to promulgate the likes of the Urukagina, the Ur-Nammu, and the Hammurabi Codes that we mentioned above. Of these, the Hammurabi Code is the one that has reached us in a more complete form and has had a remarkable impact on some aspects of the Anglo-American legal tradition.

The Hammurabi Code, composed of a preface and 282 articles of law, was promulgated by King Hammurabi, who ruled the Babylonian Empire around 1700 B.C. In the epilogue of the code, Hammurabi states that he received instructions from the sun god to establish the rule of law and justice in his realm. Hammurabi also describes his duties as a lawgiver, stating in the epilogue that, "When Marduk [the chief god] commissioned me to guide the people aright, to direct the land, I established law and justice in the language of the land, thereby promoting the welfare of the people."[9]

The 282 articles of law in the code cover subjects related to commerce and trade, family and social relationships, and crime and punishment procedures. Of interest to our subject are those articles that deal with the charges of criminality, false witness, and evidentiary rules in criminal prosecution covered in Articles 1 through 24. For example, Article 3 states that: "if anyone bring (sic) an accusation of any crime before the elders, and does not prove what he has charged, he shall, if it be a capital offense charged, be put to death."[10] Other articles depicting criminal acts of stealing and witnessing of crime are mentioned in Articles 4, 6, 7, 8, 9, 10, 11, and 12 of the code.[11]

Article 5 of the code is about the legal procedure through which a judge is to resolve a case. This article also provides an answer in case a judge has erred in his judgment of a case. It reads: "If a judge try (sic) a case, reach (sic) a decision, and present (sic) his judgment in writing; if later error shall appear in his decision, and it be through his own fault, then he shall pay twelve times that fine set by him in the case, and he shall be publicly removed from the judge's bench, and never again shall he sit there to render judgment."[12]

Article 9 is one of the longest in the code. It deals with the subject of false claim to property and fraudulent witness on behalf of the claimant. Article 9 asks what happens if merchandise is lost, but later is found in the possession of someone else.

Should we assume that the crime of theft has taken place? This is an important legal question because the accused may claim that he or she has purchased it from a merchant and may in fact be able to bring before the court the seller as his or her witness. In addition, Article 9 advises that in such a situation, "The judge shall examine their testimony—both of the witnesses before whom the price was paid, and of the witnesses who identify the lost article on oath."[13] It is only then that punishment would apply to the party found guilty of fraud.

The Hammurabi Code has been praised for its attempts to put legal equity in the ancient system of criminal prosecution and punishment that prevailed in the Middle East region. Legal equity means consistency in the application of law and punishment. Prior to the issuance of the Hammurabi Code, the notion and practice of legal equity was not universally observed in criminal prosecutions. In fact, in most of the pre-Hammurabi period, law and justice applied in an arbitrary manner. Judges took bribes and showed bias and favoritism in rendering judgments. As a general rule, harsh, inconsistent, unjust, cruel and unusual, and collective punishments applied to those who did not belong to powerful clans and families. The promulgation and application of the Hammurabi Code changed this situation by stressing the principle of "an eye for an eye, a tooth for a tooth," in relation to punishment. Therefore, it can be argued that King Hammurabi was perhaps the first lawgiver in history to install equity in the application of punitive justice.

The Hammurabi Code has played a very important role in the development of the notion of legal equity in three monotheistic faiths that arose in the Middle East: Judaism, Christianity, and Islam. These religions gave primacy to the Hammurabi Code's principle of "an eye for an eye" and thus prohibited the use of arbitrary and collective punishments, stressing instead some measure of equity in the application of punishment. The code's stress on legal equity found a central place in the Jewish Torah, the Christian Gospel, and the Islamic Koran, to be discussed shortly.

Babylonia was later conquered by the Persian emperor Cyrus the Great in 539 B.C. It remained an integral part of the Persian empire until the Arab conquest of Iran in 650 A.D. Like Egypt and Persia, the Islamized Babylonia now called *Al-Jazirah* (Iraq) was transformed into a powerful center for the spread of Islamic civilization and the Islamic legal tradition.

Ancient Israel: The Ten Commandments

Israel, the birthplace of the Jewish faith, has four thousand years of history. The Jewish people trace their roots to the patriarch Abraham who lived around 1812 B.C. Abraham is considered the founder of monotheism, which is belief in one universal god. Jews, Christians, and Muslims all give homage to Abraham as the founder of monotheism, and that is why there are doctrinal similarities between the Jewish, Christian, and Islamic concepts of law and justice.

It is beyond the scope of this book to deal with the life of the prophet Moses, whose name is almost synonymous with the Ten Commandments. Suffice it to state that Moses lived around 1392 B.C. The Jewish Bible declares Moses a prophet of God (Yahweh) whose charge was to rescue Jews from the bondage of slavery in Egypt. According to the story, once Yahweh helped Moses to deliver the Jews from bondage, he summoned Moses to Mount Sinai (located in the Sinai Peninsula in modern Egypt) to give him the Ten Commandments.

The Ten Commandments can be looked upon as the basis of criminal law in the ancient Middle Eastern legal traditions. The thrust of the Ten Commandments is that there are social acts that are in and of themselves evil. In modern criminology we call such acts *malum in se*, a Latin term describing acts that are evil by their very nature such as murder, rape, thievery, and false witness. As observed by one scholar,[14] the Ten Commandments comprise the Torah part of the Jewish Bible whereby God commanded Moses saying:

1. You shall have no other god before me;
2. You shall not make for yourself an idol, whether in the form of anything that is in heaven or above, or that is on the earth beneath, or that is in water under the earth;
3. You shall not make wrongful use of the name of the LORD, your God, for the LORD will not acquit anyone who misuses his name;
4. Remember the Sabbath day, and keep it holy;
5. Honor your father and your mother;
6. You shall not murder;
7. You shall not commit adultery;
8. You shall not steal;
9. You shall not bear false witness against your neighbor;

10. You shall not covet your neighbor's house; you shall not covet your neighbor's wife, or male or female slave, or ox, or donkey, or anything that belongs to your neighbor.[15]

Although this list is customarily presented as the Ten Commandments, the text of the biblical document contains other clauses pertaining to other aspects of law, justice, testimony, and punishment. For example, there are clauses that regulate the affairs of slaves, the incurring of debt, and marital relationships. There are also clauses that deal with crimes such as assault and battery, kidnapping, cursing, and bestiality.

Of special significance are the clauses that deal with charges of criminality and false witness. One clause addressing judges mandates the following:

- You shall not spread a false report.
- You shall not join hands with the wicked to act as a malicious witness.
- You shall not follow a majority in wrongdoing: when you bear witness in a lawsuit, you shall not side with the majority so as to pervert justice; nor shall you be partial to the poor in a lawsuit.[16]

Other clauses in the expanded version of the Commandments warn the faithful not to pervert justice, sternly warning against taking bribes or siding with wrongdoers. The Jewish Torah, because of its Ten Commandments, has exerted a powerful impact on the Western legal tradition because it has provided the theoretical basis of what is known as natural law. Natural law, the opposite of positive law, has its foundation in the "Doctrine of Creation," which is the basis of the three monotheistic religions of Judaism, Christianity, and Islam. Positive law has its foundation in a human-based rationality and logic in relation to creating rules and regulations. In the monotheistic religions, there is one universal and all-powerful God who is looked upon as the creator of the universe, including law. The gist of natural law is that God has provided human beings with a set of universal laws to regulate our social affairs. Thus, when the Torah commands Moses that, "thou shalt not murder," or "rape," or "injure," or "covet the possessions of others," these injunctions are not just for the Israelites, but apply to the whole of humanity because these are evil deeds whose commission hurts humanity regardless of race, gender, and ethnicity. These injunctions remain valid through eternity because no civilized society has ever allowed, or will ever allow, these acts to go unpunished, a legal philosophy adhered to by the Anglo-American legal tradition.

Ancient Persia: The Judge

Persia (modern-day Iran) is one of the oldest human civilizations. Persians belong to the Indo-European stock of people who migrated from the northern European steppes into the southern Asian grazing lands around 1000 B.C. In due time a faction of these Indo-European tribes arrived in the Iranian plateau to establish several world-class empires such those of the Achaemenids (550–330 B.C.), the Selucid-Partihans (331 B.C.–224 A.D.) and the Sasanids (224–642. A.D.). Persia was conquered by Muslim Arabs in the mid-seventh century A.D. to become one of the most important civilizing factors in the Islamic world.

The Persian emperors were called *Shahan-shahs,* which means "kings of kings." Like their Egyptian, Assyrian, and Babylonia counterparts, the Persian emperors had immense wealth and power and thus ruled with absolute impunity over their subjects. At the height of the Persian empire, they ruled over a vast empire that included more than fifty nations of the Old World. Pre-Islamic Persians believed in the Zoroastrian religion founded by the prophet Zarathustra, whose motto was "good deed, good thought, and good word." Thus, a true Zoroastrian was duty bound to adhere to these principles. Of special significance were the principles of righteousness, justice, and telling the truth. Founded on these principles, the Persian legal system enabled a number of competent Persian kings to gradually build a complex legal tradition. However, it was during the Sasanid period (224–642) that a distinct Persian system of criminal law, justice, and punishment reached its zenith. With the conquest of Iran by Muslim Arabs in 650 A.D., Persian legal procedures and concepts were gradually adapted to the Islamic legal tradition.

The Persian system of criminal prosecution was under the influence of the Zoroastrian religion and its priestly class, known as the *Mobads.* In criminal trials much emphasis was placed on reaching a verdict of guilt or innocence through oath-based testimony. The system had a penchant for resolving conflicts on the principle of justice, a concept and ideal that occupied an important place in the larger Persian culture and social psychology.[17] One legal scholar argues that the Persian system of criminal law resembled the Code of Hammurabi.[18] Besides adjudication of guilt through criminal law, the system followed the rationale of the Code of Hammurabi and allowed trial by ordeal.

Trial by ordeal has a long history in the world. In trial by ordeal, the guilt or innocence of the accused is determined by his or her reaction to corporal pain. If the defendant was capable of enduring such pain, he or she would be exonerated of the charges of criminality.

In the Persian legal system, and especially under the Sasanid kings, the institution of judgeship reached its most evolved form. The judges played a significant role in the adjudicative process. Thus, it was the emperor himself who appointed judges to the bench. Judges who accepted bribes faced the most horrendous form of capital punishment. Herodotus, the renowned Greek historian contemporaneous with the Achaemenids in Persia, reports examples of the Persian style of swift punishment applied to corrupt judges. In one, a judge convicted of corruption was immediately executed and then skinned. The skin was then tanned, and the king ordered it to be spread on the next judge's bench so that he, who happened to be the executed judge's son, would learn a lesson from his father's fate.[19] This stress on the importance of the judge as the central figure in the adjudicative process was passed on to both the Islamic and the Greco-Roman legal traditions.

The Greco-Roman Legal Tradition

The legal tradition founded on Greco-Roman law, also known as civil law, is one of the oldest. As the name implies, this tradition has combined the legal heritage of the ancient Greeks with that of the Romans. Synopses of each are given below, considering that some of the legal doctrines created by the Greco-Romans have had lasting impacts on the Anglo-American legal tradition.

Ancient Greece: Codes of Law

The ancient Greeks played a very important role in the development of the Greco-Roman system. The Helens, as they were known, were part of the Indo-European stock of tribes who migrated from the northern plains of Europe to the shores of the Mediterranean basin and established city-states throughout the Hellenistic world. In due time some of these city-states such as Athens, Salonika, and Sparta contributed tremendously to the civilization of the ancient world. Among such contributions, the Athenian notion of law and justice is of interest to our discussion.

The Greek legal system developed in several stages.[20] Between 900 to 700 B.C., the legal system was of a primitive nature. Laws were not codified yet, and most disputes were settled through mediation by councils of elders. Punishments were carried out by the family of the wronged party against a defendant found guilty of crime. It was during 621–550 B.C. that the Greek legal system gradually formed under Draco, Lycergu, and Solon.[21]

Draco was a king of Athens and is renowned for his law concerning homicide and the severe punishments that he designed for those who committed it. The term *draconian* means "harsh," "severe," or "cruel" and comes from Draco's legal heritage. Draco's laws were codified and most of them were incorporated into Solon's laws, to be discussed shortly.[22]

Lycergu was the king of Sparta, a Greek city-state located in Macedonia. Spartans were known for their military prowess. Unlike Draco, whose laws were codified, Lycergu's laws were not written down, but were passed orally from one generation to another. Most of Lycergu's laws concerned military matters, how to prepare children for military training, and the art of warfare.[23] As such, it is plausible to propose that they provided some procedural defense measures against charges of cowardice and treason.

Solon, succeeding Draco in 594 B.C., is the most renowned among the Greek lawgivers. Solon's tort laws were built upon those of Draco. The legal definition of tort is "any one of various, legally recognized, private injuries or wrongs which do not arise as the result of a breach of contract."[24] This is the modern definition of tort, which differentiates tort from crime. Crime is any wrong that has been proscribed by the criminal code and is punishable by the state. Under Draco, many wrongs, including murder, were considered torts. Therefore, it was tort law, rather than the criminal law, that regulated the legal affairs of Athens under Draco.

Solon, however, gradually changed these Draconian legal measures by creating four basic sets of laws. These were (1) tort laws, (2) family laws, (3) public laws, and (4) procedural laws. Solon's tort laws were similar to Draco's. Family laws covered issues concerning marriage, divorce, inheritance, child custody, and responsibilities of parents towards children and vice versa. Public laws covered the structure of the city government, services that the government provided for the public, the manner in which public officials were selected to office, and how they attended to their duties. Procedural laws provided guidelines for judges such as how to apply the law to any legal proceedings, how to determine the guilt or innocence of a defendant accused of criminality, and what witness testimonies to consider.[25]

The gradual application of Solon's four sets of laws led to the rise of legal expertise among Greek judges and prosecutors. Based on this expertise, judges and prosecutors applied the law to the facts in cases alleging violation of Solon's laws. For example, in ancient Greek city-states, one who studied family law became an expert in that area. Whenever family-related matters were to be judged, those who were known for expertise in family law would appear to testify in court. Simply put, by codifying laws that applied to different sets of social relationships, Solon took the first step in the professionalization of law among the Greeks.

Under Solon a number of courts were created to try those accused of crime. The earliest known court in ancient Greece was the *Areiopagos.* This court started as a special tribune to adjudicate the crime of homicide. The jurisdiction of the *Areiopagos* gradually extended to other crimes, making the *Areiopagos* a court of general jurisdiction. Finally, it was reorganized into four different categories known as:

- The *Prutaneion* court tried cases in which the death of a human being was caused by either animals or inanimate objects.
- The *Palladion* court dealt with involuntary homicide or the killing of non-Greek citizens.
- The *Delphinion* court dealt with justifiable homicide.
- The *Phreatto* court dealt with the criminality of those serving terms of banishment.[26]

With the conquest and annexation of Greece by the Roman Empire, the main ideas and legal doctrines behind these court structures were adapted to the Roman notion of law and justice—thus the rationale for calling it the Greco-Roman legal tradition.

Ancient Rome: The Rule of Law

Roman legal heritage was built upon three sets of laws that emerged at different times in the evolution of the Roman empire. These were (1) the laws of seven legendary kings who reigned between 753–510 B.C., (2) the laws of the Twelve Tablets, 451–450 B.C., and (3) the Justinian Code, 529 A.D. These laws were built upon one another, although each partially refined the edicts of the preceding ones.

These laws belonged to the following Roman kings:

- Romulus, 753–716 B.C.
- Numa Pompilius, 716–673 B.C.
- Tullus Hostilius, 673–640 B.C.
- Ancus Marcius, 640–616 B.C.
- Lucius Taraquinius, 616–578 B.C.
- Servius Tullius, 578–534 B.C.
- Tarquinius Superbus, 534–510 B.C.[27]

Most of these laws have reached us indirectly either through anecdotal evidence or oral tradition. A cursory reading of these laws tells us that during 753–510 B.C., the Roman kings were trying to organize the Roman economy, as well as the social and legal affairs of the empire. For example, under Romulus, Romans were divided into two general classes of free people known as the Patricians (the Roman nobility) and the Plebeians (the Roman commoners). Only members of the Patrician class were legally allowed to become priests, magistrates, and judges. The Plebeians, on the other hand, were allowed to become farmers, traders, or artisans.[28]

The social relationship between the Patricians and the Plebeians was governed by a patronage system whereby each Plebeian was allowed to choose a Patrician as his or her overlord. This was not slavery per se, but a legal form of social and economic servitude and patronage. The relationship was not one-sided, but of a reciprocal nature. As observed by one source on the subject, the Plebeians were duty bound to perform the following for their overlords:

- to contribute to the matrimonial cost of their patrons' daughters if such were needed;

- to contribute to ransom money in case of the capture of their patrons and/or of their offspring in war,
- to contribute to any fine that arose out of a private, or public judgment against their patrons;
- not to participate in any legal action against their patrons, nor to cast a vote against their patrons.[29]

In return, the Patricians were responsible for the following duties towards those under their protection:

- to interpret the law for their clients;
- to bring suit on behalf of clients when wronged;
- to support their clients in the legal action.

It is noteworthy that under King Romulus, a Plebeian found guilty of a breach of his or her responsibilities—especially of those related to politics—could be charged with the crime of treason. The crime of treason carried the penalty of death. When such a capital penalty was announced by the court, it could be carried out against the convict by anyone who wished to do so. The incentive for such vigilante type of justice was enormous because Romans worshiped a large number of gods and, to curry favor with them, sacrificed living entities (plants and animals) in temples. A convict sentenced to death was highly valued as a sacrificial item for the most feared god of the underworld: the Greek Hades worshiped as Pluto by the Romans.

King Romulus also enacted laws in relation to different aspects of Roman society. One scholar has observed that these laws regulated: (1) The administration of the government and its relationship with Roman citizens; (2) the extent of the king's power as the main judge; (3) the extent of Roman senators' power as lesser judges; (3) the responsibilities of the free citizens of Rome; and (4) the structure of power, marriage, divorce, inheritance, child custody, and the position of male and female siblings in the family.[30] After Romulus, new laws were added to enhance the structure of the Roman government and economy, as well as to regulate social and legal relationships in the kingdom.

The Twelve Tablets of Rome, 451–450 B.C., known as *Duodecium Tabularum*, together comprised the essence of Roman legal thinking in relation to justice and punishment. The Twelve Tablets, based on their subject matter, have been categorized as follows:

- Tablet I: Proceedings Preliminary to Trial
- Tablet II: Trial
- Tablet III: Execution of Judgment
- Tablet IV: Paternal Power
- Tablet V: Inheritance and Guardianship
- Tablet VI: Ownership and Possession
- Tablet VII: Real Property
- Tablet VIII: Tort and Delict
- Tablet IX: Public Law
- Tablet X: Sacred Law
- Tablet XI: Supplementary Laws
- Tablet XII: Supplementary Laws

Of interest to our subject matter are Tablets I, II, and III. These Roman tablets covered some of the procedures that the Greco-Roman legal tradition devised and passed on to the British common law legal tradition. In turn, the British common law passed these traditions to the U.S. legal system. In modern legal systems we follow some of the procedures that these tablets (I, II, and III) devised in relation to criminal prosecutions. Put together, these tablets have nineteen articles of law that cover the following in relation to defense in a criminal prosecution:

- the manner in which a defendant is summoned to a court of law to respond to the complaints of a plaintiff;
- what happens if the defendant does not show up before a court of law to respond to the charges (complaints of the plaintiff);
- what constitutes surety (bail), and who is allowed to use surety;
- what are the responsibilities of the presiding judge or magistrate towards the opposing parties in a criminal case;
- how the parties are to plead their cases;
- what happens if one party does not show up for a proceeding that has already commenced;
- what are valid excuses for not showing up for the proceedings;
- how a judgment concerning the resolution of indebtedness is executed;
- alternative dispute resolution for settling indebtedness;
- how a party to a conflict should collect evidence.[31]

The procedures prescribed by the Roman tablets are similar to the manner in which defendants are summoned to court and treated in the Anglo-American legal tradition.

British Common Law

The British common law is one of the oldest established systems of conflict resolution. The legal doctrine of defendant rights evolved in Britain through centuries of trial and error. This evolution was closely contemporaneous with the procedural development that took place in the notion of a fair trial. Simply put, the fairness of a trial depends on how a legal system handles the criminal complaint, the criminal defendant, and imposes punishment on the convicted culprit. This handling process has to be consistent, balanced, and impartial.

The Magna Carta

The Magna Carta of 1215 may be looked upon as the genesis of defendant rights in Great Britain. Clauses 14, 17, 19, 20, 21, 22, 24, 32, 36, 38, 39, 40, and 45 of that document were particularly important in providing:

- that in a criminal prosecution the defendant is entitled to receive notice (summons) as to why he or she must appear before a legal authority, as well as when and where (Clause 14);
- that instead of the King's Court, the hearing of the common pleas would take place elsewhere (in a court whose place is to be predetermined) (Clause 17);
- that the defendant (be it a baron, free man, cleric, merchant, or villein) is entitled to a reasonable amount of fine commensurate with the type of offense committed, an amount not to be ruinous of one's free-status position, of the vitality of one's business venture, or of agricultural produce and tillage (Clauses 20, 21, and 22);
- the right to be "amerced" (fined) by one's peers (Clauses 21 and 22);
- the right to be tried only in front of an authorized court (Clause 24);

- the right for a convicted felon to regain his or her confiscated land after the duration of the confiscation period
  of one year and one day (Clause 32);
- the right to be safe with respect to one's life and limbs
  (Clause 36);
- the right not to be put on trial based upon mere unsupported accusations (Clause 38);
- the right to be secure against unlawful search and
  seizure, confiscation of property, banishment or destruction unless by the judgment of one's peers in accordance
  with the law of land (Clause 39);
- the right to unadulterated, nondelayed, and nondenied
  justice (Clause 40);
- the right to stand before a court of law presided over
  only by those functionaries of the king (justiciars, constables, sheriffs, bailiffs) who are competent in the
  knowledge of the law (Clause 45).[32]

Thus, the Magna Carta recognized a set of social and legal responsibilities for the Britons. However, it took several centuries for
these legal responsibilities to take root in the British common law
tradition.

Defendant Rights, 1215–1613

The Magna Carta has been considered the first legal document to
(theoretically) give British citizens charged with crimes a set of
legal rights to defend their reputations, limbs, lives, and property
in a duly convened court of law. However, it was only in the seventeenth century that the protections of the Magna Carta were officially recognized as applying to the average British citizen. In 1613,
"Sir Edward Coke, Chief Justice under James I," writes one
scholar, "held that the Magna Carta guaranteed basic liberties for
all British citizens and ruled that any acts of Parliament which contravened common law would be void."[33] In other words, the
Magna Carta became a guiding instrument in the hands of British
criminal defense lawyers defending ordinary British citizens
charged with crime.

The Islamic Legal Tradition

The Islamic legal tradition emerged in the Middle East region in the seventh century A.D. It is a complex tradition that is known by its Arabic name, the *Sharia*. In dealing with those accused of criminality, the Islamic legal tradition tries to strike a balance between three factors: law, justice, and morality. In past centuries, many Islamic countries followed Islam's sacred law in resolving their civil and criminal conflicts. In the twentieth century, many Islamic countries abandoned the sacred law altogether and instead adopted modern constitutional laws and procedures. Some Islamic countries (e.g., Pakistan, Sudan, and Nigeria) have tried to reform their Islamic legal tradition. In the early twenty-first century, only two Islamic countries follow Islam's sacred law. These are the Islamic Republic of Iran and the Kingdom of Saudi Arabia. Before its demise, the Taliban in Afghanistan followed a strict and literalist Islamic legal tradition. The new Afghan government has moved to reform the Islamic legal tradition.

Islam's sacred law has four principal sources composed of (1) the Koran, (2) the Traditions of the Prophet Muhammad, (3) the consensus of Muslim judges on legal matters, and (4) the use of analogy in legal matters. A brief outline of the these sources is provided below. Those interested in a more detailed analysis may refer to the works cited at the end of this chapter.

The Koran

The Koran is the most important source of Islam's sacred law because Muslims believe that the text represents the laws of God. Muslims further believe that God (known as Allah in Islam) revealed divine laws to the Prophet Muhammad within a period of twenty-two years (610–632 A.D.). During this long period of revelation, Muhammad lived in the cities of Mecca (610–622) and Medina (622–632), two cities located in present-day Saudi Arabia that have played important roles in the development of Islam's legal tradition.

Muslims believe that the Koran is a divine text not penned by mortal beings, but by Allah himself. Thus, in the Islamic world any suggestion that Muhammad is the author of the Koran is considered an affront against the divinity of the text. The Koran is composed of 114 chapters. Each chapter, known as a *surah*, is composed of different rhyming verses. Each verse, called an *ayah* (which means "a sign from God"), relates to an event in the development of Islam during Muhammad's rise to prophecy. Muslims cherish these signs that the text of the Koran has provided. Some chapters of the Koran are very short, while others are very long. As a general rule, the shorter ones are believed to have been revealed in Mecca and the longer ones in Medina.

The thrust of the Koran is very similar to that of the Bible, namely that it is the word of God revealed to Muhammad for three grand purposes: (1) to morally guide humanity, (2) to show the righteous way for creating general prosperity and peace in this world, and (3) to enable the salvation of our souls in the world to come. Thus, a devout Muslim is duty bound to seek guidance from the Koran and to work diligently for universal peace and prosperity, which is achievable through law and righteous acts, coupled with noninvolvement in crime and violence. In addition, the Koran advises modesty in all aspects of social and personal affairs of daily life.

The Koran contains two basic legal instruments whose utilization by generations of Muslim jurists has enabled the Islamic world to create an elaborate and complex legal tradition. These legal instruments are what the Koran calls (1) God's Commandments (*Ahkam*), and (2) God's Boundaries and Punishments (*Hudud*). The former has functioned as the basis of the Islamic notion of tort-criminal law, the latter as the basis of an Islamic notion of penology. Together they have formed the basis of an Islamic system of justice and punishment. The Islamic field of study that comprises tort law, criminal law, punishment, and adjudication is known as *Ilm al-Qaza* and is the equivalent of Anglo-American jurisprudence. The term *Kadi,* which is the anglicized form of the Arabic *Qaazi,* refers to the Islamic judge and is a derivative of the term *Qizaaawat,* which stands for the Islamic notion of legal judgment.

The Prophet Muhammad

The Traditions of the Prophet Muhammad (the *Sunna*) is the second most important source of the Islamic legal tradition. These traditions cover both the historical acts and sayings of the Prophet. It should be noted that the Koran does not portray Muhammad as a divine entity, but praises him as a human being who heeded righteousness, sought God, helped the needy, and refrained from the evil ways of the pagan Arabs. Therefore, his actions and words have been exemplary for Muslims throughout the world. However, Muslim scholars have pointed out that not all the traditions of the Prophet are genuine because some of these traditions contradict each other and therefore are falsely attributed to him. From the time of the Prophet to the twenty-first century (a period of fourteen centuries), Muslim religious doctors have studied the traditions of the Prophet Muhammad in order to define which traditions are authentic and which are false. In due time, the religious doctors devised a methodology for this purpose.

This authentication methodology requires that any action or saying attributed to the Prophet meticulously be traced back to its originator to see if the alleged act or saying is in harmony with the realities of its time and conditions. For example, if a tradition purports that the Prophet ordered wanton acts of violence and aggression against Jewish or Christian people, this tradition is a false attribution because the Koran has specified unequivocally that the Jews and Christians are "People of the Book" who enjoy full protection of the Islamic state. No Muslim doctor of jurisprudence has ever argued that the life and properties of the People of the Book can be violated without just cause, let alone Muhammad, whom Muslims believe had a legendary sense of justice. By showing which Prophetic traditions were authentic and which ones false, Muslim jurists and doctors gradually created an Islamic legal tradition with its system of criminal prosecution and defense procedures.

The Juristic Consensus on Legal Matters

The third source of the Islamic legal tradition is the consensus of Islamic judges on legal matters. This is similar to case law through which legal precedent is established in the Anglo-American tradition. The theory is that a collective wisdom develops if there is philosophical consistency among judges. For example, how does a judge decide on the proper punishment for murder? If all preceding judges have applied capital punishment to murder, it is only logical that a new judge should follow the same course. Why? Because there has developed a collective wisdom in relation to murder: the most appropriate punishment for murder is execution of the murderer.

In the Islamic legal tradition, the rationale for utilizing juristic consensus stems from a saying attributed to the Prophet Muhammad. The Prophet is reported as having said that the community of believers does not err in its collective wisdom. In other words, if the community believes that a certain criminal act has to be codified as an indexed crime, it will do so because the community feels that such a crime inflicts a certain amount of harm on society. In other words, following the rationale behind this prophetic saying, it is logical to argue that in the Islamic legal tradition criminal law reflects communal norms, values, and mores. In time, however, the Islamic community relegated its judgment duties to those who were trained in the Islamic law, as, for example, the aforementioned *Kadi* who composed a professional class of trained judges whose main responsibility was to interpret the law and traditions in the application of justice.

The Analogy

Analogy (*Ijamaa* in Arabic), is the fourth principal source that Muslim jurists have utilized in the formation of the Islamic legal tradition. It is an act of comparing cases and situations to one another to arrive at the best course of action in relation to a legal matter. A system of analogy gradually developed as Muslim judges started facing complex legal issues as Islam expanded (through conversion and conquest) in the post-Muhammad period. To resolve many of these issues, the judges could refer to the Koran or to the Prophet's traditions. However, there were other issues that the judges had to resolve through analogous reasoning by referring to precedent set by past judges.

In modern times, the Islamic legal tradition has faced issues such as democracy, human rights, civil liberties, and representative and participatory forms of government, including the issue of cruel and unusual punishment that democratic societies have banned. The same applies to the death penalty, which most democratic countries have found against human dignity and therefore have abolished. These represent issues that have profoundly challenged the whole structure of the Islamic legal tradition.

Adjudication of both civil and criminal cases has a long history in the Islamic world. In resolving civil and criminal cases, Islamic judges and prosecutors must follow the principles that the Koran has outlined. These are:

- fairness and impartiality
- respect for privacy
- the search for the truth

- knowledge of the case and law
- the presumption of innocence
- proportionality between crime and punishment
- action, not thought
- mitigating and aggravating circumstances surrounding the crime.[34]

A synopsis of each principle is presented below. It is noteworthy that these principles have their proper names in the Koran and in the Prophet Muhammad's traditions.

The Principle of Fairness and Impartiality

An Islamic judge must be fair and impartial in the adjudicative process because both the Koran and the Prophetic traditions have stressed these aspects of a just verdict. Thus, a judge is both morally and legally bound to approach a case (civil or criminal) without any preconceived notion as to the guilt or innocence of the accused. Islamic judges are duty bound not to allow their personal feelings to influence their decisions. Neither should judges allow factors that are not relevant to a just resolution of the case influence their decisions one way or another. These include bribes and favoritism based on social or blood relationships.

The Koran states categorically that Allah watches over those who sit in judgment of others' deeds, especially the *Kadis*, the Islamic judges. Those judges, prosecutors, and witnesses who corrupt God's law, sternly warns the Koran, will face eternal punishment once they appear before God in the world to come. For example, Verse iv:136 in the Koran maintains:

> O ye who believe! Be strict in observing justice, and be witnesses for Allah, even though it is against yourselves or against parents and kindred. Whether he be rich or poor, Allah is more regardful of them both than you are. Therefore, follow not low desires so that you may be able to act equitably. And if you conceal the truth or evade it, then remember that Allah is well aware of what you do.[35]

Given the stern warnings of the Koran, judges sitting to adjudicate cases have to follow high standards of justice and morality. They must also be aware that penal measures apply only after proof has been established. The proof involves (1) eye witnesses, (2) voluntary confessions, (3) oaths, and (4) weapon(s) by means of which crime has been committed.

The Principle of Respect for Privacy

The Koran opposes surveillance for detection of unlawful and undesirable activities that people may commit in their private residences (e.g., drinking alcoholic beverages, engaging in illicit sex, or using drugs), despite the fact that these acts are strongly renounced by the text and the Prophetic traditions. Thus, one of the most immoral acts according to the Koran is to give false witness against others. Those who engage in false witness will reap the sour fruits of such vile acts, warns the Koran, a premise that has played an important role in the development of the Islamic system of criminal prosecution and defense. In the past, Islamic judges depended principally on the testimony of eye witnesses in determining the guilt or innocence of defendants, be it in civil or criminal cases. For example, to prove that a defendant engaged in the crime of illicit sex, the prosecution had to produce four eye witnesses who were persons of good reputation, capable of testifying under oath that they had seen the act with their own eyes. In fact, when it comes to the proof of illicit sex, the Koranic mechanism of establishing proof is one of the most stringent among all prevailing legal systems.

The Principle of Search for the Truth

An Islamic judge must search for the truth by allowing both the defendant and the plaintiff to present their side of the case and then carefully examining the evidence before declaring the verdict. However, the Koran is against state surveillance of the private affairs of believers and admonishes judges against evidence produced through surveillance-based investigation. In fact, the Koran advises Muslim believers (and especially spouses), to safeguard each others' private secrets. The same standard applies to confessions that have been extracted from a suspect under duress or torture. The Koran admonishes judges not to build a case against a defendant based on duress, torture, or other illegal and immoral methods. For example, the Second Caliph, Umar (r. 634–644), is reported to have adjudicated a case of alleged rape and sought legal advice from Ali, who later became the Fourth Caliph (r. 656–661). According to the case:

> A woman fell in love with an Ansari lad but could not get her way with him. She thought of a scheme. One day she took an egg, threw out its yoke and spread the white part on her cloths and legs and then went to Umar Ibn Khattab and said: this lad has ambushed me in such and such place and has raped me, and that which you see on my clothes and legs is his ejaculation. Umar accepted her complaint and attempted to punish the lad. Imam Ali who was present in the adjudication session addressed the Second Caliph [Umar] and said: haste not! Maybe this woman has concocted this scheme. Then Ali recommended for hot boiling water to be brought. Upon presentation of the water, Imam Ali recommended that part of the dress be soaked in the hot water to be tasted. Once it was found[,] through this method[,] that the stain tasted like the whites of an egg, the woman confessed to her scheme.[36]

There are similar cases cited in Islamic legal sources showing that from the time of the Prophet, a rudimentary system of truth seeking started to develop in the Islamic system of criminal prosecution and defense, becoming a full-fledged system in medieval times.

The Principle of Knowledge of the Case and Law

In particular, Islamic judges must study their cases thoroughly because it is only through a thorough study of the case that a judge is able to reach a just verdict and apply a just sentence of punishment. At the same time, judges must possess expert knowledge on the sources of the sacred law, meaning that they must be adequately trained in all sources of the sacred law.

The Principle of the Presumption of Innocence

The Koran states that if an innocent person is killed, it is as if the whole of humanity has been killed, a premise that historically has had much impact on the Islamic notion of what constitutes a just system of criminal prosecution and defense. The logical implication of this stance has been that taking life without just cause is a grave sin before Allah. This premise of the Koran has led to the Islamic legal principle of the "presumption of innocence" (*baraat*) doctrine. This principle has a specific Koranic basis stemming from the slander that some of the sworn enemies of Muhammad had leveled against his third wife, Aishah. The unfounded accusation was so devastating to the Prophet and to his household that it brought Aishah to a state of profound depression and near death. At this juncture, the heavens intervened and several verses of the Koran (xxiv: 11–20) were revealed to the Prophet admonishing those who level unfounded accusations against innocent women (e.g., Aishah).

The revealed chapter (xxiv) set, among other household-related matters, rigorous legal principles for adjudicating charges of adultery and applied harsh penalties for those who falsely accuse women of adultery. The proof mechanism requires the accuser to produce four eye witnesses who can testify under oath that they have witnessed the act of penetration between the two parties involved. The punishment for the couple, characterized by the Koran as the adulterer (*al-zaani*) and the adulteress (*al-zaaniyah*), has been specified as lashing. Nowhere in the Koran is any mention of the death penalty or stoning that applies in some Islamic countries such as Iran, Saudi Arabia, Sudan (and Afghanistan under the Taliban regime).

The Principle of Proportionality between Crime and Punishment

The Koran emphasizes the importance of maintaining proportionality between crime and punishment by adhering to the principle of "an eye for an eye and a tooth for a tooth"—and a life for a life. However, the text has improved this premise by providing compensatory measures applicable to both property and violent crimes. Wanton violence against those in the custody of an Islamic authority has been prohibited by the Koran and no one, including a slave, can be substituted for punishment on behalf of a culprit. The Koranic formula is "a man for a man, a woman for a woman, a slave for a slave" at a time that powerful men who had committed crimes substituted their slaves for punishment in their stead.

The Principle of Responsibility for One's Actions

The Koran is adamant that on the Day of Judgment, each person is responsible for his or her deeds. Accordingly, Allah will not accept intercession on behalf of others, except the intercession of a few select souls. At the same time, the Koran maintains that on the Day of Judgment, every person's good and evil deeds will be measured. Chapter xcix, Verse 6 reads: "That day mankind will issue forth in scattered groups to be shown their deeds."[37]

Verse 7 reads "And whosoever doth good an atom's weight will see it then." This is followed by Verse 8: "And whosoever doth ill an atom's weight will see it then."[38]

This position of the Koran implies that on the Day of Judgment, God will personally judge our deeds committed during our mortal days on this earth. This powerful premise of the Koran is, of course, reflected in the Islamic legal tradition. It implies that if one is charged with a crime, he or she ought to be subjected to a proper punishment only after a thorough investigation has been conducted to the satisfaction of the judge. The judge has to be a person of the highest morality and integrity. The punishment must fit the crime. Islamic jurists have argued that the Prophet Muhammad meticulously adhered to these Koranic principles in the adjudication of both criminal and civil cases.

The Principle of Action versus Thought

The Koran maintains that it is the believers' actions rather than their intentions that God will take into consideration on the Day of Judgment. The implication of this Koranic premise has been that no criminal defendant can be, or should be, found guilty of a thought that he or she has not acted upon. A person cannot be punished for ill thoughts that have not been acted upon.

The Principle of Mitigating and Aggravating Circumstances

A judge must analyze each and every shred of evidence presented to the court, including what legal literature considers the mitigating and aggravating circumstances that surround the case. Mitigating circumstances are those factors that decrease the level of the heinousness of the crime in contrast to aggravating circumstances, which do the opposite. For example, the facts that a criminal defendant shows much remorse for his or her criminal act, cooperates with the police in the investigation of the crime, and has no prior criminal record are mitigating factors. On the other hand, if a criminal defendant shows no remorse for the crime, has a long criminal record, and shows much contempt towards the police, the victim, and the court, such are aggravating circumstances. In all legal traditions, including the Islamic tradition, judges have taken mitigating and aggravating circumstances into consideration.

In sum, the Prophet Muhammad has consistently been portrayed as an Islamic model of a just judge, whose adjudication guidelines Muslim caliphs and judges have followed as civil and criminal cases were brought before them. However, in modern times justice has been in a sorry state in many Islamic countries, and that is one main reason why so many Islamic countries have adopted modern secular laws and procedures.

Commonalities between the Four Legal Traditions

A systematic study of the four legal traditions outlined above shows that all have recognized that the overall legitimacy of a tradition depends on the degree to which the principles of fairness and consistency can be maintained in the application of law and justice. In theory, they have recognized the importance of creating procedural laws that enable defendants to rebut charges of criminality and to explain their sides of the story. That is why in the four prevailing legal traditions discussed above procedural safeguards have been codified so that fairness in criminal prosecutions can be observed, at least in theory. Many countries have constitutions in which the responsibility for the determination of the guilt or innocence of a criminal defendant has been assigned to the legal system.

Differences between the Four Legal Traditions

In reality, however, there are profound differences between the four legal traditions based on the degree to which each has procedurally applied fairness to the actual trial proceedings. Simply put, it is not enough to have a modern constitution in which a lot of homage is given to justice and equity and claiming that a country's legal system accepts the notion that the accused has a right to defend himself or herself against charges of criminality. What is of paramount importance is what procedurally and substantively takes place in a court of law. How scrupulously do judges, prosecutors, police, and governmental authorities observe the procedural safeguards inserted in the law to expedite a criminal defendant's progress through the justice system?

Notes

1. See Hamid R. Kusha, *The Sacred Law of Islam: The Case of Women's Treatment in the Islamic Republic of Iran's Criminal Justice System* (London, UK: Ashgate, 2002).

2. Lloyd Duhaime, "The Time Table of World Legal History," pp. 1–9, available at: http://www.duhaime.org./hist.html.

3. *Ibid.*, pp. 1–5.

4. John R. Wilson, "Authority and Law in Ancient Egypt," in Herbert J. Liebesny, *The Law of the Near & Middle East: Readings, Cases, & Materials* (Albany, NY: State University of New York Press, 1975), p. 5.

5. Mark Andrews, "Law and the Legal System in Ancient Egypt," p. 1, available at http://www.touregypt.net/featurestories.html.

6. *Ibid.*

7. *Ibid.*, p. 2.

8. *Ibid.*, pp. 2–3.

9. James B. Pritchard, ed., *Ancient Near Eastern Texts Relating to the Old Testament*, p. 165, cited in Liebesny, p. 5.

10. *Ibid.*

11. L. W. King, trans., *The Avelon Project: The Code of Hammurabi*, p. 3, available at http://www.yale.edu/law.web/avelon/medieval/hamcode.html.

12. *Ibid.*, pp. 3–4.

13. *Ibid.*, p. 3.

14. *Ibid.*, p. 3.

15. Paul Brians, "The Law: Exodus," in *Crash Course in Jewish History*, pp. 1–6, available at http://www.aish.com.

16. *Ibid.*, pp. 1–2.

17. *Ibid.*, p. 3.

18. A. T. Olmsted, *History of the Persian Empire* (Chicago, IL: University of Chicago Press, 1959).

19. Parviz Sanei, *Criminal Law,* vol. 1 (Tehran, Iran: Ganj-e Daanesh Publications, 1995), p. 82.

20. *Ibid.*, p. 80.

21. Ancient Greek Legal System, pp. 1–5, available at http://www.crystallinks.com/greeklaw.html.

22. *Ibid.*

23. *Ibid.*, pp. 1–2.

24. Duhaime, p. 4.

25. Wesley Gilmer Jr., *The Law Dictionary,* 6th ed. (Cincinnati, OH: Anderson, 1986), p. 321.

26. Ancient Greek Legal System, pp. 1–3.

27. Ancient Greek Legal System, p. 4.

28. L. W. King, pp. 1–9.

29. *Ibid.*, pp. 1–2.

30. *Ibid.*, pp. 1–2.

31. *Ibid.*, pp. 2–3.

32. *Ibid.*, pp. 1–11.

33. *Ibid.*, pp. 1–3.

34. Howard, Dick A.E., *Magna Carta: Text and Commentary,* rev. ed. (Charlottesville: University of Virginia Press, 1998), p. vii.

35. Frank Shmalleger, *Criminal Justice Today: An Introductory Text for the 21st Century,* 6th ed. (Upper Saddle River, NJ: Prentice Hall, 2001), p. 121.

36. See for example Wael B. Hallaq, *A History of Islamic Legal Theories: An Introduction to Sunni usual al-fiqh* (Cambridge, UK: Cambridge University Press, 1997); Muhammad Khalid Masud, Brinkley Messick, and David S. Powers, *Islamic Legal Interpretation: Muftis and Their Fatwas,* (Cambridge, MA: Harvard University Press, 1997); Bernard G. Weiss, *The Search for God's Law: Islamic Jurisprudence in the Writings of Sayf al-Din al-Amidi* (Salt Lake City: University of Utah Press, 1992).

37. Mirza Tahir Ahmad, *The Holy Qur'an,* vol. 2 (New York: Mostazafan Foundation, 1984) p. 571.

38. Muhammad Hussain Saket, *Nahad-e Daadrasi Dar Islam,* p. 83, cited from Muhammad Albaji, *Mathal 'Aliya Min Qaza al-Islam* (Tunisia, Al-Maktab al-Sharqiyah, 1376 Hijri), al-Tab al-Awal, pp. 74–79, fn. 82.

5

Key People, Cases, and Terms

This chapter briefly discusses a number of important personalities and events in relation to the development of defendant rights in the Anglo-American legal tradition.

Benton v. Maryland (1969)

This case addressed the issue of due process. The Supreme Court, citing the Fourteenth Amendment, decided that a criminal defendant's right against being placed in double jeopardy as expressed by the Fifth Amendment applies to trials in both state and federal courts.

Blackmun, Harry Andrew (1908–1999)

Harry Andrew Blackmun, associate justice of the U.S. Supreme Court from 1970 to 1994, has been praised as a "judicial giant."[1] President Richard Nixon appointed Blackmun to the high Court in 1970 when Blackmun was already sixty-one years old. He served the Court for twenty-four years, writing some of the most enduring and controversial opinions such as *Roe v. Wade* (1973), which legalized abortion in this country. He also played an important role in the enhancement of civil liberties and of due process, despite the fact that he was supposed to be a conservative. Gradually, he shifted to the liberal wing of both the Burger and Rehnquist Courts. By the time of his retirement in 1994,

Blackmun had won the reputation of being one of the most liberal justices of the Court.[2]

Blackmun was born in Nashville, Illinois, in 1908. He later moved to the Minneapolis-St. Paul area, where in grade school he met the future chief justice Warren Burger, with whom he would serve on the high Court until Burger's retirement in 1983. After high school, Blackmun went to Harvard University for a B.A. degree in mathematics, which he received in 1929. In 1932, he received a law degree from Harvard Law School. Between 1932 and 1933, he worked as a clerk for the United States Court of Appeals for the Eighth Circuit. After a brief stint teaching at the Mitchell College of Law in St. Paul, Blackmun joined a Minneapolis law firm to practice law for the next sixteen years. In 1950, he joined the prestigious Mayo Clinic in Rochester, Minnesota, as a legal counsel.[3]

In 1959, President Dwight Eisenhower appointed Blackmun to the Eighth Circuit Court of Appeals to replace Judge John Sanborn. In that capacity, Blackmun proved his legal acumen and sense of justice. In 1970, President Richard Nixon nominated Blackmun to the Supreme Court after the Senate Judiciary Committee rejected two of his previous nominees, Clement F. Haynsworth Jr. of South Carolina and G. Harrold Carswell of Florida. "In his decisions, Blackmun generally voted against expanding the rights of criminal suspects but cast liberal votes in cases pitting the right of individuals against those of government." Blackmun's decisionmaking strategy can be summarized as one of resisting any attempts to expand criminal suspects' rights counterbalanced by support of individual liberties.[4] Despite this legacy, there is common consensus that Blackmun was instrumental in the enhancement of defendant rights and various aspects of due process. After twenty-four years of serving the high Court with distinction, Blackmun retired in 1994. In 1999, Blackmun died at the age of ninety following hip-replacement surgery at a Virginia hospital.

Blackstone, Sir William (1723–1780)

Sir William Blackstone played an important role in the evolution of the British legal system. This evolution was important for the further development of defendant rights in the British system of criminal prosecution. Blackstone was a jurist, judge, and lecturer in law. Through his writings and activities Blackstone advocated the philosophy of the rule of law.

Blackstone published his lectures in a four-volume publication titled *Commentaries on the Laws of England.* It took him four years (1765–1769) to finish this monumental work. The work gave to British laypersons and to the American colonies a text of the laws of England that was easy to read and to understand. The first volume, composed of eighteen chapters and one appendix, covered the "Rights of Persons"; the second volume, comprising thirty-two chapters, covered the "Rights of Things"; the third volume, composed of twenty-seven chapters and three appendices, covered "Private Wrongs," or the law of torts; and finally, volume four, comprising thirty-three chapters, one appendix, a supplement, and an index, covered "Public Wrongs,"[5] or crimes.

Burger Court (1969–1986)

Chief Justice Warren Earl Burger was appointed by President Nixon on 21 May 1969. Under Burger, although the Supreme Court was cognizant of the importance of due process, it nevertheless applied a more conservative view regarding due process. Although it is the prosecution that must prove that the defendant charged with a crime has indeed committed the criminal act, during Burger's tenure, the Court started shifting the bulk of the burden of proof to the shoulders of those criminal defendants who claimed that the police had violated their rights during search and seizure activities. Whereas during the Warren Court, the exclusionary rule applied when the defense showed that due process had been violated by the police, under Chief Justice Burger, the application of the exclusionary rule became more restricted, a process that continued under the Rehnquist Court.

Chimel v. California (1969)

This case addressed the issue of warrantless search and seizure activities. The Supreme Court decreed that if a search is incidental to the arrest of a suspect, the police are allowed to conduct a warrantless search of the suspect's immediate surroundings. However, there is a limit to what is legally permissible in such warrantless searches, the high Court warned, giving the example of a suspect's residence as being off-limits to such search activities.

Coke, Sir Edward (1552–1634)

Sir Edward Coke played an important role in the development of defendant rights in the British system of criminal prosecution. Coke promoted the idea that all British citizens were entitled to defend their good names, lives and limbs, and property in a court of law regardless of their social status. Coke was a prominent English jurist with a remarkable career in service to the state. He entered Parliament in 1589. In the same year, Coke was elected Speaker of the House of Commons. He was appointed attorney general in 1593 and chief justice of Common Pleas in 1606. In 1613, Sir Edward Coke became the chief justice of England.[6]

As chief justice, Coke interpreted the British common law more in line with the doctrine of legal equity. The doctrine of legal equity maintains that no one is above the law. Therefore, when a law is violated, justice applies regardless of one's social status, be the perpetrator a prince or a pauper. In addition to his attempts to bring legal equity to the British legal system, Coke was against the exercise of the arbitrary powers of the British monarchs. One example was the monarch's investiture powers. This allowed the monarchs arbitrarily to arrest any persons they wished, to confiscate property, or to impose unjust taxes. It also allowed the monarchs to house soldiers in the private residences of citizens during peacetime. This situation prevailed despite the fact that the Magna Carta had prohibited a good number of these arbitrary measures.

Under James I (r. 1603–1625), the British legal system went through turmoil. The hub of the crisis centered on whether the protective clauses of the Magna Carta applied to all British citizens. Sir Edward Coke rejected the legal elitist position of those British social thinkers and lawyers who argued that the protective clauses of the Magna Carta applied only to the British nobility. Instead, Coke argued that the "original intent" of the Great Charter was to make the protective clauses inclusive. This meant that all British citizens could claim the benefit of the Charter's protections, and not just the upper classes. This enhancement of defendant rights for all citizens was perhaps one of Coke's greatest legal accomplishments. Unfortunately, this position won Coke much enmity from British royal circles. These circles conspired against him and had Coke dismissed from the bench in 1616.[7] However, Coke later outmaneuvered his adversaries. In 1620, he was elected to the House of Commons where he continued to work hard for promoting legal equity for all British citizens. This activity culminated in 1628 when Coke sponsored the famous Petition of Right, another measure that expanded legal rights to a greater proportion of the British population.

Duncan v. Louisiana (1968)

In this case, the U.S. Supreme Court decreed that when charged with the commission of a serious crime, a criminal defendant in state court has the same Sixth Amendment right to a jury trial as he or she would have had if tried in federal court, through operation of the due process clause of the Fourteenth Amendment.

Elkins v. United States (1960)

This case addressed the issue of whether evidence gathered by state authorities through illegal search and seizure methods is admissible in federal court for prosecution purposes. The Supreme Court held that it is not. This case put a decisive end to what was known as the "silver platter" doctrine, which had allowed federal prosecutors to take advantage of evidence seized illegally by state authorities to convict defendants in federal court.

English Bill of Rights (1689)

In 1689 the British Parliament passed a legal measure known as the English Bill of Rights. The main purpose of the measure was to limit the centuries-old doctrine of the "divine right of the king." This doctrine gave absolute powers to British monarchs. Although it was important for the kings to use their order-setting powers to bring criminal and deviant acts under control, such control often meant disregard for procedural justice, and abuses of innocent persons followed. By 1689, English citizens had developed a sense of entitlement to fairness in proceedings involving government action.

By restricting the sovereign's range of powers, the English Bill of Rights played an important role in the enhancement of defendant rights in the British system of criminal prosecution. Later, the American legal tradition followed the English Bill of Rights in its own version of the American Bill of Rights.

The official title of the English Bill of Rights was "An Act Declaring the Rights and Liberties of the Subjects, and Setting the Succession of the Crown."[8] The text of the act enumerates the excesses and illegal actions of the deposed king, James II, as follows:

- suspending laws, or executing laws, without the assent of the British Parliament;
- creating a commission in order to create a court named the Court of Commissioners for Ecclesiastical Causes without proper authority for such undertaking;
- inappropriate levying of money for the Crown despite the Parliament's monetary provisions for the same purpose;
- maintenance of an standing army during the time of peace and without proper authorization from the Parliament;
- disarming of some Protestant subjects of the sovereign at the same time that the followers of the Pope were illegally allowed to carry their arms;
- violation of the freedoms in relation to Parliamentarian electoral law;
- usurpation of some of the prosecutorial powers of the British Parliament.[9]

The English Bill of Rights also described corrupting acts of the monarch. These were manipulation of the jury system and the imposition of excessive bail, fines, and cruel and unusual punishments on British subjects. James II utilized his sovereign powers to influence the legal system through these corrupting practices in direct violation of the laws and statutes of the land.[10]

Having enumerated the deposed monarch's illegal acts, the Bill of Rights decreed that:

- the crown could not arbitrarily declare laws null and void without the consent of the British Parliament;

- tribunals such as the Court of Commissioners for Ecclesiastical Causes created without the expressed authority of the British Parliament were illegal;
- the crown could not levy, for its expenses, various forms of taxes on British subjects despite the British Parliament's provision of funds for such expenses of the crown;
- British subjects were to have the right to petition the king without facing any adverse official repercussions;
- the crown could not maintain a standing army during time of peace and without the consent of the British Parliament;
- Protestant subjects were allowed to keep arms for defensive purposes;
- freedom of participation in Parliamentarian elections was to be restored;
- Parliamentarian freedoms such as the freedom of speech, debate, and proceeding were to be recognized and such freedoms were not to be questioned in any form or manner outside the halls of the British Parliament;
- excessive bail, or fines, would not be imposed nor cruel and unusual punishments;
- in cases of high treason, the jury was to be impaneled from freeholders;
- fines and forfeitures imposed without convictions were declared illegal;
- the sessions of Parliament would be held frequently so that British subjects' grievances could be heard and amended.[11]

In short, the English Bill of Rights, as precursor to the American Bill of Rights, limited the arbitrary powers of the British monarchs. The bill also forced the British monarchy to acknowledge the indispensable legislative role and power of the British Parliament. By limiting the power of the monarchs, the British legal system took a major step in the direction of the rule of law rather than persons. This philosophy maintains that everyone must be considered equal before the law. It was in the structural context of this philosophy that defendant rights found its institutional place in the Anglo-American legal tradition.

Escobedo v. Illinois (1964)

This case addressed the issue of the right to counsel. Concentrating on the Sixth Amendment's stipulation that criminal defendants are entitled to legal counsel when interrogated by the police, the high Court decreed that police must inform suspects of that right. Confessions obtained by the police without a suspect's knowledge of that right are illegal and may not be used in trial proceedings.

Exceptions to Probable Cause

This exception to the exclusionary rule applies when police officers believe that danger to life or property is imminent and therefore that they must intervene without any warrant. The concept of probable cause as a legal restriction was originally inserted in the Fourth Amendment to stipulate that any search and seizure activity must be based on a valid warrant obtained by the police. Under normal circumstances, the police present probable cause of criminality to a judge or magistrate and obtain a warrant to search specified premises and seize specified types of evidence found there.

Fourth Lateran Council (1215)

The Fourth Lateran Council of 1215 was an important event in the development of defendant rights in the Anglo-American legal tradition. The council, held in Rome, was called into session by the Vatican under Pope Innocent III. There were important issues that the pope wanted to address. One issue related to the overall relationship of the Catholic churches to the emerging states in medieval Europe.[12]

A large number of both religious and state functionaries representing various Christian denominations and European states attended the council. The council members discussed a wide range of issues. At the end of the session, the council issued seventy-nine directives or "canons." Canon 18 is of interest to our discussion of the development of defenses against charges of criminality. It decreed that:

- the members of the clergy were no longer entitled to pronounce, or to execute, a sentence of death;
- the members of the clergy were no longer permitted to preside as judges over criminal cases that were "extreme" [capital cases];
- the members the clergy were no longer allowed to conduct the rituals of trial by ordeal be it by hot or cold water, or hot iron.[13]

These prohibitions were important for the procedural development of a secular criminal prosecution. For example, trial by ordeal was a form of defense against charges of criminality. Its historical roots go far back to very ancient legal traditions. The rationale for trial by ordeal was rooted in the belief that only an innocent person would voluntarily go through the excruciating pain of physical ordeal to prove that he or she was innocent of the charges of criminality.

Gideon v. Wainwright (1963)

This case addressed the issue of the right to legal counsel. The question raised was whether the states were obliged to provide legal counsel to those who could not afford to hire their own defense lawyers. The Supreme Court decided that the due process clause of the Fourteenth Amendment applied to both state and federal criminal defendants. Because of this application, the Sixth Amendment's guarantee of legal counsel to those charged with serious crime applies to state criminal defendants as well as federal, and states are obligated to provide legal counsel for criminal defendants who are unable to afford it themselves.

Good-Faith Exception

This exception to the exclusionary rule applies when police officers acting in good faith in their search and seizure activities later find out that they have made procedural mistakes. The question arises as to what to do with such tainted evidence. Under the Warren Court, such evidence would automatically have been thrown away as inadmissible based on a liberal interpretation of the exclusionary rule. Under the Burger and Rehnquist Courts, much more restrictive application of the exclusionary rule has been the norm.

Griffin v. California (1965)

In this case, the U.S. Supreme Court decided that a criminal defendant's right against self-incrimination, as stipulated by the Fifth Amendment, is violated when a presiding judge or prosecuting attorney makes comments implying that the defendant's refusal to take the witness stand for self-defense purposes is evidence of his or her guilt.

Hoyt v. Florida (1961)

This case addressed the issue of whether the state of Florida could categorically exclude women from jury duty on the grounds that women should not be distracted from their responsibilities towards home and family. The U.S. Supreme Court agreed with the state of Florida and rejected the plaintiff's argument that such an exclusion violated the equal protection guarantee of the Fourteenth Amendment.

Katz v. United States (1967)

The U.S. Supreme Court decided in this case that any form of electronic surveillance of a criminal suspect is a search and seizure activity subject to the requirements of the Fourth Amendment. In the past the Court had argued otherwise, setting a precedent in *Olmstead v. United States* (1928).

Kerr v. California (1963)

This case addressed the issue of whether different legal standards apply to state and federal search and seizure activities. The Supreme Court decided that the standards of legality as prescribed by the Fourth Amendment are the same in both state and federal jurisdictions.

King Edward III's Declarations (1368)

King Edward III (r. 1327–1377) played an important role in the enhancement of defendant rights.[14] He achieved this through his declarations concerning the Magna Carta. Edward III decreed that (1) the codes of the Magna Carta carried the force of law, (2) no law superseded the codes of the Magna Carta, and (3) the text of the Magna Carta had to be readily accessible to the general public so that the public would be aware of its contents.[15] The laypersons' knowledge of their legal rights and responsibilities is quite important. Such knowledge made the enforcement of the Magna Carta's provisions much easier. In due time, the idea that a criminal defendant is entitled to procedural rights became an accepted legal norm in the Anglo-American tradition.

Klopfer v. North Carolina (1967)

This case addressed the issue of due process. The U.S. Supreme Court decreed that a criminal defendant's right to a speedy trial as expressed in the Sixth Amendment applies to both state and federal prosecutions.

Magna Carta (1215)

As discussed in previous chapters, the Magna Carta played an important role in the rise and codification of defendant rights in the Anglo-American legal tradition. The Magna Carta reaffirmed the traditional freedoms that the English Church enjoyed in England during the reign of the Anglo-Saxon monarchs but also moved law and justice in a more secular direction by limiting the jurisprudential powers of the clergy.

The clauses of the Magna Carta were complementary to some canons of the Fourth Lateran Council, as for example Canon 18. This canon prohibited the use of trial by ordeal. It also gave primacy to various procedures through which the guilt or innocence of defendants could be determined in a court of law.

Mallory v. United States (1957)

This case addressed the issue of due process. Mallory was arrested for rape and interrogated continuously for seven hours until he confessed. He was not told of his right to counsel, his right to remain silent, or his right to a preliminary examination before a magistrate. The Supreme Court held that this treatment violated Mallory's Fifth Amendment rights and constituted "unnecessary delay" in bringing him before a judicial officer to determine whether charges were warranted.

Mapp v. Ohio (1961)

This landmark case held for the first time that the Fourth Amendment prohibition against unreasonable searches and seizures was applicable to state proceedings through the due process clause of the Fourteenth Amendment. It also held that the exclusionary rule was the remedy for police misconduct in this area. Henceforth, evidence seized in violation of the Fourth Amendment would be excluded from state criminal trials.

Marshall, Thurgood (1908–1993)

Thurgood Marshall played a central role in the Civil Rights movement and is considered one of the most important advocates of civil liberties during his long tenure as an associate justice of the U.S. Supreme Court (1967–1981). He was born in Baltimore, Maryland, in 1908. His grandfather was a slave whose plight deeply affected Justice Marshall's thoughts and deeds, including his activism in the Civil Rights movement.

In 1930, Marshall graduated from Lincoln University in Chester, Pennsylvania. In 1933, he received a law degree from Howard University in Washington, D.C. Prior to that, he had applied to the University of Maryland Law School, but was rejected because of his race. This rejection deeply impacted Marshall's social conscience, strengthening his resolve to fight against the social and legal injustices of his time. It was with this determination that Marshall, once having become a lawyer, set to work to eradicate discriminatory laws and regulations that prevented the progress of socially maligned segments of American society, be they white or black, throughout the nation.

In 1934, Marshall started working for the Baltimore branch of the National Association for the Advancement of Colored People (NAACP). In 1935, he successfully sued the University of Maryland Law School to admit a young African American student named Donald Gaines Murray. In *Murray v. Pearson,* Marshall argued that the denial of Murray's application by the University of Maryland, a state institution, deprived him of the equal protection of the law guaranteed by the Fourteenth Amendment. Marshall, the young lawyer, won his first major civil rights case arguing that, "What's at stake here is more than the rights of my client. It's the moral commitment stated in our country's creed."[16]

In 1936, Marshall went to New York to become the assistant special counsel for the NAACP in New York City. Between 1940 and 1954, Marshall won a number of important cases that he argued before the U.S. Supreme Court. These included cases such as *Chambers v. Florida* (1940), *Smith v. Allwright* (1944), *Shelly v. Kraemer* (1944), two cases of *Sweatt v. Painter* (1950), *McLaurin v. Oklahoma State Regents* (1950), and *Brown v. Board of Education* (1954). Of these cases, *Smith v. Allwright* put a decisive end to the system of "whites only" political primaries in the South, and *Brown v. Board of Education* dismantled the "separate but equal" legal rationale for racial segregation in public schools in the United States.[17]

In 1961, Marshall won the case of *Garner v. Louisiana,* in which racial segregation in public places was found to be unconstitutional by the Supreme Court. In the same year, President John F. Kennedy nominated Marshall to the Second Circuit Court of Appeals. Between 1961 and 1965, Marshall wrote 112 decisions, none of which were overturned by the Supreme Court.[18]

In 1967, President Lyndon B. Johnson appointed Marshall to the Supreme Court. He was the first African American to be appointed to the nation's highest bench. He served as an associate justice until 1991. He passed away in 1993 at the age of eighty-four. Through his indefatigable energy, foresight, and thirst for justice, Thurgood Marshall played an important role in the U.S. Supreme Court as a promoter of due process of which defendant rights is an important constituent.

Miranda v. Arizona (1966)

The U.S. Supreme Court decided in this landmark case that suspects in police custody must be informed of their constitutionally protected rights against self-incrimination. These include the rights to remain silent and to have legal counsel for their defense.

Nix v. Williams (1984)

This case addressed the issue of incriminating evidence obtained by the police when suspects in custody are not informed of their *Miranda* rights.[19] The case involved the abduction of a ten-year-old girl, Pamela Powers, from a YMCA in Des Moines, Iowa, on 24 December 1968. The suspect, Williams, was spotted leaving the YMCA carrying a wrapped bundle to his car, which later turned out to be the body of Pamela. Williams was arrested in Davenport and charged with the abduction and murder of the little girl. While being transferred to Des Moines, Williams was enticed by one of the accompanying police detectives to think about what he had done to the little girl on Christmas Eve. The detective told Williams that the body would be discovered in any case, but the Christian thing to do was to lead them to the place where Williams had disposed of it. Williams obliged this request and led the two police detectives to the remains of the girl. In February 1969 Williams was indicted for the crime of first-degree murder.

At the time of the conversation that led to the discovery of Pamela's body, the local police had already put out 200 volunteers to search the area where the police thought Williams could have dumped the body and other incriminating evidence. However, the above conversation, which ultimately led to Williams's indictment, took place without the presence of his defense lawyer, who had been retained by Williams in Davenport. The detectives had promised Williams's lawyer that they would not question him en route to Des Moines.

At the first trial, which took place in 1969, the defense made a motion for the suppression of the evidence on the grounds that the police had violated Williams's Sixth Amendment rights by engaging him in an incriminating conversation without the presence of legal counsel. The trial court denied the motion and allowed the incriminating evidence to be presented to the jury.

The first trial resulted in the conviction of Williams of the crime of first-degree murder.

The defense appealed the trial court's decision to the Iowa Supreme Court, which affirmed the lower court's decision. The case finally reached the U.S. Supreme Court, which decided that the police had indeed violated the defendant's Sixth Amendment rights as they had obtained the incriminating evidence through a conversation without the presence of the defendant's legal counsel. Thus, the Court decreed that in a new trial, the contents of the conversation were to be excluded from the proceedings. However, the prosecution could introduce as evidence the remains of the victim and their location of discovery, on the grounds that the body would ultimately have been discovered by the 200 volunteers involved in the search process.

In the second trial, which took place in 1977, the prosecution did not make any reference to the tainted conversation the police officers had with Williams en route to Des Moines, nor to Williams's role in the discovery of Pamela's body, but used the location and remains of the victim as evidence pointing to Williams's culpability in the crime. The second trial jury also found Williams guilty of the crime of first-degree murder. He was sentenced to life imprisonment. Williams again appealed to the Iowa Supreme Court, which again affirmed the lower court's decision on the grounds that the body would have been found regardless of Williams's collaboration and therefore the exclusionary rule did not apply in this case.

In 1980, Williams sought relief in federal court. Subsequently, the United States District Court for the Southern District of Iowa issued a writ of habeas corpus. A writ of habeas corpus is a legal instrument whose purpose is to investigate the reasons for the imprisonment of a person, be it in the state or federal systems. After conducting its own independent investigation, the district court agreed with the Iowa Supreme Court, deciding that there were enough independent sources that would inevitably have led to the discovery of the victim's body. Therefore, the exclusionary rule did not apply in this case. The case reached once again the U.S. Supreme Court, which agreed with the district court that the discovery of the victim's body was "inevitable" because the police had put out a large number of searchers for that purpose and they were moving in the right direction.

The *Nix v. Williams* case opened up a new chapter in the manner in which the Burger Court applied the exclusionary rule to regulate police search and seizure activities. It followed a liberal view of due process in relation to defendant rights in criminal prosecution. Being more on the side of the "law and order"philosophy than the Warren Court, the Burger Court applied exceptions to the exclusionary rule and therefore gave the police more leverage in their search and seizure activities. This new leverage given to police was followed by other "law and order" measures that further eroded the parameters of the exclusionary rule. Among such measures mention can be made of the "good faith" exceptions that one legal scholar has characterized as, "the largest loophole in the exclusionary rules. . . . which has been actively explored by all three branches [of the government]."[20]

Petition of Right (1628)

The Petition of Right of 1628 was an important document that enhanced civil liberties in Britain. It also played some role in the development of defendant rights in the Anglo-American system of criminal prosecution. The Petition of Rights was initiated by Sir Edward Coke. It was a product of Coke's legal activism in the House of Commons of the British Parliament. This petition sought to curtail some of the excesses of the monarch Charles I (r. 1625–1649). Among other things, the Petition of Right demanded that "no British subject shall be imprisoned without cause."[21]

Plain View Exception

This exception to the exclusionary rule applies when police officers come across incriminating evidence that is in their plain view while they are conducting a legal search. For example, if during a search of a suspect's residence, the police were to see drug paraphernalia spread conspicuously around the living room, they could seize it as evidence without a warrant.

Pointer v. Texas (1965)

In this case, the U.S. Supreme Court decided that the right to confront and cross-examine witnesses as stipulated by the Sixth Amendment applies to criminal defendants prosecuted in state courts as well as federal courts through incorporation by the due process clause of the Fourteenth Amendment.

Rehnquist Court (1986–Present)

William Rehnquist was appointed chief justice of the Supreme Court by President Ronald Reagan in 1986. The two terms of President Reagan ushered in a new era of social and legal conservatism. The high Court under Rehnquist started chipping away some of the more liberal and controversial aspects of due process. For example, the Rehnquist Court gave more weight to the "law and order" philosophy in the application of law enforcement. The police were given more discretionary leverage in their search and seizure activities. The more conservative judges and prosecutors followed the Court's conservatism in interpreting criminal law. In trial procedures, for example, a good number of exceptions to the exclusionary rule entered into both the state and federal criminal prosecution systems.

Robinson v. California (1962)

In this case, the U.S. Supreme Court ruled that the Eighth Amendment ban on cruel and unusual punishment applies to the states through the due process clause of the Fourteenth Amendment. The question addressed by the high Court was whether the state of California could make the mere state of being addicted to narcotic drugs a criminal offense (as opposed to possession or sale of such substances). The Court decided that it could not and found California in violation of the Eighth Amendment's ban on cruel and unusual punishment.

Terry v. Ohio (1968)

This case addressed the issue of "reasonableness" in search and seizure activities. The Supreme Court decided that it is legal for police to stop, question, and "frisk" a person who the police officer reasonably believes is acting suspiciously. This is a lower standard than probable cause. Such a frisking does not violate a suspect's Fourth Amendment rights.

Trial by Ordeal, Prohibition of (1215)

Trial by ordeal had a religious rationale to its application. This rested on the belief that guilt or innocence was a matter whose importance was far beyond the day-to-day existence of one's mortal being. It concerned the future of one's salvation in the next world. In medieval Europe, a person accused of crime had to clear his or her good name. Otherwise, he or she would be excommunicated from the church, which in turn would condemn such a person to eternal damnation in the world to come. This was a powerful belief that kept the church in a very powerful social and legal position in relation to both the state and individuals. Therefore, it was of prime importance to allow a criminal defendant to prove his or her innocence by every means possible. Trial by ordeal served this purpose. Once trial by ordeal was prohibited, medieval legal traditions had to devise other means and procedures for defense purposes.

Trop v. Dulles (1958)

This case addressed the issue of cruel and unusual punishment in relation to those who desert the ranks of the American armed forces during time of war. The question raised was whether the threat of denaturalization or expatriation of a defendant charged with desertion constituted cruel and unusual punishment. The U.S. Supreme Court decided that it did and that the Eighth Amendment's ban on cruel and unusual punishment applied. At the same time, the decision addressed the propriety of the methods of execution, namely, that it ought to meet "evolving standards of decency" to avoid being seen as cruel or unusual.

Ullmann v. United States (1956)

This case addressed the issue of self-incrimination. The question raised was whether a witness who has been given immunity from prosecution can use his or her Fifth Amendment right against self-incrimination to refuse to testify. The U.S. Supreme Court decided that when such immunity is granted, the Fifth Amendment privilege against self-incrimination cannot be utilized.

United States v. Leon (1984)

This landmark case raised the issue of whether the Fourth Amendment's exclusionary rules applied to evidence obtained by the police that turned out to be illegal even though the police claimed that they acted in good faith. The case involved the arrest of Alberto Leon, a resident of Burbank, California, in 1981. The arrest was the outcome of a long investigation of a number of small drug dealers and their operations in the area. Leon was in touch with these drugs dealers and used them for drug-pushing purposes. Leon was known to the police for his prior drug-smuggling activities and had been arrested by the Burbank police in 1980. Based on evidence obtained from informants, the Burbank police sought a search warrant for the search of residential houses that Leon and his associates used for drug-pushing purposes. Because of the sensitive nature of the investigation and the amount of time the Burbank police had put into the case, the detective in charge of the investigation, Officer Cyril Rombach, made sure that the detailed and long affidavit presented to the judge to obtain a search warrant was carefully prepared, checked, and scrutinized by several deputy district attorneys.

Upon arrest of the suspects and their indictment based on the charges of conspiracy to possess and to distribute cocaine, the defense filed a motion for the suppression of evidence on the ground that the affidavit did not establish probable cause for arrest. After an evidentiary hearing, the district court agreed to partially suppress the evidence on the grounds that the affidavit was indeed insufficient to establish probable cause. However, the district court did not suppress all evidence seized because the defense had not challenged the legality of all of it. The district court also held that Officer Rombach had acted in good faith in obtaining the search warrant. This judgment of the district court was due to the fact that Officer Rombach had taken every precautionary measure in preparing the affidavit so that it would stand up to stringent legal standards. However, the district court did not agree with the government's premise that the Fourth Amendment's exclusionary rule should not apply because the officer had acted in good faith. Therefore, the court suppressed the evidence against Leon, but not against the other suspects. The government appealed the decision of the district court to the Court of Appeals for the Ninth Circuit, which affirmed the lower court's decision. The government appealed the court of appeals decision to the Supreme Court, asking it to decide "[w]hether the Fourth Amendment exclusionary rule should be modified so as not to bar the admission of evidence seized in reasonable, good-faith reliance on a search warrant that is subsequently held to be defective."[22]

In simple terms, the government was asking the Supreme Court to reconsider the exclusionary rule of the Fourth Amendment based on a good-faith criterion. If a police officer acted in good faith, the incriminating evidence should not be excluded from presentation, even if the police turned out to be on shaky legal grounds. Siding with the government, the Supreme Court upheld the good-faith exception to the exclusionary rule without making the Amendment null and void altogether.

In short, it could be argued that under the Warren Court, the exclusionary rule of the Fourth Amendment has been gradually chipped away as the Burger Court moved away from due process and more in the direction of the "law and order" philosophy.[23] Under the Rehnquist Court, a strategic shift seems to have been made to the primacy of law and order at the expense of due process.

United States v. Wade (1967)

Addressing the issue of the right to counsel, in this case the U.S. Supreme Court decided that a criminal defendant may not be forced to participate in a lineup without the presence of his or her attorney, and that any identification of the suspect made in a lineup under such circumstances must be excluded from evidence at a subsequent criminal trial.

U.S. Bill of Rights (1791)

The American Bill of Rights played an important role in the development of defendant rights in the American system of criminal prosecution. The American Bill of Rights comprises the first ten amendments to the Constitution of the United States. Of these amendments, the Fourth, Fifth, Sixth, and Eighth have played an important role in the establishment of due process in the American system of criminal prosecution. Due process is one of the main ideals of the American notion of justice. It requires that a person suspected of crime be accorded certain procedural rights beginning even before arrest, during the course of a trial, and after conviction.

U.S. Circuit Court of Appeals Act (1891)

The American court system is divided into state and federal components. At the federal level, district courts try cases that involve federal crimes. There are ninety-four federal district courts scattered throughout the United States, with each state having at least one. The circuit courts are the federal appellate courts, which review appeals from the district courts. There are twelve circuit courts, each of which has appellate jurisdiction over those district courts that geographically have been organized under their jurisdictions. For example, the federal district courts of California, Oregon, Washington, Idaho, Montana, Nevada, Arizona, Hawaii, and Alaska (in addition to Guam and the Northern Mariana Islands) are organized under the Ninth Circuit Court of Appeals, which convenes in San Francisco, California. This means that if a federal case is tried in any district of these states, the verdict can only be appealed to the Ninth Circuit. Before the enactment of the Circuit Court of Appeals Act of 1891, the district judges also acted as appellate judges. Therefore, they had to travel around their circuits to preside over federal appeals cases. In other words, district judges acted in the capacity of both trial and appellate judges. This situation was less than ideal. Not only did the judges suffer from crushing workloads and the fatigue of travel, but it is not generally a sound legal practice to allow a trial judge to also act as an appellate judge. The reason is that these are two very different functions. A trial is an adjudication largely of the facts of the case. An appeal is a judicial review of the case. It focuses more on the procedures that the trial judge followed during the trial and the law that he or she applied. An appeals court is quite pointedly required to refrain from resifting the factual evidence presented at the initial trial, with very few exceptions. The theory is that the trial judge and the jury were in a better position to evaluate the factual evidence, seeing as they did the demeanor of the witnesses and parties firsthand. Unless an appellate court were prepared to retry every case from the beginning (a costly and time-consuming proposition), it must necessarily rely on the written record of the trial and hence be one step removed from the immediacy of the proceedings. The record is, however, sufficient to examine whether the procedures followed by the trial judge comported with the requirements of the Constitution and whether the law applied to the case was correct. Thus, appellate judges must be specialists in the minutiae of legal procedures, while trial judges must be more adept at managing the flow of the trial's many steps, at making quick calls on the propriety of proffered proofs or testimony, and at handling the people involved with some diplomacy. Thus, separation of trial and appellate functions is more efficient and doubtless results in a greater likelihood of delivering justice to the parties.

The separation between adjudication and appeal was achieved (at the federal level) through the Circuit Court of Appeals Act. The purpose of the Act was to "establish circuit courts of appeals and to define and regulate in certain cases the jurisdiction of the courts of the United States, and for other purposes."[24] Composed of fifteen sections, the act organized the administrative, managerial, and financial aspects of the federal circuit courts. It also prescribed the manner in which cases tried in district courts would proceed to the appellate circuit courts. Thus, the act played an important role in giving order to the federal appeal procedure.

U.S. Constitution (1787)

The U.S. Constitution is a remarkable legal document that has helped, among other things, the procedural and substantive development of defendant rights in the American system of criminal prosecution. One essential feature of the American Constitution is its stress on human dignity. The intellectual thrust of the constitution is that human dignity can only be preserved when liberty, the rule of law, justice, and tolerance of others are respected. The American Constitution maintains that laws are created by "We the People." These laws are put at the service of the common people for the just resolution of conflicts. These laws also express the community's compassion for the downtrodden among us.

U.S. Judiciary Act (1789)

The Judiciary Act of 1789 played an important role in the creation of the U.S. court system. It also advanced the development of defendant rights in federal criminal prosecutions. Prior to the passing of the Judiciary Act of 1789, the American judiciary followed the British court system. The British legal system had evolved through centuries, and as a result of this long experience, British judges and prosecutors tried cases in an orderly and expedient manner. The same professionalism applied to British criminal defense lawyers. By contrast, the American colonial legal system was adopted from the British legal tradition in a relatively short period of time. Because of the shortness of its evolution, the American legal system did not have a stable structure. Likewise, the American colonial judiciary was not experienced to adjudicate cases in the manner that the British judiciary did. The purpose of the Judiciary Act of 1789 was to systematically address some of the organizational shortcomings of the American colonial judiciary.

The Judiciary Act of 1789 was composed of thirty-four sections and was entitled, "An Act to establish the Judicial Courts of the United States."[25] It organized the following aspects of the American court system:

- judicial power
- judicial review
  * jurisdiction
  * the schedule of the U.S. Supreme Court
  * the size of the U.S. Supreme Court
  * the workload of the U.S. Supreme Court

These regulatory aspects of the Judiciary Act of 1789 were followed by other judiciary acts in 1801, 1802, 1817, 1837, 1863, 1867, 1869, and 1925. These acts gradually enhanced the manner in which the American criminal justice system applied the justice process to those accused of the commission of crime.[26]

War on Terrorism after 11 September 2001

With the 11 September 2001 terrorist incidents in New York and Washington, D.C., the American system of criminal defense and prosecution has entered a new phase of its evolution. The strategic question raised in the post–September 11 period is whether the American constitutional notion of defense against charges of criminality (or terrorism) makes the war on terrorism ineffective at best or impossible at worst. This is because those who engage in a war of terror against American citizens, military personnel and installations, or legitimate American interests (be it around the world or in this country) are not ordinary criminal suspects. To effectively stamp out this type of insidious activity, which is far more dangerous and destructive than traditional criminal activities, there are those who argue that suspects of terrorism must be treated differently than suspects of traditional crime. The latter do not deserve the constitutional amenities that are accorded to traditional criminal defendants. This new legal thinking is expressed in the USAPATRIOT Act of 2001.

Warren Court (1953–1969)

On 30 September 1953, President Dwight D. Eisenhower nominated Earl Warren as chief justice of the Supreme Court. He was confirmed by the Senate early the following year. Warren served as chief justice until 1969. The Warren Court has been praised for its activism on behalf of individual rights and support for due process. It was in large part during the Warren Court that the various protective measures of the Fourth, Fifth, Sixth, Eighth, and Fourteenth Amendments were institutionalized in the American criminal justice system at both state and federal levels.

Between 1954 and 1969, the Warren Court made, among others, the following landmark decisions related to defendant rights:

- Self-incrimination: *Ullmann v. United States*, 1956;
- Due process: *Mallory v. United States*, 1957;
- Cruel and unusual punishments: *Trop v. Dulles*, 1958;
- Search and seizure: *Elkins v. United States*, 1960;
- Search and seizure: *Mapp v. Ohio*, 1961;
- Equal protection: *Hoyt v. Florida*, 1961;
- Cruel and unusual punishment: *Robinson v. California*, 1962;
- Right to counsel: *Gideon v. Wainwright*, 1963;
- Search and seizure: *Kerr v. California*, 1963;
- Right to counsel: *Escobedo v. Illinois*, 1964;

- Due process: *Pointer v. Texas,* 1965;
- Self-incrimination: *Griffin v. California,* 1965;
- Self-incrimination: *Miranda v. Arizona,* 1966;
- Due process: *Klopfer v. North Carolina,* 1967;
- Search and seizure: *Katz v. United States,* 1967;
- Right to counsel: *United States v. Wade,* 1967;
- Due process: *Duncan v. Louisiana,* 1968;
- Search and seizure: *Terry v. Ohio,* 1968;
- Due process: *Benton v. Maryland,* 1969;
- Search and seizure: *Chimel v. California,* 1969.[27]

Notes

1. "Judicial giant" Blackmun dead at 90. March 4, 1999, available at http://www.cnn.com/US/9903/04/blackmun.02.

2. *Ibid.*

3. "Harry Andrew Blackmun," in *Congressional Quarterly's Guide to the U.S. Supreme Court,* p. 864.

4. "Judicial giant."

5. "Blackstone's Commentaries on the Laws of England," available at http://www.yale.edu/lawweb/avalon/blackstone/blackstone.htm, pp. 1–7.

6. "Sir Edward Coke," available at http://www.aug.edu/delta_chi/coke.html.

7. Goldwin Smith, *A Constitutional and Legal History of England* (New York: Dorset Press, 1990), pp. 305–313.

8. "English Bill of Rights," in *Encyclopedia Americana,* vol. 3 (New York: Grolier, 1996), p. 743.

9. "English Bill of Rights, December 16, 1689," available at http://www.constitution.org/eng/eng_bor.tx, p. 1.

10. *Ibid.*

11. *Ibid.*, p. 2.

12. "Fourth Lateran Council (1215)," Catholic Encyclopedia website, available at http://www.newadvent.org/cathen/09018a.html.

13. Lateran IV, Canon 18, available at http://www.intratext.com.

14. Dick A. E. Howard, *Magna Carta: Text and Commentary,* rev. ed. (Charlottesville: University of Virginia Press, 1998), pp. 24–25.

15. *Ibid.*

16. The African American Registry, *Murray v. Pearson* ruling, available at http://www.aargistry.com.

17. Thurgood Marshall biography, available at http://www.chnm.gmu.edu.

18. *Ibid.*

19. See David M. O'Brien, *Constitutional Law and Politics,* vol. 2, pp. 892–897.

20. Louis Fisher, *American Constitutional Law,* vol. 2, p. 836.

21. "Petition of Right," Columbia Electronic Encyclopedia website, available at http://www.bartleby.com.

22. O'Brien, p. 898. See also *United States v. Leon,* in Louis Fisher, *American Constitutional Law,* vol. 2, pp. 847–850.

23. Fisher, p. 836.

24. "Circuit Court of Appeals Act of 1891," in Elder Witt, ed., *Congressional Quarterly's Guide to the U.S. Supreme Court,* (Washington, DC: Congressional Quarterly Press, 1979), pp. 957–959.

25. "Judiciary Act of 1789," in *Congressional Quarterly's Guide to the U.S. Supreme Court,* pp. 949–956.

26. *Ibid.*

27. *Congressional Quarterly's Guide to the U.S. Supreme Court;* Fisher; and Lloyd L. Weinreb, *Leading Constitutional Cases on Criminal Justice.*

6

Documents and Data

Every year a large number of crimes and misdemeanors are committed in the nation, leading to the apprehension and detention of suspects by state and federal law enforcement officers. The arrested suspects go through what is known as the criminal justice process. It is composed of a number of interconnected sequential steps that lead to either acquittal or conviction in a court of law. In prosecuting those charged with criminality, the American courts follow a meticulous procedure at both the state and federal levels. The process is governed by two types of laws: procedural and substantive.

Criminal Procedure and Defense

The procedural laws lay out the procedures through which the trial proceedings unfold. These address the following matters:

- how a criminal defendant is brought before the court,
- how criminal charges are explained to the criminal defendant,
- how a criminal defendant pleads to the charges of criminality (e.g., guilty, not guilty, nolo contendere),
- how incriminating and exculpatory evidence is presented to the court,
- what the legal bases are for procedural objections and the manner in which each party lodges objections to any aspect of the proceedings.

These and similar procedures are all described by the procedural laws. According to the U.S. Constitution, a criminal defendant is entitled to all the procedural amenities of due process. This entitlement applies to both state and federal prosecutions. Violation of these legal procedures may lead to the dismissal or retrial of the case.

Crime Classifications

In the American legal system the substantive laws lay out the nature, form, and classification of acts whose commission may entail punishment. At the most abstract level, undesirable social acts can be classified as:

- felonies
- misdemeanors
- infractions

In the above classification, there is a descending order of what is known as the "degree of social harm" resulting from the action. Social harm is measured along a continuum. For example, murder inflicts the most harm on victims and their survivors. By contrast, a petty theft inflicts much less harm than murder. Therefore, undesirable social acts are classified based on the degree of social harm they inflict.

Felonies are the most serious category of crime, followed by misdemeanors and infractions. The more severe the charge leveled against a defendant, the more severe the punishment is likely to be if the defendant is convicted.

Felonies, misdemeanors, and infractions lend themselves to yet another level of classification. For example, all felonies can be divided into two general types as either (1) violent crimes or (2) property crimes. Violent crimes are those committed against a person. Crimes such as homicide, assault, rape, and robbery are committed against persons. Property crimes are those that are committed against property such as burglary, theft, arson, and larceny. Each category is subdivided further in both state and federal criminal codes. These codes define what constitutes each offense, its elements, and the sanctions applied to it.

This precision in American criminal codes allows criminal defendants to be cognizant of the charges that they face during a criminal prosecution. At the same time the precision in the criminal code allows experienced criminal defense lawyers to devise appropriate defense strategies in court. Vague, imprecise, and arbitrary criminal codes make an effective defense more difficult on the one hand. On the other hand, vagueness and imprecision in a criminal law is a gift for defense lawyers because such laws can be challenged as unconstitutional. Criminal laws must be precise in defining the elements of crime so that citizens can know how to tailor their behavior. Imprecise criminal codes render the application of the justice process arbitrary. For example, first-degree murder must be defined in the most precise manner so that it can be differentiated from second- or third-degree murder. Vague criminal codes are devoid of such precision in the definition of crime categories and therefore allow for the intrusion of arbitrary procedures in trial.

The U.S. Constitution and Criminal Defense

In the United States, both the federal and state governments have their criminal codes. These criminal codes have to be harmonious with the American Constitution's legal checks and balances. These checks and balances, as already discussed in previous chapters, are codified in Amendments Four, Five, Six, Eight, and Fourteen. The purpose of these amendments is to ensure that criminal defendants receive fair treatment. The full text of these amendments is given below.[1]

The Fourth Amendment (1791)

The right of the people to be secure in their persons, houses, papers, and effects, against unreasonable searches and seizures, shall not be violated, and no Warrants shall issue, but upon probable cause, supported by Oath or affirmation, and particularly describing the place to be searched, and the persons or things to be seized.

The Fifth Amendment (1791)

No person shall be held to answer for a capital, or otherwise infamous crime, unless on a presentment or indictment of a Grand Jury, except in cases arising in the land or naval forces, or in the Militia, when in actual service in time of War or public danger; nor shall any person be subject for the same offence to be twice put in jeopardy of life or limb; nor shall he be compelled in any criminal case to be a witness against himself, nor be deprived of life, liberty, or property, without due process of law; nor shall private property be taken for public use, without just compensation.

The Sixth Amendment (1791)

In all criminal prosecutions, the accused shall enjoy the right to a speedy and public trial, by an impartial jury of the State and district wherein the crime shall have been committed, which district shall have been previously ascertained by law, and to be informed of the nature and cause of the accusation; to be confronted with the witnesses against him; to have compulsory process of obtaining witnesses in his favor, and to have the Assistance of Counsel for his defence.

The Eighth Amendment (1791)

Excessive bail shall not be required, nor excessive fines imposed, nor cruel and unusual punishments inflicted.

The Fourteenth Amendment (1868)

Section 1. All persons born or naturalized in the United States, and subject to the jurisdiction thereof, are citizens of the United States and of the State wherein they reside. No State shall make or enforce any law which shall abridge the privileges or immunities of citizens of the United States; nor shall any State deprive any person of life, liberty, or property, without due process of law; nor deny to any person within its jurisdiction the equal protection of the laws.[2]

Criminal Defense Data

Depending on the nature of the charges leveled against them, criminal defendants are judicially processed in federal, state, juvenile, or military courts in the United States. The relevant data pertaining to the judicial processing of criminal defendants can be accessed through print and electronic sources. These multifaceted sources are partially provided by the following state and federal agencies:

- The Administrative Office of the U.S. Courts
- The Bureau of Justice Statistics
- The U.S. Sentencing Commission
- The Office of Juvenile Justice and Delinquency Prevention
- The Executive Office for the U.S. Attorneys
- The Court of Appeals for the Armed Services

In the rest of this chapter, data pertaining to criminal defenders and prosecution provided by these agencies are discussed, preceded by a brief explanatory section for each agency.

The Administrative Office of the U.S. Courts

The Administrative Office of the United States Courts was created by an act of Congress. It is the main support agency responsible for the administration of the federal court system. The main responsibilities of the office can be delineated as follows: (1) to obtain adequate funding for the judiciary from Congress, and (2) to develop, implement, and support new management techniques and technologies for the federal courts throughout the nation.[3]

Next to the Administrative Office of the U.S. Courts is the Federal Judicial Center (FJC) in Washington, D.C. Its main responsibility is to facilitate education and research. In 2002, the FJC was involved in projects aimed to help increase the public's understanding of the judicial process, as well as enhance the education of federal judges and court personnel. In addition, the FJC is responsible for providing research outlets and publications in relation to the following: judicial ethics, the development of technology in the litigation process (e.g., discovery and information on civil litigation), and the development of alternative dispute resolution on the federal level.

Criminal prosecution and defense data can be obtained from both print and electronic media disseminated by the Administrative Office of the U.S. Courts.[4]

The Bureau of Justice Statistics

The Bureau of Justice Statistics (BJS) was established on 27 December 1979, under the auspices of the Justice System Improvement Act. The act itself was part of the Public Law 96-157. The bureau, as a component of the Office of Justice Program (OJP), operates under the U.S. Department of Justice.

The BJS defines its mission in these words, "To collect, analyze, publish and disseminate data on crime, criminal offenders, victims of crime, and the operation of the justice systems at all levels of the government."[5] The data, accordingly, helps both federal and state authorities and policymakers in designing crime-fighting and preventing strategies. The BJS collects data on the following topics:

- Administration of law enforcement agencies and correctional facilities
- Prosecutorial practices and policies
- State court case processing
- Felony convictions
- Characteristics of correctional populations
- Criminal justice expenditures and employment
- Civil case processing in state courts
- Special studies in other criminal justice topics[6]

There is a huge amount of data that these agencies regularly collect. They utilize different research and collection methods. The end products are distributed to the public by means of both print and electronic communications networks. Examples of data collection means pertaining to courts and sentencing statistics include the following: (1) the National Judicial Reporting Program, (2) the State Court Processing Statistics, (3) the State Court Statistics Project, (4) the Survey of Court Organization, (5) the Civil Justice Survey of State Courts, and (6) the National Survey of Indigent Defense Systems.[7]

The BJS also distributes a wide range of statistical data on criminal offenders. These include data on subjects such as:

- Lifetime likelihood of going to state or federal prison
- Characteristics of state prison inmates
- Characteristics of jail inmates
- Comparison of federal and state prison inmates
- Recidivism
- Sex offenders
- Child victimizers
- Inmate victimizers
- Use of alcohol by convicted offenders
- Women offenders.[8]

The collected data are tabulated and analyzed. The results are then published in the form of reports, studies, and news sheets made available to the general public. These data are also given to state and federal authorities to give them a better grasp of the complex factors that operate in the American crime and justice scenes.

In short, the data collected and analyzed by the BJS help federal and state authorities in several ways, such as giving advice on: (1) how to devise preventive measures against crime commission, (2) how to devise criminal justice reform strategies, (3) how to improve steps in the application of the justice process, and (4) how to better determine the guilt or innocence of criminal defendants.

The U.S. Sentencing Commission

The U.S. Sentencing Commission was created in 1984 under the auspices of the Comprehensive Crime Control Act, Public Law 98-473.[9] This act gave statutory authority to the commission to achieve sentencing policies and practices for the federal criminal justice system so that those convicted of federal crimes would not be subjected to unfair and inconsistent punishments. Accordingly, the commission was charged with revamping sentencing guidelines in order to meet the criteria of sentencing as set forth in Section 3553 (a) (2) of Title 18 of the United States Code.[10] This section specifies that the court must consider several criteria as it determines a particular sentence to impose.

According to the commission, the sentence imposed must reflect the seriousness of the crime. At the same time, the sentence must be severe enough to offer adequate deterrence to criminal conduct. It should also provide protection for the public against further criminal conduct of the offender. Finally, the guidelines maintain that the sentence must be structured in a constructive way. This means that the sentence must be conducive to the educational, vocational, and medical needs of the convicted criminal. This is because these factors are needed for the rehabilitation of the convict within the penal institution.

The sentencing guidelines and their implementation are of relevance to the issue of defendant rights.[11] When the guidelines are not followed in the sentencing phase, a criminal defendant may appeal the legality of his or her confinement. This is legally done through the application for what is known as a writ of habeas corpus. It allows a judge to determine whether a criminal defendant is being imprisoned illegally.

The Office of Juvenile Justice and Delinquency Prevention

The Office of Juvenile Justice and Delinquency Prevention (OJJDP) was created in 1974 after Congress passed the Juvenile Justice and Delinquency Prevention Act. The act committed the federal government to undertaking a number of important reforms in the prosecution and incarceration of juvenile offenders. These reforms included measures such as separating juvenile offenders from adult criminals. In order to achieve its goals, the act allowed the federal government a more active role in the juvenile justice system.

The juvenile justice system in the United States has historically promoted the idea that state and local communities should actively be involved in the implementation of preventive measures against juvenile delinquency and crime. To this end, the act of 1974 made available much needed research money to state and local communities. The act also established the OJJDP. Its purpose was to institutionalize more effectively the federal presence in the American juvenile justice system. In addition, the act of 1974 created the National Institute for Juvenile Justice and Delinquency Prevention (NIJJDP). The main functions of the NIJJDP have been to: (1) conduct research, (2) collect relevant statistics, and (3) evaluate the effectiveness of various delinquency prevention programs and measures.

The Office of Juvenile Justice Delinquency Prevention has taken a leading role in funding research in the field of juvenile crime and delinquency. The OJJDP has funded various research studies and methodologies to address the most pressing issues of juvenile delinquency and justice in the nation. For example, as of May 2001, the following subjects related to the social causes and consequences of juvenile violence have been studied and reported by the OJJDP:

- Research on very young offenders
- Program research on the causes and correlates of delinquency
- Juvenile transfers to criminal court
- Juveniles in corrections
- Youth gang research
- Diversion from juvenile court
- National statistics on juvenile offenders and victims.[12]

The Executive Office for the U.S. Attorneys

The United States attorneys are the legal authorities responsible for prosecuting federal crimes. There are ninety-four of them located in all fifty states and the territories of the nation. The Executive Office for the U.S. Attorneys (EOUSA), created on 6 April 1953, is the main administrative body that liaises between the Department of Justice in Washington, D.C., and the ninety-four U.S. attorneys scattered throughout the nation. The EOUSA provides technical and advisory help to the U.S. attorneys concerning matters such as policy development, administrative management, direction, and oversight. It also helps the U.S. attorneys to coordinate their activities with other state and federal agencies as they carry out their prosecutorial responsibilities.[13]

The Executive Office for the U.S. Attorneys, through one of its educational agencies named the National Advocacy Center (NAC), is also involved in the training and education of federal, state, and local prosecutors and litigators. The program is called advocacy and litigation management. This is a very important educational program for those authorities involved in the general prosecution of criminal defendants in the American justice system. One important training program relates to the management of the flow of criminal case filing in both state and federal courts.

The orderly management of criminal case filing impacts the manner in which such cases are prosecuted in both state and federal courts. This, in turn, relates to one important right of criminal defendants in the American ideal of justice: namely, that justice delayed is justice denied to a criminal defendant. As discussed in Chapter 4, the Sixth Amendment mandates, among other things, the right to a speedy trial.

The U.S. Court of Appeals for the Armed Services

The U.S. Court of Appeals for the Armed Services is an appellate court. As the name implies, its main duty is to process appeals made to it from those members of the U.S. armed forces prosecuted in courts-martial. A court-martial is a military tribunal that has original jurisdiction over crimes committed by U.S. military personnel, which include the uniformed personnel of the army, navy, air force, marines, and the coast guard.

The military tribunal's prosecutorial jurisdiction is based on the Uniform Military Code of Justice (UMCJ). The UMCJ defines different aspects of the tribunal, its jurisdiction, its personnel, and the manner in which the military tribunal operates. Every year a committee known as the Code Committee on Military Justice (CCMJ) gives an annual report to the Senate, the House of Representatives, the secretary of defense, and the secretary of transportation, as well as to the secretaries of the army, navy, and air force. This annual report, among other information, contains statistics on the number of appellate cases filed, processed, and pending.

Criminal Prosecution Data

In this section, statistical data in relation to several areas of prosecution and incarceration of criminal defendants is presented. The data comes from public information sources that are maintained and operated by some of the agencies already discussed above.

Convictions in State and Federal Courts

This data set gives us important information about the number of adult criminal defendants convicted in both state and federal courts. The data sheds light on the overall efficacy of state and federal criminal justice systems. The data can also be utilized for comparative purposes. As of the end of 1998, the data revealed:

- 1998 was the first year state and federal courts convicted a combined total of nearly 980,000 adult felons.
- Between 1990 and 1998 the number of felony convictions increased 12 percent in state courts.
- State courts convicted almost 928,000 adults of a felony in 1998. The general trend has been upwards since 1990.
- Sixty-eight percent of those convicted of a felony in 1998 were sentenced to incarceration.
- Almost two-thirds of defendants charged with a felony in the 75 most populated counties in May 1996 were released from jail pending disposition of their case.
- Thirty-one percent of those who were released were rearrested for a new offense or did not show for a court date or violated some other condition of their pre-trial release.[14]

The data in relation to one's "lifetime likelihood of going to State or Federal prison" statistically measures factors whose absence, or presence, may lead to a higher chance of incarceration. These factors are related to chances of imprisonment at either state, or federal penal institutions. This is an important statistical measure for reforming the manner in which these systems of prosecution operate. For example, by studying this measure one can assess the overall efficacy of hired criminal defense lawyers versus appointed legal defense for indigents. Thus, if it can be shown that (1) both state and federal prosecution systems put a disproportionate number of indigent white and minority criminal defendants in prison and (2) both systems suspend the sentences of those criminal defendants who are represented by hired defense lawyers, then it might be concluded that the lifetime likelihood of going to prison is a function of income level rather than race. If this can be shown, then a giant step for reform-

ing the systems of criminal prosecution could be taken throughout the nation through reform measures in indigent defense funds
and system.

On the other hand, this measure can also be used for comparative purposes. One example is to use this measure to answer the
following question: Is the combination of racial, social, and economic factors of a criminal defendant related to his or her lifetime
chance of going to prison? It is highly probable that those criminal
defendants who come from the lower social and economic strata
have a higher lifetime likelihood of going to both state or federal
prison than those who come from the higher economic and social
strata of American society. One reason for this has to do with the
kind of criminal defense lawyers that the two groups can afford to
hire. Another reason has to do with the recurring cycles of economic downturns that impact the two groups differently.

The following statistical information applies to the lifetime
likelihood of going to prison:

- If recent incarceration rates remain unchanged, an estimated 1 of every 20 persons (5.1 percent) will serve time
  in a prison during their lifetime.
- Lifetime chances of a person going to prison are higher
  for men (9 percent) than for women (1.1 percent), blacks
  (16.2 percent) and Hispanics (9.4 percent) than for
  whites (2.5 percent).
- Based on current rates of first incarceration, an estimated 28 percent of black males will enter state or federal prison during their lifetime, compared to 16 percent
  of Hispanic males and 4.4 percent of white males.[15]

Characteristics of State Prison Inmates

This data set gives information about the race, gender, ethnic origin, and education of criminal defendants convicted and sentenced to state prisons. In addition, statistical data is given about
the type of crimes for which the defendants have been found
guilty. As of 2001, the following applied in this regard:

- Women were 6.6 percent of the state prison inmates in
  2001, up from 6 percent in 1995.

- Sixty-four percent of prison inmates belonged to racial or ethnic minorities in 2001.
- An estimated 57 percent of inmates were under age 35 in 2001.
- About 4 percent of state prison inmates at the end of 2001 were not U.S. citizens.
- Altogether, an estimated 57 percent of inmates had only a high school diploma or its equivalent.
- Among the state prison inmates in 2000:
  —nearly half were sentenced for a violent crime (49 percent)
  —a fifth were sentenced for a property crime (20 percent)
  —about a fifth were sentenced for a drug crime (20 percent).[16]

Characteristics of Jail Inmates

This data set gives information about the race, gender, ethnic origin, and education of those criminal defendants who are placed in jail. Jail is different from prison. The primary function of a jail is for detention purposes, whereas prison is for incarceration of more than one year (technically one year plus one day). There are other important differences between the two. Inmates incarcerated in prisons are entitled to a number of constitutional rights and protections different than those in jails. Prisons are much more structured, with elaborate bureaucratic rules and regulations than jails. The data set utilized below gives information about those who have been placed in jail because they either have committed a crime whose penalty is a jail term or they have temporarily been placed in jail waiting for trial. This is because there are criminal defendants who cannot post the required deposit of money for bail, or are denied bail because of the severity of the crime, or because they are a flight risk. In addition, this report also gives statistical data about the type of crimes for which defendants have been found guilty. In the 1990s, the following applied to jail inmates:

- Women comprised 10 percent of the local jail inmates in 1996, unchanged from 1989.

- Forty-eight percent of jailed women reported having been physically or sexually abused prior to admission; 27 percent had been raped.
- Sixty-three percent of jail inmates belonged to racial or ethnic minorities in 1996, up slightly from 61 percent in 1989.
- Twenty-four percent of jail inmates were between the ages of 35 and 44 in 1996, up from 17 percent in 1989.
- Over a third of all inmates reported some physical or mental disability.
- About 8 percent of local jail inmates were not U.S. citizens.
- Altogether, 54 percent of inmates had only a high school diploma or its equivalent.[17]

Comparing Federal and State Prison Inmates

A comparison between federal and state prison inmates can shed light on the race, gender, ethnic origin, and type of offense that distinguish federal prison inmates from state prison inmates. State prison inmates compose about 90 percent of the total inmate population. This is a percentage that has remained almost constant in many decades of the past century. This is because the bulk of the crimes committed in the United States have been violations of state codes that are processed in state jurisdictions. On the other hand, the bulk of the federal arrests and convictions are related to illicit drug activities. These differences are important for comparative research concerning the overall differences between those criminal defendants who end up in federal and those who end up in state penal institutions. As of 2000, the following applied in this regard:

In 1997, federal inmates were more likely than state inmates to be

- women (7 percent versus 6 percent)
- Hispanic (27 percent versus 17 percent)
- age 45 or older (24 percent versus 13 percent)
- with some college education (18 percent versus 11 percent)
- noncitizens (18 percent versus 5 percent).[18]

In 2000, an estimated 57 percent of federal inmates and 21 percent of state inmates were serving a sentence for a drug offense; about 10 percent of federal inmates and 49 percent of state inmates were in prison for a violent offense. Violent offenders accounted for 53 percent of the growth in state prison between 1990 and 2000, drug offenders accounted for 59 percent of the growth in federal prisons.[19]

Recidivism

Recidivism means the tendency to repeat criminal behavior, even after conviction and punishment. One who repeatedly engages in crime is a recidivist, or simply a repeat offender. Gathering statistical data about recidivism is important because it sheds light on whether punishing criminal offenders actually deters them from committing crimes in the future.

A high recidivism rate in any jurisdiction suggests that either (1) the general deterrence mechanism does not function properly in that jurisdiction, or (2) that the jurisdiction lacks effective social support programs (e.g., educational, legal, economic, law enforcement, communal, etc.) to promote law-abiding life styles. In the 1990s, the following applied:

- Of the 272,111 persons released from prisons in 15 states in 1994, an estimated 67.5 percent were rearrested for a felony or serious misdemeanor within 3 years, 46.9 percent were reconvicted, and 25.4 percent resentenced to prison for a new crime.
- The 272,111 offenders discharged in 1994 accounted for nearly 4,877,000 arrest charges over their recorded careers.
- Within 3 years of release, 2.5 percent of released rapists were resentenced for another rape, and 1.2 percent of those who had served time for homicide were arrested for a new homicide.
- On any given day in 1994 there were approximately 234,000 offenders convicted of rape or sexual assault under the care, custody, or control of corrections agencies; nearly 60 percent of these sex offenders are under conditional supervision in the community.

- The median age of the victims of imprisoned sexual assaulters was less than 13 years old; the median age of rape victims was about 22 years.
- An estimated 24 percent of those serving time for rape and 19 percent of those serving time for sexual assault had been on probation or parole at the time of the offense for which they were in state prison in 1991.[20]

Use of Alcohol by Convicted Offenders

Alcohol consumption may lead to intoxication. Intoxication can lead to violence, crime, or other antisocial behavior. Alcohol use plays an important causal role in criminal behavior. The data presented below is related to the age, gender, race, ethnic origin, and prior criminal record of those arrested while under the influence of alcohol and sheds light on an important category of criminal defendants. In the 1990s, the following facts applied:

- Among the 5.3 million convicted offenders under the jurisdiction of corrections agencies in 1996, nearly 2 million, or about 36 percent, were estimated to have been drinking at the time of the offense. The vast majority, about 1.5 million, of these alcohol-involved offenders were sentenced to supervision in the community—1.3 million on probation and more than 200,000 on parole.
- Alcohol use at the time of the offense was commonly found among those convicted of public-order crimes, a type of offense most highly represented among those on probation and in jail.[21]

Women Offenders

This data set sheds light on criminal offenses committed by American girls and adult women. Historically speaking, crime has been committed predominantly by males throughout the world. Women's criminal activities have been of a sexual nature, expressed usually in the form of female prostitution and, in modern times, pornography.

In the United States, the decades of the 1960s and 1970s saw major changes in the overall American crime scene. These decades witnessed dissent, social upheavals, and even crime generated by complex social and political events. These included the so-called sexual revolution, the women's liberation movement, the civil rights movement, and the hippie counterculture movement. In addition, these decades witnessed impacts of the infiltration of illicit drugs into large urban centers, coupled with the experimentation with marijuana of thousands of middle-class, suburban adolescents. Finally, a large number of American women from different social strata entered into the job market. Put together, these complex social events brought a new dynamic into the American arena of crime, criminal defense, and prosecution.

This data set gives us a comparative yardstick to measure the social and economic factors of a gender-based universe of crime and criminal defendants. As of 2000, the following facts applied:

- In 1998 there were an estimated 3.2 million arrests of women, accounting for 22 percent of all arrests that year.
- Based on self-reports of victims of violence, women accounted for 14 percent of violent offenders, an annual average of about 2.1 million violent female offenders.
- Women accounted for about 16 percent of all felons convicted in state courts in 1996: 8 percent of convicted violent felons, 23 percent of property felons, and 17.5 percent of drug felons.
- In 1998 more than 950,000 women were under correctional supervision, about 1 percent of the U.S. female population.[22]

Indigent Defense

In the United States, those criminal defendants with financial means can afford the price of legal defense as they proceed through the American justice system. The American criminal defense industry is represented by a hierarchy of professionals of which attorneys at law are only the tip of the iceberg. Private investigators, expert witnesses, forensic specialists, psychiatrists, doctors, public relations flacks, and consultants of all stripes vie for a piece of the criminal defense industry pie. These people's services can be retained from the very beginning of the process until the very end. Those who cannot afford the price tag are left vulnerable to the negative realities of the American system of conflict resolution.

One stark reality of this system is that competent defense is like any other commercial product that has to be purchased within the context of a market mechanism. The mostly indigent minorities who live in large urban areas of the United States are ill equipped to navigate the adversarial process through which legal guilt or innocence is determined. This is despite the fact that state and federal indigent defense funds are institutionalized for indigent criminal defense purposes. In addition, there are institutions for legal help such as the Public Defender's Office that operate throughout the states defending indigents charged with crime.

The Bureau of Justice Statistics reported the following facts in relation to indigent defense as of 1996:

- States and localities use several methods for delivering indigent defense services: public defender programs, assigned counsel, and contract attorney systems.
- Twenty-eight percent of state court prosecutors reported that their jurisdictions used public defender programs exclusively to provide indigent counsel.
- In 1990 states and local governments spent approximately $1.3 billion on public defender services. In 1979 this figure was about $300 million.
- About three-fourths of the inmates in state prisons and about half of those in federal prisons received publicly provided legal counsel for the offenses for which they were serving time.
- In 1992 about 80 percent of defendants charged with felonies in the nation's 75 largest counties relied on public defenders or on assigned counsel for legal representation.
- Little current information is available regarding the workload, staffing, procedures, or policies for indigent defense services across the nation.[23]

As of the year 2000, the following pertained to the provision of indigent defense services throughout the nation based on the Bureau of Justice Statistics Bulletin:

- An estimated $1.2 billion was spent on indigent criminal defense in the nation's 100 most populous counties during 1999, with about 73 percent spent by public defender programs, 21 percent by assigned counsel programs, and about 6 percent on awarded contracts.
- Indigent criminal defense expenditures in the largest 100 counties comprised 3 percent of all local criminal justice expenditures and 16 percent of judicial expenditures in these counties.
- County governments provided 60 percent and state governments 25 percent of total funding used by indigent criminal defense service providers.
- Indigent criminal defense providers in the 100 most populous counties received an estimated 4.2 million cases in 1999.
- Public defenders handled about 82 percent of these 4.2 million cases, assigned counsel attorneys about 15 percent, and contract attorneys about 3 percent.
- Over 12,700 individuals were employed by public defender programs in the largest 100 counties in 1999. Half of the 123 public defender programs had 33 or more assistant public defenders.
- In 1999, over 30,700 attorneys received appointments through assigned counsel programs to represent indigent defendants. Half of the 126 assigned counsel programs had 109 or more appointments.
- Over 1,000 contracts for indigent defense services were administered in the top 100 counties during 1999.[24]

Federal Criminal Prosecution and Defense

In this section, data on federal criminal prosecution and defense are provided from the Executive Office for U.S. Attorneys. The data sets are of a longitudinal nature. Longitudinal data allows researchers to compare and contrast the fluctuation patterns of the subject under study over a period of time. For example, Table 6.1 depicts longitudinal data on criminal defendants processed by the U.S. attorneys between 1980 and 2000. This data set gives an idea of the role of the grand jury in the federal court system.

TABLE 6.1

Grand Jury Proceedings and Criminal Cases Filed and Terminated by U.S. Attorneys, 1980–2000

Year	Grand Jury Proceedings	Cases Filed	Terminated
1980	16,592	26,088	NA
1981	16,794	25,830	NA
1982	17,064	26,106	NA
1983	17,765	27,462	NA
1984	17,487	27,292	NA
1985	17,094	27,059	NA
1986	20,111	31,012	NA
1987	19,263	31,593	30,547
1988	20,184	33,294	29,582
1989	23,203	34,865	29,322
1990	23,925	36,042	32,204
1991	25,943	38,374	33,834
1992	25,470	35,263	33,161
1993	25,757	36,995	35,809
1994	20,714	33,307	32,231
1995	22,856	36,878	32,829
1996	22,449	38,250	34,882
1997	25,209	39,291	34,634
1998	30,734	47,277	40,746
1990	32,474	50,779	48,423
2000	34,055	52,887	48,308

Source: Sourcebook of Criminal Justice Statistics, 2001, p. 399.

Although no data are given for the category of "terminated" between 1980 and 1986, for the remaining years for which data have been given, one discerns that there has been a close correlation between criminal cases filed by the federal grand jury and cases terminated in the federal court system. However, it is also noteworthy that there is a gradual divergence between the two categories (of filed and terminated) as we approach the year 2000, a divergence that perhaps implies that the federal court system's docket is becoming clogged as the number of cases filed by the federal grand jury increases.

The second longitudinal data set presented in Table 6.2 depicts criminal cases filed in the U.S. district courts. The U.S. district courts are federal courts of general jurisdiction that try criminal cases involving federal crimes. Table 6.2 categorizes federal crimes committed between 1993 and 2001. The fluctuation in the overall number of federal crimes as depicted by Table 6.2

TABLE 6.2
Criminal Cases Filed in U.S. District Courts by Offense, 1993–2000

Offense	1993	1994	1995	1996	1997	1998	1999	2000
Misc. general offenses	11,838	12,414	11,114	10,462	10,386	10,856	11,747	12,544
Fraud	7,575	7,098	7,414	7,633	7,874	8,342	7,654	7,788
Drug laws	12,238	11,369	11,520	12,092	13,656	16,281	17,483	17,505
Larceny/theft	3,322	3,337	3,431	3,674	3,299	3,590	3,514	3,414
Forgery/ counterfeiting	1,059	1,093	1,001	987	1,156	1,346	1,292	1,203
Embezzlement	1,857	1,575	1,368	1,284	1,172	1,397	1,315	1,200
Immigration laws	2,487	2,595	3,960	5,526	6,677	9,339	10,641	12,150
Federal statutes	2,200	2.084	2,403	2,317	2,158	2,363	2,241	2,844
Robbery	1,789	1,520	1,240	1,365	1,453	1,448	1,295	1,258
Assault	523	563	561	540	527	629	529	665
Motor vehicle theft	349	335	267	232	189	182	189	199
Burglary	141	139	63	65	70	89	72	59
Homicide	181	195	295	344	348	384	383	370
Sex offenses	337	359	412	623	690	777	893	944
Liquor, IRS	6	2	3	2	2	0	3	9
Total	45,802	44,678	45,053	47,146	49,655	57,023	59,251	62,152

Note: In the original document, the categories of miscellaneous general offense, federal statutes, and robbery have been broken down into sub-categories, which I have omitted above.

Source: Data from *Sourcebook of Criminal Justice Statistics,* 2001, page 403.

allows researchers to test different hypotheses as to the efficacy of the federal court system and its operational dynamics. For example, the data on drug crimes, drug-related arrests, and drug-related prosecutions can give us some ideas as to whether the American "war on drugs" is succeeding.

Table 6.3 sheds light on criminal cases commenced, terminated, and pending in U.S. district courts between 1982 and 2001. Ideally speaking, criminal cases should be disposed of in the most just and yet expeditious manner. To expedite the resolution of cases in federal courts, Congress passed the Speedy Trial Act of 1974. The act mandates that a case be judicially disposed of within a maximum of 180 days. The speedy trial requirement is expressed in the Sixth Amendment to the U.S. Constitution.

The data presented in Tables 6.1, 6.2, and 6.3 (pertaining to judicial processing of criminal defendants in 1980–2000) is taken from the *Source Book of Criminal Justice Statistics 2001.* The *Source*

TABLE 6.3
Criminal Cases Commenced, Terminated, and Pending
(Judgeship Authorized in U.S. District Court), 1982–2001

Case commenced	Judgeship authorized	Cases per judgeship	Number	Drug cases	Terminated	Pending
1982	515	32,682	63	4,218	31,889	16,659
1983	515	35,872	70	5,094	33,985	16,546
1984	515	36,845	72	5,606	35,494	19,938
1985	575	39,500	69	6,690	37,139	22,299
1986	575	41,490	72	7,893	39,328	24,453
1987	575	43,292	75	8,878	42,287	25,263
1988	575	43,607	76	10,603	41,878	28,776
1989	575	45,792	80	12,342	2,933	32,666
1990	575	46,568	81	11,547	3,296	35,308
1991	649	47,123	73	11,954	43,073	35,562
1992	649	48,366	75	12,833	44,147	34,078
1993	649	46,786	72	12,238	44,800	28,701
1994	649	45,484	70	11,369	45,129	26,328
1995	649	45,788	71	11,520	41,527	28,738
1996	647	47,889	74	12,092	46,499	32,156
1997	647	50,363	78	13,656	46,887	37,273
1998	646	57,691	89	16,281	51,428	40,277
1999	646	59,923	93	17,483	56,511	42,966
2000	655	62,745	96	17,505	58,102	47,677
2001	655	62,708	94	18,425	58,718	51,667

Source: Data from *Sourcebook of Criminal Justice Statistics,* 2001, page 401.

Book of Criminal Justice Statistics is published by the Department of Justice, the Executive Office for the U.S. Attorneys. It covers all conceivable information from the state and federal components of the American criminal justice system.

State-level Prosecution

The complexity of defendant rights in the United States is compounded by the fact that each state has its own criminal justice system composed of its own police, courts, and corrections departments. The operations of all these institutions—although subject to the requirements of the U.S. Constitution—nevertheless function independently and differently from one state to another. For example, California's criminal justice system is radically different from that of North Dakota. The former, with an ethnically and culturally diverse populace with a high crime rate, can afford to experiment with different policing strategies, penal institutions, and legal philosophies to better control crime. California is a pioneer in what we may consider legal activism, resulting in the most imaginative criminal defense strategies that the U.S. legal tradition has devised. An example is the defense of the ex-football player, O. J. Simpson in 1995.

North Dakota on the other hand, is one of the least populated states with a rather homogeneous culture and the lowest rate of crime in the nation. Both states adhere to U.S. constitutional checks and balances, but here ends the similarity between the two states' criminal justice systems. The differences between the two states' criminal justice systems are profound in terms of their structure and operational dynamics. For example, the California Criminal Code is quite complex, covering a wide range of felonies, misdemeanors, and city and county ordinances, including a comprehensive victims' bill of rights. In addition, the state has twenty-seven codes regulating different aspects of social life in California. Naturally, the more legal and regulatory codes there are, the more complex the social and legal relationships become. An example is California's victims' bill of rights, a measure inserted in Article 1, Section 28 of the California Constitution. It reads:

> The people of the State of California find and declare that the enactment of comprehensive provisions and laws ensuring a bill of rights for victims of crime, including safeguards in the criminal justice system to fully protect those rights, is a matter of grave statewide concern. The rights of victims pervade the criminal justice system, encompassing not only the right to restitution from wrong-doers for financial losses suffered as a result of criminal acts, but also the more basic expectation that persons who commit felonious acts causing injury to innocent victims will be appropriately detained in custody, tried by the courts, and sufficiently punished so that the public safety is protected and encouraged as a goal of highest importance. Such public safety extends to public primary, elementary, junior high, and senior high school campuses, where students and staff have the right to be safe and secure in their persons. To accomplish these, broad reforms in the procedural treatment of accused persons and the disposition and sentencing of convicted

persons are necessary and proper as deterrents to criminal behavior and to serious disruption of people's lives.[25]

In contrast, North Dakota has a much simpler criminal code and court system. Its victim rights legislation provides the following rights to victims of crime:

• To receive prompt notice of the inmate's release from custody, including work release program, community residential program or transfer to mental health facility.
• To be informed of the parole and pardon process, including notice of any pending review.
• To submit a written statement to the parole board and pardon advisory board concerning the impact of the crime. Victims of violent crime may, at the board's discretion, personally appear to give a statement.
• To be notified of the parole board and pardon of advisory board's decision.
• To be notified of protection available in cases of intimidation.
• To be informed of appropriate and available community services.[26]

Thus, the fact that California has made victims' rights a constitutional matter provides victims much leverage in terms of services. North Dakota's notification process affords fewer services to crime victims. The differences between the two states approach to the issue of victim rights impacts the manner in which disputes are resolved in each jurisdiction.

Juveniles Prosecuted in State Criminal Courts

As of March 1997 the Bureau of Justice Statistics reported the following in its "Selected Findings" concerning the prosecution of juvenile defendants in state courts:

• Nationwide, 94 percent of State court prosecutors' offices had responsibility for handling juvenile cases.
• Among prosecutors' offices handling juvenile cases, almost two-thirds transferred at least one juvenile case to criminal court in 1994. Of these offices, 37 percent transferred at least one aggravated assault case, 34 per-

cent at least one burglary case, 34 percent at least one robbery case, and 32 percent at least one murder case.

- Nineteen percent of prosecutors' offices handling juvenile cases had written guidelines about the transfer of juveniles to criminal court.
- States have developed mechanisms to permit proceeding against alleged juvenile offenders as adults in criminal court. These mechanisms include judicial waivers, concurrent jurisdiction statutes, and statutorily excluding certain offenses from juvenile court jurisdiction.
- The percentage of petitioned cases judicially waived to criminal court has remained relatively constant at about 1.4 percent since 1985. In 1994, 12,300 juvenile cases were judicially waived.
- From 1985–1991 property offenses comprised the largest number of cases judicially waived. Since 1991 violent

TABLE 6.4
Characteristics of Waived Cases, 1987–1996

	1987	1992	1996
Total Cases Waived	6,800	10,300	10,000
Most Serious Offenses			
Person	28%	39%	47%
Property	55	41	37
Drugs	9	11	14
Public order	7	12	15
Gender			
Male	95%	96%	95%
Female	5	4	5
Age at Time of Referral			
Under 16 years	7%	12%	15%
16 or older	93%	87%	85%
Race/Ethnicity			
White	57%	47%	51%
Black	41	50	46
Other	2	3	3
Predisposition Detention			
Detained	58%	53%	51%
Not detained	42	47	49

Note: Numbers may not add to 100% due to rounding.

Source: Data from *OJJDP Fact Sheet* 99, April 1999.

offenses have outnumbered property offenses as the most serious charge.

- Currently no national data describe the number of juvenile cases processed in criminal court under concurrent jurisdiction or statutory exclusion provisions.[27]

Table 6.4 is taken from the Office of Juvenile Justice and Delinquency Prevention. It shows juvenile defendants whose status has been waived, allowing their cases to be transferred from juvenile to adult criminal court to be prosecuted as adults. The waiver is because of the severity of the crime alleged against the juvenile, causing such change of legal venue. The change of venue from juvenile to adult criminal court is important because it shows that the American juvenile justice system is perhaps incapable of rehabilitating and/or effectively deterring a segment of American youth from involvement in serious crime.

Notes

1. George C. Edwards, Martin P. Wittenberg, and Robert L. Lineberry, *Government in America: Brief Version*, 3rd ed. (New York: Longman, 1997), pp. 328–329.

2. *Ibid.*, p. 330.

3. Ralph Mecham, "2002 Year-End Report on the Federal Judiciary," in *The Third Branch: The Newsletter of the Federal Courts* (2003). Available at http://www.uscourts.gov/ttb/indx/html.

4. *Ibid.*

5. Bureau of Justice Statistics website. Available at http://www.ojp/bjs/aboutbjs.htm.

6. *Ibid.*

7. *Ibid.*

8. *Ibid.*

9. Dean J. Champion, ed., *The U.S. Sentencing Guidelines: Implications for Criminal Justice* (New York: Praeger, 1989), pp. 247–249.

10. *Ibid.*

11. *Ibid.*

12. *OJJDP Research Report 2000* (Washington, DC: Office of Juvenile Justice and Delinquency Prevention, May 2001), Table of Contents.

13. "Year-End Report on the Federal Judiciary," 2002. Available at http://www.uscourts.gov/ttb/jan03ttb/page4.html.

14. "Courts and Sentencing Statistics," Bureau of Justice Statistics website. Available at http://www.ojp.usdoj.gov/bjs/stsent.htm.

15. "Criminal Offenders Statistics," Bureau of Justice Statistics website. Available at http://www.ojp.usdoj.gov/bjs/crimoff.htm.

16. *Ibid.*

17. *Ibid.*

18. *Ibid.*

19. *Ibid.*

20. *Ibid.*

21. *Ibid.*

22. *Ibid.*

23. K. Steven Smith and Carol J. DeFrances, "Indigent Defense," NCJ 158909, (Washington, DC: U.S. Department of Justice, Bureau of Justice Statistics, 1996), p. 1.

24. Carol J. DeFrances and Marika F.X. Litras, "Indigent Defense Services in Large Counties," NCJ 184932 (Washington, DC: U.S. Department of Justice, Bureau of Justice Statistics, 1999), p. 1.

25. Cliff Roberson, *California Criminal Codes,* second ed., (Incline Village, NV: Copper House Publishing Co., 2000), p. 42.

26. Victim Service Program at web page: http://www.state.nd.us/docr/parole/victim_program.html.

27. U.S. Department of Justice, Bureau of Justice Statistics, *Juveniles Prosecuted in State Courts, 1994* (Washington, DC: Government Printing Office, 1997).

.

7

Agencies and Organizations

U.S. Advocacy Organizations

All-American Legal Forms and Research
3312 Scottsville Road
Lafayette, TN 37083
Phone: (615) 666–8882
E-mail: clgammon@justice.com
Website: http://www.firms.findlaw.com/allamericanlegal/
  index.htm

All-American Legal Forms and Research is a nonprofit organization dedicated to "empowering" U.S. citizens in regard to legal matters. The organization believes that there are legal procedures that do not require the paid services of a professional attorney. Based on this rationale, this organization acts in the capacity of a legal research and clearinghouse. It provides, free of charge, legal information on the United States federal and state codes, statutes, laws, and regulations. It also provides information on caselaw and the meanings of legal terms and doctrines. In addition, All-American Legal Forms and Research, as the name implies, provides all those legal forms required for writing a legally acceptable will or a petition to court. The expenses of the organization are paid through private donations. These services are important, maintain the founders of All-American, because they enable low-income citizens to have some control over their legal destiny as they get entangled with the U.S. justice system. Naturally, the organization's services are invaluable for those criminal defendants who may want to act as their own defense attorneys.

American Bar Association (ABA)
One Elk Street
Albany, NY 12207
Phone: (518) 463-3200

The American Bar Association was established on 21 August 1878, in Saratoga Springs, New York. It has played a significant role in articulating the goals and professional standards of the legal profession in this country. Those charged with crimes or misdemeanors, or anyone who is in need of the services of a lawyer may consult their state bar association to get, free of charge, referrals to such services.

Because of the continuous efforts of the ABA, the U.S. legal profession has gradually become systematized, making law a reputable and rewarding profession. To practice in any branch of law in this country, one has to go through arduous academic training in an accredited law school to get a three-year J.D. (juris doctorate) degree. After getting the degree, one has to pass a written examination administered by the state bar association in the state in which one intends to practice law. The prospective lawyer can then get a license to practice law in that state. At all times, a lawyer must adhere to a set of principles enunciated by the gatekeeper of the profession, the American Bar Association. The ABA has also played an important organizational role in development of "indigent defense," the purpose of which is to help low-income or indigent defendants to pay their legal defense costs.

American Civil Liberties Union (ACLU)
125 Broad Street, 18th Floor
New York, NY 10004
Website: http://www.aclu.org

Founded in 1920 by a number of civil libertarian activists, the ACLU has played a prominent, and at times controversial, role in the direction that the U.S. legal profession has taken in the twentieth century and beyond. The ACLU is a nonprofit organization. It is dedicated to preserving the basic civil liberties that the U.S. Constitution has provided for U.S. citizens and others who live in this country. The ACLU has contributed to the national debate over the range of liberties that U.S. citizens enjoy. In particular, the ACLU has been involved in a legal battle against restrictions that local, state, and federal governments have tried to impose on the exercise of rights guaranteed by the Constitution. For example, after the tragic events of 11 September 2001, the Bush administration presented to Congress a multitude of bills that if passed, the ACLU believes, would severely curtail basic freedoms in this country. Examples include the USAPATRIOT Act, which facilitates local, state, and federal police agencies in arresting, searching, detaining, and interrogating suspects without observing long-standing safeguards designed to protect citizens from arbitrary and groundless government intrusion into their lives, as well as allowing the police to extend the search to see if the suspect has any connections to domestic or international terrorism.

The ACLU is against this proposed legislation and finds it unconstitutional because it allows the police to arbitrarily fish for incriminating evidence by leaping from investigating the probable cause of criminality to a probable cause of linkage to international terrorism. In other words, under the new proposed legislation, any criminal suspect is also a potential suspect of domestic or international terrorism. This legal reasoning is contrary to the ideal of the presumption of innocence in the U.S. system of criminal prosecution.

The ACLU has objected to the Bush administration's other crime-fighting and crime-control projects, such as the Defense Department's Total Information Awareness Project (TIA). If implemented, the TIA would allow the Defense Department's supercomputers to monitor, on a continuous basis, each and every electronic transaction, communication, Internet surfing connection, and chat room comment of the average U.S. citizen. The administration's justification for such intrusive, continuous, and en mass surveillance of the U.S. population is to fight domestic and international forms of terrorism. The rationale is that through this surveillance, the Defense Department would be able to discover patterns of activity suggestive of terror plots. This computer-based surveillance would enable the authorities to locate and identify prospective terrorists as well.

The ACLU is of the opinion that these types of intrusive surveillance are in violation of the Fourth Amendment. In short, the ACLU is dedicated to the safeguarding of America's basic constitutional liberties of which the right to be secure in one's home, papers, and effects against government intrusion constitutes a significant one.

Association of Federal Defense Attorneys
16000 Ventura Boulevard, Suite 500
Encino, CA 91436
Phone: (818) 998-2706
Fax: (818) 998-8427
Website: http://www.afda.org

Established in 1989, the Association of Federal Defense Attorneys (AFDA) represents the professional interests and concerns of federal criminal defense lawyers. In particular, the AFDA specializes in the following areas: federal criminal trial and appellate litigation; representing witnesses before federal grand juries; defense of paralegal civil and criminal proceedings; and providing consultation services to defense attorneys on federal criminal cases.

Attorney Find
96 Chalet Court
Lake Saint Louis, MO 63367-2028
Phone: (636) 561-0755
E-mail: Visibility@primary.net
Website: http://www.attorneyfind.com

Attorney Find is a legal firm referral service that provides the names, addresses, and areas of expertise of law firms and attorneys throughout the United States and in other nations of the world. The service gives pertinent legal and organizational information on seventy areas of legal practice. In return for a fee, U.S. and international law firms and attorneys use FindLaw to advertise their services to the public.

Center for Law and Social Policy
Phone: (202) 906-8013
E-mail: jhutchin@clasp.org
Website: http://www.clasp.org

Composed of lawyers and experts on policy issues, the Center for Law and Social Policy (CLASP) is a recently established national nonprofit organization. It conducts research on U.S. law and social policy issues such as education, child health and welfare, reproductive health, and other relevant issues. Insofar as legal services are concerned, the Center provides such services funded by the Legal Services Corporation (LSC). These include training and material related to the criminal defense and civil representation of LSC's indigent clientele.

Equal Justice America
3010 Fox Chase Drive
Midlothian, VA 23112
Phone: (804) 744-4200
Fax: (804) 744-6789
E-mail: info@equaljusticeamerica.org
Website: http://www.equaljusticeamerica.org

Equal Justice America (EJA) is a nonprofit corporation established in 1993 to enhance civil legal representation for low-income clients. The founders of Equal Justice America believe that there is an urgent and dire need for adequate legal representation for indigent or low-income people in civil cases. Since its inception, the EJA has placed law students in different legal organizations and agencies throughout the country to help those who need legal representation in civil legal matters. The rationale for EJA's activism has been endorsed by the American Bar Association. The latter has estimated that in the 1990s, a large percentage of the poor did not get adequate legal representation in civil matters brought before courts in this country. Besides placement of law students as interns, the EJA has provided grant money (more than $2 million) and more than 250,000 hours of free legal services to its indigent or low-income clientele.

Foundation for Criminal Justice
c/o NACDL
1150 18th Street, NW, Suite 950
Washington, DC 20036
Phone: (202) 872-8600
Fax: (202) 872-8690
E-mail: assist@nacdl.org
Website: http://www.nacdl.org/public.nsf/freeform

The Foundation for Criminal Justice (FCJ) is a newly established (2002) nonprofit affiliate of the National Association of Criminal Defense Lawyers (NACDL). Its expressed ideal is to expedite the support of basic fairness in the U.S. criminal justice system. To achieve this ideal, the foundation engages in active protection of the U.S. Bill of Rights. In addition, the foundation stresses that the Bill of Rights must be applied to the justice process in order to enhance due process in relation to all citizens regardless of their social and economic standing. The FCJ, through its legal activism supported by voluntary public donations, seeks to enhance those legal services that its parent organization, the NACDL, has availed to its clientele.

Innocence Project Northwest

University of Washington Law School
1100 NE Campus Parkway
Seattle, WA 98105-6617
Website: http://www.law.washington.edu/ipnw

The Innocence Project Northwest (IPNW) was founded in 1997 at the University of Washington Law School. It is a nonprofit legal-help project developed by a group of concerned lawyers and forensic pathologists. The foundation and its professionals believe that a good number of criminal convictions are regularly obtained based on evidence that would not stand the test of a vigorous authentication process. Based on its research, the Innocence Project advocates have reached the conclusion that about 10 percent of U.S. prison inmates are innocent of the crimes of which they have been convicted. This percentage corresponds to nearly 200,000 inmates. The Innocence Project is especially important for those indigents who have been convicted of capital crimes and are facing either long-term incarceration or execution.

Mexican American Legal Defense and Educational Fund (MALDEF)

140 E. Houston Street, Suite 300
San Antonio, TX 78205
Phone: (210) 224-5476
Fax: (210) 224-5382
Website: http://www.maldef.org

The Mexican American Legal Defense and Education Fund (MALDEF) is a national organization dedicated to facilitating the legal and educational needs of Mexican Americans. It was first established in San Antonio, Texas, in 1968. The MALDEF has opened up chapters in large metropolitan cities with sizeable Mexican American communities, such as Atlanta, Houston, Albuquerque, Chicago, Los Angeles, Sacramento, Phoenix, and Washington, D.C. Despite having made tremendous social, economic, and political strides, Mexican Americans still face enormous educational and legal challenges. Therefore, the MALDEF provides much-needed and valuable legal and educational help to the poorer sections of the Mexican American communities.

National Archive of Criminal Justice Data
ICPSR, Institute for Social Research
P.O. Box 1248
Ann Arbor, MI 48106
Phone: (800) 999-0960
Fax: (734) 998-9825
E-mail: nacjd@icpsr.umich.edu

Established in 1978, the National Archive of Criminal Justice Data is a crime and justice clearinghouse. It is sponsored by the Bureau of Justice Statistics, which operates as an agency of the U.S. Department of Justice. The National Archive of Criminal Justice Data provides a wealth of information about crime and justice in this country, including data on various aspects of criminal defense. The data are collected by both academic and government-based agency researchers who conduct research in criminology, criminal justice, and social problem fields. In addition, there are those institutions that survey public attitudes about social issues. For those interested in criminal defense processes, reference should be made to Sections 4, 5, and 6 of the National Archive of Criminal Justice Data.

National Association of Criminal Defense Lawyers (NACDL)
1150 18th Street, NW, Suite 950
Washington, DC 20036
Phone: (202) 872-8600
Fax: (202) 872-8690
E-mail: assist@nacdl.org
Website: http://www.nacdl.org

The National Association of Criminal Defense Lawyers (NACDL) was founded in 1958. It represents a segment of the U.S. criminal defense lawyer establishment composed of 10,400 members organized in 80 affiliated criminal defense organizations scattered throughout the United States and the rest of the world. The primary purpose of the NACDL is twofold: (1) to act in the capacity of a permanent organization of criminal defense lawyers, and (2) to facilitate the legal representation of criminal defendants to the fullest extent of the law and in the most competent manner possible. Besides its private lawyers, the NACDL membership cadre also includes public defenders, active military defense counsel, law professors, and judges who believe in the basic fairness of the justice process as idealized in the Bill of Rights of the U.S. Constitution.

The NACDL also provides information on legal assistance to its members, advising them how to prepare oral arguments for court appearances or how to access legal experts in forensic-based evidence gathering, forfeiture-based police abuses, or in criminal justice ethics. One of the most valuable services of the NACDL is its indigent defense service, which among other things, sustains programs such as the aforementioned Innocence Project Northwest.

National Capital Area
1400 20th Street, NW, Suite 119
Washington, DC 20036
Phone: (202) 457-0800
Website: http://www.aclu-nca.org

The National Capital Area (NCA) is a newly established affiliate of the ACLU whose focus is the nation's capital city, Washington, D.C. Based on the NCA's electronic website, Washington, D.C., is fast becoming a city under very intrusive electronic surveillance that allows the Metro Police and other federal agencies located there to monitor every aspect of daily life in the city. The NCA is of the opinion that D.C.'s "spy cameras are a step toward totalitarianism" in this country.

How this intense surveillance would impact the U.S. system of criminal prosecution is yet to be seen. What is certain is that a number of legal experts consider such intrusion as not boding well for the future of civil liberties in this country. The same concerns have been raised by criminal defense lawyers, who argue that this unchecked intrusion may gradually erode the lawyer-client privilege that allows communications between the two to remain confidential. The privilege applies to information that a client gives to his or her lawyer. A judge is not legally allowed to compel a lawyer to divulge this privileged information. However, intrusive electronic surveillance is capable of breaching the most private conversation, making it almost impossible to keep secret. This is the gist of the NCA's concerns.

National Lawyers Guild
143 Madison Avenue, 4th Floor
New York, NY 10018
Phone: (212) 679-5100
Fax: (212) 679-2811
E-mail: nlgo@nlg.org
Website: http://www.nlg.org

The National Lawyers Guild (NLG) is a left-leaning, progressive, and nonprofit association of lawyers. It is dedicated to the U.S. ideal of justice for all regardless of race, gender, religion, or economic status. The association believes that justice is inherently linked to the social and economic structure of U.S. society. One main purpose of the association is to promote justice for and the civil rights of the working men and women in this country. The association is keen on preserving the civil liberties of Americans, especially since the tragic events of 11 September 2001 in New York, Pennsylvania, and Washington, D.C.

Through referrals, the association also helps those who need legal assistance in relation to immigration, civil rights issues, and the U.S. criminal justice system. Besides a number of national projects (e.g., NLG Post 9/11 Project, NLG Immigration Project, NLG National Police Accountability Project), the association has created an extensive website with links to many national and international organizations and associations dedicated to the enhancement of civil liberties or the defense of those accused of political crimes in nondemocratic societies around the world. The NLG has its chapters in the states of Minnesota, Michigan, Vermont, Massachusetts, New York, Georgia, New Mexico, California, and Washington.

National Legal Aid and Defender Association
1625 K Street, NW, Suite 800
Washington, DC 20005
Phone: (202) 452-0620
Fax: (202) 872-1031
E-mail: s.mayuga@nlada.org
Website: http://www.nlada.org

The National Legal Aid and Defender Association (NLADA) was established in 1911. It is the largest nonprofit organization dedicated to the advocacy of equal justice for all Americans. It provides a wide range of legal services to those who cannot afford their costs, be it in the handling of criminal or civil cases. The electronic website of the NLADA in its fact sheet section explains that the National Legal Aid and Defender Association is composed of two types of member organizations: (1) those that provide direct assistance and services in the arena of public defense, and (2) those that provide such legal services pro bono.

The NLADA fact sheet explains that the services are delivered in three ways to low-income clients through: (1) the public defender model, (2) the assigned counsel model, or (3) the contract model.

International Agencies and Organizations

International Association of Democratic Lawyers
Rue Brialmont 21
1210 Brussels, Belgium
Phone: (322) 223-33-10
E-mail: szmukler@ciudad.com.ar
Website: http://www.iadllaw.org

The International Association of Democratic Lawyers (IADL) is a nongovernmental organization (NGO). It was created in 1946 in Paris, France. Its main purpose is to help the United Nations to achieve some of its goals as articulated in the Charter of the United Nations. The IADL believes that to achieve its goals, there is a need for cooperation, contact, and good will, as well as better understanding among lawyers and their associations throughout the world. In addition, the IADL believes that governments and their agencies need to respect human rights and adhere to the rule of law. Both of these processes take shape through organizational independence of the judiciary. It is only through unencumbered functioning of an independent judiciary that legal professionalism develops. And that, in turn, promotes equity and justice in the application of law.

The IADL from its inception has continuously pressured the United Nations General Assembly to pass internationally binding legislation against the violation of human rights. It believes that the bulk of human rights violations take place in developing countries that do not have independent judiciaries and therefore do not adhere to the philosophy of the rule of law in their criminal defense and prosecution systems.

International Commission of Jurists
P.O. Box 216
81a Avenue de Chatelaine
1219 Geneva, Switzerland
Phone: 41 (0) 22-929-38-01
E-mail: info@icj.org
Website: http://www.icj.org

The International Commission of Jurists (ICJ) is affiliated with the United Nations. The commission is composed of sixty lawyers who are dedicated to the ideal of the universality of human rights. The commission is also dedicated to the philosophy of the just and equitable application of law throughout the world. The commission monitors the situation of human rights around the world through a process of fact finding that includes observing trial procedures and investigating alleged violations of human rights in different countries. It publishes documents dealing with these issues and sponsors studies about different legal systems, including how they operate and how they apply law and justice. The commission also disseminates much information through its electronic website for those who are interested in comparative and international legal research.

International Court of Justice
Peace Palace
2517 KJ The Hague
The Netherlands
Phone: 31 (0) 70 302-2323
Fax: 31 (0) 70 364-9928
E-mail: information@icj-cij.org
Website: http://www.icj-cij.org/icjwww/igeneralinformation.
  htm

This is the official judicial organ of the United Nations. Its main duty is to resolve disputes between nations who have appealed to it for arbitration and have accepted its jurisdiction. It is composed of fifteen judges elected for terms of nine years. For further reference on various aspects of the International Court of Justice, see also *Germain's International Court of Justice Research Guide* at http://www.lawschool.cornell.edu

International Crime and Justice Research Institute
Viale Maestri del Lavoro
10–10127 Turin
Italy
Fax: 39 (011) 63-13-368
E-mail: internship@uniciri.it
Website: http://www.un.org/Pubs/whatsnew/unicjri.htm

The UN International Crime and Justice Research Institute (UNICJRI) was established in 1968. The authorization for the creation of the UNICJRI came through Resolution 1086 B (XXXIX). This resolution also authorized the creation of the United Nations Social Defense Research Institute (UNSDRI). The main purpose of the resolution was to combat both juvenile and adult criminality on an international basis. The UNICJRI has funded many research projects, some of which have dealt with the issues of victimization, criminal prosecution, and defense in developing countries of the world.

International Criminal Court
Division of Common Services
P.O. Box 19519
2500 The Hague
The Netherlands
Phone: 31 (70) 515-8515
Fax: 31 (70) 515-8555

The idea to create the International Criminal Court dates back to December 1948. In that year the General Assembly of the United Nations passed a resolution (No. 260) expressing the need for such a legal body to prosecute a category of crime that is known as crimes against humanity. These are crimes that are so grave that they impact the whole of humanity. Examples include the acts of genocide, war crimes, use of weapons of mass destruction, and the systematic rape of women and young girls during war or regional conflicts. The main purpose of crimes against humanity is to terrorize, intimidate, subjugate, or liquidate a group of people who are of a different race, ethnicity, or religion. For example, genocide involves the systematic attempts by a state to mass murder a group of people for social and political reasons.

At the same time, the United Nations authorized a commission composed of international lawyers to study how to organize such a judicial body. The commission studied various complex legal and organizational issues in the early 1950s. However, the General Assembly did not follow through until 1989 when ethnic cleansing erupted (first in Africa and in 1993 in the former Yugoslavia). Finally, in 1998 the International Criminal Court was officially inaugurated by the United Nations. Its legal jurisdiction covers the so-called core crimes. These include genocide, crimes against humanity, and war crimes. Because of the complexities involved in the investigation, prosecution, and defense of those charged with the commission of core crimes, many legal and procedural issues need further research and organizational fine-tuning for the ICC to become fully operational as desired by the court's charter.

Crimes against humanity are difficult to prosecute because they involve different state authorities and agencies involved in different stages of the commission of such crimes, as well as complex chains of command—all of which give perpetrators the opportunity to point fingers elsewhere. Therefore, it is difficult to find one culprit to charge him or her with the crime. In most cases, there are top state officials who should be indicted, pursued, and brought to justice through international legal cooperation.

8

Print and Nonprint Resources

Print Resources

Books on the United States

Barak, Gregg, Jeanne M. Flavin, and Paul S. Leighton. *Class, Race, Gender and Crime.* Los Angeles, CA: Roxbury Publishing Company, 2001. 302 pages.

Written from a critical perspective, this book explores the relationship between four factors: race, class, gender, and crime. Gregg et al. argue that the configuration of these factors determines the manner in which justice is applied to those who get entangled with the U.S. criminal justice system. The central tenet of the book is that those who come from the privileged white social strata of U.S. society are treated differently by the criminal justice system than those from nonprivileged and minority classes. The authors propose that gender also plays an important part in the process. Because of this differential treatment, qualitative differences exist between privileged and nonprivileged members of U.S. society when it comes to defense in a court of law. From this perspective, this book allows the reader to appreciate both the positive and negative aspects of the U.S. system of criminal defense and prosecution. The authors make a convincing case that a defendant's race, gender, and class play an important role in the manner in which he or she receives, or does not receive, justice in America.

Baumgartner, M. P., ed. *The Social Organization of Law.* 2d ed. San Diego, CA: Academic Press, 1999. 435 pages.

This book brings together twenty-one research articles and essays about sociological factors that play a role in the organization of the law and legal tradition. The book highlights the historical development of the concept and practice of criminal defense. In a nutshell, this collection can shed light on the complexity of the U.S. notion of criminal defense in a court of law.

Biskupic, Joan, and Elder Witt. *The Supreme Court and Individual Rights.* 3rd ed. Washington, DC: Congressional Quarterly, Inc., 1996. 360 pages.

Composed of five chapters and reference materials, this book gives a detailed picture of the U.S. court system and its relation to the individual and society at large. The reference section provides material about the Supreme Court justices, explains how to read a court citation, and includes a glossary of legal terms and a select bibliography.

Cole, George F., and Marc G. Gertz, eds. *The Criminal Justice System: Politics and Policies.* 7th ed. Belmont, CA: Wadsworth, 1998. 506 pages.

This book is a collection of research articles written by leading scholars in the field of criminal justice. It offers a number of chapters dedicated to various aspects of criminal prosecution and defense in the U.S. criminal justice system. The editors believe that, although U.S. justice has gone through significant changes in recent years, politics still plays a significant role in the operational dynamics of the criminal justice system, a premise that thematically links twenty-eight chapters of the book. On the general subject of criminal prosecution and defendant rights, the reader will find much valuable information in Chapters 10 through 21, which compose Parts III, IV, and V of the book.

del Carmen, Rolando V. *Criminal Procedure: Law and Practice.* 3d ed. Belmont, CA: Wadsworth, 1995. 521 pages.

This book, composed of fourteen chapters and two appendices, gives a detailed picture of the U.S. court system, its operational dynamics, and the legal processes through which the guilt or innocence of those charged with the commission of crime is established.

It explores a wide range of Supreme Court cases in relation to police search and seizure, booking, interrogation, and surveillance activities, the abuse of which provides the basis for the bulk of the civil liability lawsuits that are filed against police in this country.

DeLeon, Angelo, and Gary H. Weddle, eds. *A Summary of U.S. Supreme Court Decisions for the Criminal Justice Community*. Fresh Meadows, NY: Looseleaf Law Publications, Inc., 1998. 238 pages.

The editors of this book have compiled U.S. Supreme Court decisions covering issues related to law enforcement at both the state and federal levels. Students of defendant rights in America will find this book a useful reference in researching caselaw relevant to the Fourth, Fifth, Sixth, and Eighth Amendments to the Constitution of the United States. These Amendments lie at the core of due process in the U.S. criminal court system.

Dorne, Clifford, and Kenneth Gewerth, eds. *American Juvenile Justice: Cases, Legislation and Comments.* Bethesda, MD: Austin and Winfield Publishers of Legal Commentary, 1995. 1,226 pages.

U.S. juvenile crime is to some extent different from adult crime. That is why juvenile crime is handled under a different justice system. Dorne and Gewerth discuss the rise of the U.S. juvenile justice system from its beginnings to the present time. The authors give a wealth of information about the system, how it operates, and the manner in which juvenile defendants are adjudicated in the structurally complex and organizationally varied state juvenile justice systems throughout the nation. Of special significance is the recognition that the treatment of juvenile defendants must differ from that of adult offenders. For example, the treatment of a juvenile in the adult criminal justice system would be much harsher if the case is waived from juvenile court to the adult criminal justice system. In short, this book provides a comparative reference with which to explore the juvenile justice system's treatment of this country's young offenders.

Elias, Stephen, Mary Randolph, Barbara Kate Repa, and Ralph Warner, eds. *Legal Breakdown: 40 Ways to Fix the Legal System.* Berkeley, CA: Nolo Press, 1990. 88 pages.

This collection of research essays succinctly explains some of the most problematic aspects of the U.S. legal system and then offers what the editors consider forty pragmatic ways to reform it. Although no specific section is devoted to defendant rights per se, a number of the reform proposals would certainly help defense procedure. The proposals include such measures as taking simple actions out of court, simplifying legal documents in terms of filing procedure and the jargon used in them, making the courthouse user friendly, adding self-help court clerks, providing legal help for the poor, eliminating biases from the court, reforming the jury system, and others.

Fisher, Louis. *American Constitutional Law, Volume 2, Constitutional Rights.* 3d ed. Durham, NC: Carolina Academic Press. 1,249 pages.

Fisher's second volume of *American Constitutional Law* is a valuable reference book for the issue of criminal defense in the U.S. court system. Chapter 13 of this volume is entitled "Rights of the Accused" and covers the legal, procedural, and structural aspects of defense in both the state and federal court systems. The chapter also covers Supreme Court decisions concerning these aspects of trial.

Fuller, John R. *Criminal Justice: A Peacemaking Perspective.* Needham Heights, MA: Allyn and Bacon, 1998. 312 pages.

Fuller wants to explain U.S. criminal justice from a new perspective known as "peacemaking criminology." This new perspective has a radically different view as to what constitutes criminal prosecution and defense. The theoretical gist of peacemaking criminology is that the U.S. justice system has traditionally approached the issue of crime from a "war on crime" mentality. Under this approach, those who commit crime have been identified as the enemy of law and order. In contrast, the peacemaking approach tries to understand why people commit crimes, use violence, or consume illicit drugs. This strategic shift, argue peacemaking criminologists, would change the whole dynamics of criminal prosecution and defense in America. This book provides a valuable tool with which to compare the more traditional books available in the criminal justice field.

Gabbidon, Shaun L., Helen Taylor Greene, and Vernetta D. Young, eds. *African American Classics in Criminology and Criminal Justice.* Thousand Oaks, CA: Sage Publications, Inc., 2002. 399 pages.

Composed of twenty-three essays and research articles, this collection gives an insight into the thought of both past and contemporary African American scholars and social critics in regard to race, crime, law, and justice in this country. The book explores the ideas of thinkers like Ida B. Wells Barnett, W. E. B. Du Bois, Monroe N. Work, E. Franklin Frazier, and Earl R. Moses, whom the authors have characterized as the pioneers of African American classicism in criminology and criminal justice. Part 2 of the book is devoted to contemporary classics, which include the works of writers such as A. Leon Higginbotham Jr., Robert Staples, Darnell F. Hawkins, Vernetta D. Young, Daniel E. Georges-Abeyie, and others. Although the book does not provide specific information on the subject of defendant rights, nonetheless, many chapters deal with the issue of the unequal treatment of African American criminal defendants in the U.S. criminal justice system.

Kadish, Sanford H., and Stephen J. Schulhofer. *Criminal Law and Its Processes: Cases and Materials.* 5th ed. Toronto, Canada: Little, Brown and Company, 1989. 1,280 pages.

This book by two leading legal scholars is composed of nine chapters. The authors tackle the complex nature of the U.S. legal tradition, showing how different forms of crime are defined and how legal guilt is established. In doing so, the authors explain in some detail how the process of defense against charges of criminality unfolds in a court of law. This book, due to the wealth of cases it covers, can be considered a source book for both general knowledge and research. In particular, Chapter 1 entitled "How Guilt Is Established" can shed light on the main subject of the present book, defendant rights.

O'Brien, David M. *Constitutional Law and Politics, Volume Two, Civil Rights and Civil Liberties.* 3d ed. New York: W. W. Norton and Company, 1997. 1,520 pages.

This casebook of the U.S. Constitution and Bill of Rights gives a wealth of information about caselaw, the factors involved in the interpretation of constitutional law, and various civil and political rights that citizens of this country enjoy, including the fundamental right of defense against charges of criminality. This basic right, together with legal processes and cases related to it, is covered in Chapters 7, 8, 9, 10, and 12 of the book.

Reid, Sue Titus. *Criminal Law.* 5th ed. New York: McGraw-Hill, 2001. 459 pages.

This book explores in some detail U.S. criminal law. The author also explores various types of crimes (both property and violent) committed throughout the United States, detailing as well defense procedures, concepts, and strategies that criminal lawyers utilize in this country.

Reiman, Jeffrey. *The Rich Get Richer and the Poor Get Prison: Ideology, Class, and Criminal Justice.* Needham Heights, MA: Allyn and Bacon, 1998. 226 pages.

Writing from a critical perspective, Reiman in this controversial book argues that the U.S. justice system is a product of the manner in which the U.S. class structure operates to endow the upper and middle classes with much prestige, power, and wealth and to inflict much injustice and poverty on the working class and the racial and ethnic minorities who compose the bulk of the underprivileged in this country. As far as defendant rights are concerned, Reiman argues that the rich, because they can afford competent criminal defense lawyers, get a much better deal from the justice system. The poor and the racial and ethnic minorities are financially deprived and therefore unable to hire competent criminal defense lawyers. Nor is the U.S. public defender's office capable of providing such services for the poor, who end up going to prison.

Rush, George E. *The Dictionary of Criminal Justice: With Summaries of Supreme Court Cases Affecting Criminal Justice.* 5th ed. Guilford, CT: Dushkin/McGraw-Hill, 2000. 444 pages.

As the title indicates, this dictionary of criminal justice provides the meanings of legal terms used in the Anglo-American legal tradition. It also includes summaries of Supreme Court cases concerning the protections embodied in the Fourth, Fifth, Sixth, Eighth, and Fourteenth Amendments to the U.S. Constitution.

Souryal, S. Sam. *Ethics in Criminal Justice: In Search of Truth.* Cincinnati, OH: Anderson Publishing Co., 1992. 389 pages.

Writing from a strongly moral perspective, Souryal argues that ethics ought to play a central role in any system of criminal justice, especially in those modern ones that attempt to apply justice on an equal footing to all. After giving the historical background of the field of ethics and its endemic relationship to justice, Souryal explores the requirements for the application of ethics to the U.S. criminal justice system. Although no chapter is specifically devoted to the subject of defendant rights per se, the book makes an important contribution to the notion that every criminal justice agency has ethical obligations when dealing with criminal defendants. In particular, Souryal applies his methodology to the police, highlighting the crucial role that police play in the application of the justice process in the nation.

Stuckey, Gilbert B., Clif Roberson, and Harvey Wallace. *Procedures in the Justice System.* Upper Saddle River, NJ: Prentice Hall, 1998. 434 pages.

This book explores the legal procedures that unfold in the U.S. justice system as a criminal defendant proceeds through the various stages of trial. The appendices are devoted to an outline of trial procedure (Appendix A), the issue of insanity (Appendix B), and various motions in the evidentiary process.

Sulton, Anne T., ed. *African-American Perspectives: On Crime Causation, Criminal Justice Administration, and Crime Prevention.* Newton, MA: Butterworth-Heinemann, 1996. 220 pages.

This book, composed of fifteen research articles, contains selections by African American practitioners and scholars. The authors present African American perspectives as to why crime is committed in this country, as well as commentary on how African Americans who get entangled with the U.S. criminal justice system are treated by the police, the courts, and the corrections institutions. Besides explaining various social, economic, political, and epistemological factors involved in crime causation, some aspects of the social and legal discrimination that operates in the U.S. criminal justice system are discussed, giving some research-based insight as to why African American criminal defendants get the adverse treatment by the system that they do.

Urofsky, Melvin I. *A March of Liberty: A Constitutional History of the United States.* New York: McGraw-Hill Publishing Company, 1988. 969 pages.

This is a historical account of the rise of U.S. constitutional law from its English roots to the time of the Reagan administration in the 1980s. In addition, the book traces the historical background of the U.S. legal tradition and its legal procedures, including the liberties that U.S. citizens have gradually attained during a long process of evolution. Comprising forty-one chapters, an epilogue, and appendices, the book offers those interested in defendant rights especially relevant material in Chapters 24, 29, 31, 32, 33, 34, 36, 39, and 40. The book has a long list of the Supreme Court cases in its Index of Cases.

Walker, Samuel, Cassia Spohn, and Miriam DeLone. *The Color of Justice: Race, Ethnicity and Crime in America.* 2d ed. Belmont, CA: Wadsworth, 2000. 306 pages.

This book comprises ten chapters in which the authors attempt to explain the complex relationship that exists between race, ethnicity, crime, and criminal defense in the United States. The authors marshal a wide range of statistical information about the African American and Hispanic American communities to explore why a disproportionate number of youths from these racial and ethnic minorities get entangled with crime and, therefore, with the criminal justice agencies in this country. The term *color of justice,* argue the authors, implies that U.S. justice is neither color-blind nor racist. U.S. justice is applied through a complex legal process in which a defendant's social, economic, political, and communal abilities and privileges, or lack thereof, play a significant role in the unfolding of his or her fate. Those who can afford the expenses of competent criminal defense lawyers, and are sophisticated enough to recognize the complexity of the U.S. legal system, fare much better than those who are indigent in terms of both economic resources and social and educational savvy. Chapters 5 and 6 of the book are especially relevant to defendant rights.

Weinreb, Lloyd L., ed. *Leading Constitutional Cases on Criminal Justice.* New York: Foundation Press, 1995. 1,178 pages.

As a classic among legal sources, this book covers leading Supreme Court decisions in relation to the investigation and prosecution of crime. The cases relate to due process of law (five cases); arrest, search, and seizure (fifty-one cases); electronic surveillance, agents, informers, and entrapment (six cases); the right to counsel (ten cases); the privilege against self-incrimination (twenty-one cases); preliminary examination of suspects (three cases); the right to speedy trial (two cases); plea bargaining (three cases); the right to trial by jury (four cases); trial (ten cases dealing with issues of fairness, right to confronting witness etc.); and double jeopardy (four cases). This book should be considered an important reference for those interested in the Supreme Court's rationale for its decisions on different aspects of defendant rights.

Books on Other Countries

Adler, Freda. *Nations Not Obsessed with Crime.* Littleton, CO: Fred B. Rothman and Company, 1983. 204 pages.

A classic of the series put out by the Comparative Criminal Law Project of the Wayne State University Law School, this monograph covers select countries in Western Europe (Switzerland and Ireland), Eastern Europe (Bulgaria and the German Democratic Republic), Latin America (Costa Rica and Peru), Africa (Algeria), the Middle East (Saudi Arabia), and Asia and the Pacific Rim (Nepal and Japan) to compare and contrast how crime is controlled informally and through criminal justice systems in these countries. One common denominator for selection of these socially and culturally diverse countries has to do with the fact that none is characterized by much crime or violence. This is in part due to the efficacy of the informal means that these countries employ in keeping their respective societies from falling into the grip of crime and violence. This, in turn, allows the formal means of crime control (i.e., the criminal justice systems) of these countries to better serve the cause of justice, despite the fact that none of these countries provide as broad a set of legal rights as the U.S. justice system. Though obviously dated (the countries of Eastern Europe are no longer communist states and Saudi Arabia is facing new challenges with politically motivated violence, among other changes), this book provides an excellent methodology for those interested in the comparative study of the social, cultural, and legal factors involved in both informal and formal means of crime control.

Barak, Gregg, ed. *Crime and Crime Control: A Global View.* Westport, CT: Greenwood Press, 2000. 259 pages.

This book comprising fifteen chapters of research articles written by area experts from different countries gives a global perspective on how crime is committed and controlled in developing parts of the world. A number of the articles also explore the structure and the operations of various countries' criminal justice systems, including some aspects of criminal defense and legal dynamics in the developing parts of the world. This is a timely and excellent reference book for comparative purposes.

Bellamy, J. G. *The Criminal Trial in Later Medieval England: Felony before the Courts from Edward I to the Sixteenth Century.* Toronto, Ottawa, Canada: University of Toronto Press, Inc., 1998. 208.

This is an excellent historical record of the rise and systematization of the criminal trial in medieval Britain and under British common law. The book is composed of four chapters, two appendices, and a glossary of legal terms used in medieval England. The book gives a detailed picture as to how medieval British jurists conceived of crime, what constituted the role of the jury in legal deliberations, and how criminal trials proceeded in court. This book is highly recommended for those interested in the historical linkage between the British and U.S. legal traditions, including the two systems' views of defendant rights.

Foglesong, Todd S., and Peter H. Solomon Jr. *Crime, Criminal Justice, and Criminology in Post-Soviet Ukraine.* Washington, DC: U.S. Department of Justice, 2001. 111 pages.

Ukraine was one of the most important among the fifteen republics of the Soviet Union. This research monograph commissioned by the National Institute of Justice, provides valuable information about crime and its social dynamics in the post-Soviet era in Ukraine, including some aspects of justice and criminal prosecution.

Kusha, Hamid R. *The Sacred Law of Islam: A Case Study of Women's Treatment in the Islamic Republic of Iran's Criminal Justice System.* Aldershot, England: Ashgate Publishing Company, 2002. 314 pages.

This book, composed of nine chapters and thirty-seven tables showing a wide variety of crime, violence, and illicit drug-use data, is divided into two parts. Part one traces the historical development of Islam's sacred law based on a wealth of primary and secondary sources. The second part explores Iran's criminal justice system (both secular and Islamic), its history, and its crime-control strategies. In addition, the Iranian criminal justice system's treatment of women's criminality is discussed and documented. Chapters 5, 6, and 7 include sections on the manner in which criminal defendants have been treated in both the pre-and post-1979 eras.

Nagel, Stuart S., ed. *Handbook of Global Legal Policy.* New York: Marcel Dekker, Inc., 2000. 520 pages.

Devoted to a global analyses of legal policy in Africa, Europe, Asia, and North and Latin America, this book comprises twenty-five chapters written by various prominent legal scholars. Of special significance for defendant rights are Chapter 3, entitled "The Public Prosecutor, Criminal Law, and the Rights of Accused in Japan: Yet to Strike a Balance?" authored by Masaki Koyama; Chapter 5, "Legal Reform and Minority Rights in China," by Barry Sautman; Chapter 6, "Legal Aid Services and Human Rights in the People's Republic of China," by Qizhi Luo; Chapter 9, "New Times, a New Paradigm: Mapping the Interactions of the Legal System, Judges, Lawyers, and Regime Changes in Post-Communist Europe," by Carl F. Pinkele; Chapter 12, "The Influence of Expert and Non-Expert Members of Juries: The Spanish Jury as an Illustration," by Martin F. Kaplan and Ana M. Martin; Chapter 23, "A Challenge to Reform: How Competing Views of Children's Nature Have Influenced the United States Supreme Court's Determination of the Legal Status of Accused Juveniles," by Joyce Dougherty; and Chapter 24, "Domestic Implications of Terrorism in the United States: 1972–1999," by Jorg Brehetfeld.

Obi, N. Ignatius Ebbe, ed. *Comparative and International Criminal Justice Systems: Policing, Judiciary and Corrections.* Newton, MA: Butterworth-Heinemann, 1996. 224 pages.

This book brings together a wealth of research articles written by legal scholars and criminal justice practitioners exploring various aspects of law, crime, and criminal justice systems that operate in the Americas (United States, Brazil), Northern Europe (United Kingdom, Denmark), Africa (ex-British colony of West Africa, Sierra Leon, Nigeria), and Asia (People's Republic of China, Japan).

Office of International Criminal Justice at the University of Illinois at Chicago. *The Criminal Procedure Law of the People's Republic of China.* 1999.

This book provides an English translation of the criminal procedure law of the People's Republic of China for those interested in learning more about legal modernization efforts in China. In addition, the text provides premodernization China's legal code and procedures next to the modern ones, making the book a valuable tool for comparative research.

Orucu, Esin, Elspeth Attwooll, and Sean Coyle, eds. *Studies in Legal Systems: Mixed and Mixing.* London: Kluwer Law International, 1996. 360 pages.

This book examines the degree to which legal systems around the world can be categorized as mixed or mixing. The authors are of the opinion that a mixed legal system is structurally built on different legal concepts and procedures borrowed from other systems. Mixing systems, on the other hand, are in the process of integrating and combining elements from other systems and therefore are in flux. Composed of twenty chapters written by legal scholars from different countries, the book covers the legal systems of the Basque region of Spain, Australia, Sri Lanka, the Russian Federation, Hong Kong, Israel, South Africa, Algeria, Malta, Japan, Slovenia, and Germany. These chapters cover subjects such as court structure, legal procedures, and defendant rights as they explore each country's legal system.

Rounds, Delbert, ed. *International Criminal Justice: Issues in a Global Perspective.* Needham Heights, MA: Allyn and Bacon, 2000. 306 pages.

Composed of twenty-two chapters written by legal scholars, this book covers a number of issues related to the international crime scene and criminal justice systems throughout the world. The underlying theme linking the chapters is that no criminal justice system is an isolated and autonomous structure. This means that crimes that occur on the international scene such as illegal sales of arms to terrorist groups, drug trafficking, financial fraud and money laundering, and persistent human rights violations do impact the efficacy of democratic societies' criminal justice systems.

Smith, Goldwin. *A Constitutional and Legal History of England.* New York: Dorset Press, 1990. 565 pages.

For those interested in British constitutional and legal history, Smith provides an excellent narrative and detailed picture of the subject in this book. Of special significance for defendant rights in the common law legal tradition, Chapters 5, 6, 7, 8, and 9 in particular explore the roots of British notions of law, crime, order, and their corresponding constitutional checks and balances.

Terrill, Richard J. *World Criminal Justice Systems: A Survey.* Cincinnati, OH: Anderson Publishing Co., 1999. 662 pages.

The title is a bit misleading because this survey covers only seven criminal justice systems—those of England, Canada, France, Sweden, Japan, Russia, and China. Despite this shortcoming, the survey does an excellent job in detailing the components of these countries' criminal justice systems, including the issue of legal defense in criminal court. The survey provides a tool to compare and contrast other systems of legal defense.

U.S. Government Publications

In the United States there exist numerous government agencies that disseminate data on many aspects of law, crime, and justice, including data on how data itself affects the application of justice. For example, the Bureau of Justice Statistics (BJS) of the U.S. Justice Department publishes bulletins, fact sheets, and special reports on many aspects of this country's criminal justice system. The BJS website (http://www.ojp.usdoj.gov/bjs) allows data to be downloaded free of cost. Below, BJS's criminal defense-related publications and data resources are listed by their titles followed by the order number of each document.

Compendium of Federal Justice Statistics 2000. NCJ 194067.

This document describes the manner in which the U.S. federal justice system and a number of agencies process criminal defendants in the system, including those who have already been prosecuted, convicted, incarcerated, and sentenced to probation, parole, or other forms of supervision.

Contract Cases in Large Counties: Civil Justice Survey of State Courts, 1992. NCJ 156664.

Written as a special report, this document presents data on the disposition of 366,000 legal contract cases covering 1.3 million litigants in state courts of general jurisdiction in what the document describes as the nation's seventy-five largest counties in 1992.

Contract Trials and Verdicts in Large Counties, 1996. NCJ 179451.

This report presents research results on legal contract cases that have been disposed of either by jury or bench trials conducted in the nation's seventy-five largest counties in 1996.

Defense Counsel in Criminal Cases, 2000. NCJ 179023.

Written as a position paper, this report examines issues related to legal representation in both federal district court and large state jurisdictions. In addition, some aspects of legal representation sought by local jails and federal and state prisons are examined.

Drugs and Crime Facts, 1994. NCJ 154043.

Although this report in principal summarizes 1994 data on drug-related crime and other aspects of drug usage, it also includes prosecution data on drug offenders, giving some insights as to how drug-related criminal prosecution proceeds in both federal and state courts.

Federal Criminal Appeals, 1999. NCJ 185055.

This document describes appeals made to the federal appellate courts because of challenges made to trial courts' sentences.

Federal Criminal Case Processing, 2001: With trends 1982–2001. NCJ 189737.

This is an annual publication whose purpose is to give the public and criminal researchers statistics concerning stages through which defendants go in the federal justice system.

Federal Habeas Corpus Review: Challenging State Court Criminal Convictions, 1995. NCJ 155504.

Habeas corpus cases are those in which prisoners challenge the validity of their detentions, sentences, or convictions. This report examines a sample of such habeas corpus cases in eighteen federal district courts located in nine selected states (Alabama, California, Florida, Indiana, Louisiana, Missouri, New York, Pennsylvania, and Texas).

Felony Defendants in Large Urban Counties, 1998. NCJ 187232.

Based on a representative sample gathered from data collected from the seventy-five largest counties in the nation, this report describes the steps that felony defendants go through as they face criminal prosecution. Those readers interested in longitudinal analysis can obtain similar reports pertaining to 1992, 1994, and 1996 from the Bureau of Justice Statistics.

German and American Prosecutions: An Approach to Statistical Comparisons, 1998. NCJ 166610.

This report provides statistical comparisons between the German and American systems of prosecution. The statistics relate to charging, conviction, and sentencing rates for a number of selected crimes prosecuted in Germany and in the United States.

Immigration Offenders in the Federal Criminal Justice System, 2000. NCJ 191745.

Based on data collected between 1985 and 2000, this report describes the number of immigration offenders who have been prosecuted in the federal criminal justice system in this period.

Indigent Defense, 1996. NCJ 158909.

Based on the findings of different reports and surveys of the BJS, this report contains various information concerning the defense of indigent people accused of crimes in the United States.

Indigent Defense Services in Large Counties, 1999. NCJ 158909.

Based on data gathered from the nation's 100 most populous counties, this report describes how indigent defense services are managed and delivered in these counties.

Juvenile Delinquents in the Federal Criminal Justice System, 1997. NCJ 163066.

This report covers fives areas related to those juveniles whose delinquent acts have brought them into the federal justice system. The report: (1) describes juveniles processed in the federal criminal justice system; (2) gives the number of juveniles charged with acts of delinquency; (3) describes the offenses of the juveniles; (4) gives statistical information on the proportion of juvenile delinquents processed in the system; and (5) describes the sanctions that have been imposed on such juvenile delinquents.

Juvenile Felony Defendants in Criminal Courts, 1998. NCJ 165815.

This document provides data on juvenile felonies from two related sources. One source is the 1990, 1992, and 1994 State Court Processing Statistics (SCPS) program. The other is the court data compiled by the National Center for Juvenile Justice (NCJJ).

Juveniles Prosecuted in State Criminal Courts, 1997. NCJ 164265.

This report gives a combination of findings from two sources. One source is the 1994 BJS National Survey of Prosecutors, which contains statistical information about juveniles prosecuted in the nation's state criminal courts. The other data is from the National Center for Juvenile Justice, which conveys information about juveniles prosecuted in state criminal courts.

Noncitizens in the Federal Criminal Justice System, 1984–94. NCJ 160934.

This report describes the offenses and number of noncitizens prosecuted in the federal criminal justice system between 1984 and 1994. It also includes the sanctions applied to those convicted in the system.

Prosecutors in State Courts, 2001. NCJ 193441.

This report conveys various findings from the 2001 National Survey of Prosecutors. The research involved 2,341 prosecutors' offices that tried felony cases in state courts of general jurisdiction, compiling various data as to how the offices of state prosecutors operated.

Spouse Murder Defendants in Large Urban Counties, 1995. NCJ FS000127. Executive Summary: NCJ 156831. Full Report: NCJ 153256.

Written as a fact sheet, this report discusses how courtroom players composed of prosecutors, judges, and juries handle defendants accused of the murder of their spouses. The report discusses each case history and its outcome and outlines differences in handling these types of crimes from other violent crimes.

State Court Organization, 1998. NCJ 178932.

This report, highlighting the organizational structure of the nation's court system, is the fourth of its kind prepared through a collaborative effort by the Bureau of Justice Statistics and the National Center for State Courts. In addition to each state's court structure, it also describes the federal court system.

State Court Prosecutors in Large Districts, 2001. NCJ 196020.

This report is based on the 2001 National Survey of Prosecutors (NSP) whose purpose was to gather data on the manner in which chief prosecutors handled felony cases in state courts of general jurisdiction. The main denominator for inclusion was districts whose population is 500,000 or more.

State Court Sentencing in Small Districts, 2001. NCJ 196020.

This report is based on the 2001 National Survey of Prosecutors (NSP) whose purpose was to gather data on the manner in which chief prosecutors handled felony cases in state courts of general jurisdiction. The main denominator for inclusion was districts whose population is less than 250,000.

State-Funded Indigent Defense Services, 1999. NCJ 188464.

This report is based on data from the 1999 National Survey of the Indigent Defense System that was conducted in twenty-one states. The common denominator among these states was the fact that the state governments fully funded all aspects of the indigent defense services.

What Is the Sequence of Events in the Criminal Justice System, 1998? NCJ 168629.

This is an excellent guide for those who want a schematic view of the steps a criminal defendant takes as he or she enters the justice system and proceeds through its various stages. It updates information from the original flowchart devised by the President's Commission on Law Enforcement and the Administration of Justice in 1967.

Other Resources

National Archive of Criminal Justice Data, ICPSR. Institute for Social Research, P.O. Box 1248, Ann Arbor, MI: National Archive of Criminal Justice Data, 2001. 655 pages.

The National Archive of Criminal Justice Data (NACJD) was established in 1978. It is sponsored by the Bureau of Justice Statistics (BJS), which is an agency of the U.S. Department of Justice. The main goal and mission of the NACJD is to facilitate research and data collection related to the U.S. criminal justice system. This research is done under the auspices of the Inter-university Consortium for Political and Social Research (ICPSR). Both the NACJD and the ICPSR are headquartered in the institute for Social Research at the University of Michigan, Ann Arbor. The ICPSR was founded in 1962 in its capacity as a research consortium comprising 350 colleges and universities dedicated to research in many fields including criminal justice.

The NACJD data is compiled yearly and divided into different sections. The data of the year 2001 includes the following: attitude surveys (section i); community studies (section ii); corrections (section iii); court case processing (section iv); courts (section v); criminal justice system (section vi); crime and delinquency (section vii); official statistics (section viii); police (section ix); victimization (section x); drugs, alcohol, and crime (section xi); and computer programs and instructional packages. There is additional data on the criminal justice system, including indexes of principal investigators, titles, and study numbers.

Prosecution and Defense Strategies in Domestic Violence Felonies in Iowa, 1989–1995. ICPSR 2811.

The study, sponsored by a grant from the U.S. Department of Justice, National Institute of Justice, was done by Carolyn C. Hartley and Roxann Ryan. The purpose of the study was to provide an in-depth analysis as to what trial strategies prosecutors and defense attorneys employ in domestic violence felonies in the state of Iowa. The study sought to collect data on (1) what constituted evidentiary constraints in domestic violence cases, (2) the manner in which prosecutors presented domestic violence cases in court, (3) the manner in which prosecutors prioritized their evidence, and (4) what strategies and evidence defense counsel utilized in countering the prosecutors and their evidence. The data was composed of all felony domestic violence cases in the state of Iowa between 1989 and 1995.

Source Book of Criminal Justice Statistics–1994. Albany, NY: The Hindelang Criminal Justice Research Center, 1994. 701 pages.

The Bureau of Justice Statistics is an affiliate of the U.S. Department of Justice. The Bureau has been authorized by the Justice System Improvement Act of 1979, passed by Congress, to undertake appropriate research activities in order to improve, among other things, the U.S. public's access to data on crime and justice issues.

Pursuant to this authorization, the bureau annually compiles a document entitled *Sourcebook of Criminal Justice Statistics.* It contains a huge data set covering six sections. Section 1 is "Characteristics of the Criminal Justice System"; Section 2 is "Public Attitudes towards Crime and Criminal-Justice Related Topics"; Section 3 is "Nature and Distribution of Known Offenses"; Section 4 is "Characteristics and Distribution of Persons Arrested"; Section 5 is "Judicial Processing of Defendants"; and finally, Section 6 is "Persons under Correctional Supervision."

Section 5, related to judicial processing of both adult and juvenile defendants, covers a multitude of statistics related to legal processing in both state and federal court systems. This section enables applied research into the manner in which criminal cases are filed, processed, and disposed of in state and federal courts. In addition, the section provides statistics on criminal defendants by U.S. attorneys in the federal judicial districts.

The World Factbook of Criminal Justice Systems, 1996. U.S. Department of Justice, Bureau of Justice Statistics Clearinghouse, P.O. Box 179, Annapolis Junction, MD 20701–0179, website: http://www.ojp.usdoj.gov/bjs; e-mail:askbjs@ojp.usdoj.gov.

Prepared through a BJS grant, this book provides information about criminal justice systems that operate in different countries. For those who want to compare and contrast the U.S. criminal justice system's handling of criminal defendants with other systems, this book is a valuable research tool and reference.

Periodicals

American Criminal Law Review
600 New Jersey Avenue, NW
Washington, DC 20001
Phone: (202) 662-9250
E-mail: aclr@georgetown.edu
Website: http://www.law.georgetown.edu/journals/aclr/
  overview.htm

Published four times a year, the *American Criminal Law Review* is one of the most prestigious and often cited among the nation's law journals. It gives coverage to important developments in U.S. constitutional and criminal law. Subscription fee for United States: $30; International: $38.00; Single issues may be ordered for $10.

American Journal of Comparative Law
University of California at Berkeley
School of Law, Boalt Hall
Berkeley, CA 94720
Phone: (510) 643-6115
Fax: (510) 643-2698
Website: http://www.comparativelaw.org/Jou-edit.htm

The journal is one of the several publications of the American Society of Comparative Law (ASCL), formerly the American Association for the Comparative Study of Law. Founded in 1951, the purpose of the ASCL is to facilitate research on comparative law in the United States. That is why the ASCL launched the publication of the *American Journal of Comparative Law* in 1952. The journal, published annually, gives coverage to issues related to both U.S. and foreign legal traditions, including issues related to criminal defense and prosecution procedures. Subscription fee for United States: $30; International: $32.

American Journal of International Law
The American Society of International Law
2223 Massachusetts Avenue, NW
Washington, DC 20008
Phone: (202) 939-6000
Fax: (202) 797-7133
E-mail: services@asil.org
Website: http://www.asil.org

This journal is one of the main publications of the American Society of International Law founded in 1906. The society was created to study and advance the use of international law. Published quarterly since 1907, the *American Journal of International Law* is one of the most prestigious and established journals on legal research. It features articles, editorials, and comments on legal issues and offers studies, innovative proposals, and ideas related to various aspects of international law and legal processes that different traditions use throughout the world, including in criminal prosecutions. In addition, national and international court decisions are included in the journal. Subscription fee for U.S. nonmembers: $165; International nonmembers: $200.

Cardozo Journal of International and Comparative Law
Benjamin N. Cardozo School of Law
Yeshiva University
55 Fifth Avenue
New York, NY 10003
Phone: (212) 790-0200
Fax: (212) 790-0264
E-mail: lawinfo@ymail.yu.edu
Website: http://www.cardozo.yu.edu

The purpose of the *Cardozo Journal of International and Comparative Law,* first published in 1992, was to study the many legal, political, and social changes that were taking place in Europe in the 1990s. It was originally named the *New European Law Review.* The journal publishes a variety of scholarly articles and comments concerning the international legal scene, including developments that have affected defense in criminal courts in different legal traditions as, for example, the scourge of international terrorism and regional conflicts. Subscription fee: Institutions: $27.

Crime and Justice International: Worldwide News and Trends
Office of International Criminal Justice, Publication
1333 S. Wabash, Box 53
Chicago, IL 60605
Phone: (800) 521-3044
Fax: (312) 413-0485
E-mail: rschlo2@uic.edu
Web site: http://www.acsp.uic.edu

Published eleven times a year, the journal provides a wealth of information on crime and justice, including defendant rights on a global basis. It is of an applied nature directed to an audience composed of criminal justice professionals and scholars. Subscription fee: $59; Individual issues: $6.

International and Comparative Law Quarterly
The British Institute of International and Comparative Law
Oxford University Press
Great Clarendon Street
Oxford, OX2 6DP
United Kingdom
Phone: 44 (0) 1865 353561
Fax: 44 (0) 1865 353485
E-mail: willisf@oup.co.uk
Website: http://www.oup.co.uk

The *International and Comparative Law Quarterly* is one among several legal research journals that the British Institute of International and Comparative Law publishes. It covers a wide range of subjects related to public international law, comparative law, and legal procedures—including criminal defense and prosecution as well as subjects related to human rights and European Union law and legal procedures.

International Criminal Justice Review
College of Health and Human Sciences
Georgia State University
P.O. Box 4018
Atlanta, GA 30302-4018
Phone: (404) 651-3660
E-mail: icjr@gsu.edu
Website: http://www.gsu.edu/icjr

Located at Georgia State University's College of Public Health and Human Sciences, this peer-reviewed journal publishes articles and book reviews dedicated to the explanation and analyses of what the editors have characterized as "system-wide trends and problems on crime and justice issues throughout the world." Published annually, the articles are of both applied and theoretical natures. Individual subscription fee: $18; Institutions: $25.

International Law in Brief
The American Society of International Law
2223 Massachusetts Avenue, NW
Washington, DC 20008
Phone: (202) 939-6000
Fax: (202) 797-7133
E-mail: services@asil.org
Website: http://www.asil.org/ilibindex.htm

As a core publication of the American Society of International Law, this journal, prepared by the editors of *International Legal Materials,* explores recent and important developments in international law and its legal procedures, including in criminal defense and prosecutions. It is published electronically, free of subscription fee.

International Legal Materials
The American Society of International Law
2223 Massachusetts Avenue, NW
Washington, DC 20008
Phone: (202) 939-6000
Fax: (202) 797-7133
E-mail: services@asil.org
Website: http://www.asil.org

As another publication of the American Society of International Law, this journal is published biannually since 1962. As the name implies, the journal covers full texts of treatises, judicial decisions, arbitrations, and national and international legislative acts and documents. The journal is a primary source tool for those doing comparative research in legal matters, including criminal defense and prosecution. Members: $120; International: $180; Nonmembers: $215; International nonmembers: $275.

Journal of Criminal Justice Education
Academy of Criminal Justice Sciences
Department of Sociology
Colorado State University
Fort Collins, CO 80523-1784
Phone: (970) 491-2191
Fax: (970) 491-2191

E-mail: jcje@lamar.colostate.edu
Website: http://www.acjs.org

As one of the several official publications of the Academy of Criminal Justice Sciences, one of the biggest criminal justice research associations in North America, this journal publishes articles on educational aspects of criminal justice, including issues related to criminal defense and prosecution.

The National Journal of Criminal Defense
National Criminal Defense College
c/o Mercer Law School
343 Orange Street
Macon, GA 31207
Phone: (478) 746-4151
E-mail: webber@ncdc.net
Website: http://www.deryld.home.mindspring.com

Until 1983, this journal was affiliated with the National College of Criminal Defense (NCCD) in Houston, Texas. With the closure of the NCCD in 1983, its task was taken up by the Mercer Law School in Macon, Georgia. Thus, the journal is now affiliated with the Mercer Law School. It publishes criminal defense- and prosecution-related articles and comments.

Nonprint Resources

Nonprint sources include documentary films, newsreels, and videotapes that depict different aspects of the U.S. criminal justice system. Criminal trial and defense procedures are discussed and critiqued by panels of legal experts and criminal justice practitioners. In this section, some nonprint sources are presented.

Videotapes and DVDs

Amendments 5–8: The Justice Amendments
Type: video, color
Length: 15 minutes
Date: 1998
Cost: $119 (#GAA996)
Source: Insight Media

2162 Broadway
New York, NY 10024-0621
Phone: (800) 233-9910
Fax: (212) 799-5309
Website: http://www.insight-media.com

In the U.S. system of criminal trials, defendants are entitled to a number of constitutional rights that are expressed in what are known as the Justice Amendments. These are Amendments Four, Five, Six, and Eight of the U.S. Constitution. This video briefly probes into the history of these justice amendments and discusses the rights that they stipulate for criminal defendants.

An Angry Man? The Trial of Jamil Abdullah Al-Amin
Type: video, color
Length: 23 minutes
Date: 2003
Cost: $89.95 (#HFU30078)
Source: Films for the Humanities and Sciences
          P.O. Box 2053
          Princeton, NJ 08543-2053
Phone: (800) 257-5126
Fax: (609) 275-3767
Website: http://www.film.com

This video documentary sheds light on the life, career, and trial of an ex–Black Panther member, H. Rap Brown, who converted to Islam and took the name Jamil Abdullah Al-Amin. Prior to his conversion, he was a radical civil rights activist. Afterwards, he got notoriety for being accused of the murder of a sheriff's deputy in Atlanta. The documentary examines the murder case in the course of which ABC News correspondent Ted Koppel discusses it with former U.S. Ambassador to the United Nations, Andrew Young. The case is important for the issue of defendant rights because there is concern whether the case can be prosecuted without prejudice because of Mr. Al-Amin's radical Muslim views.

Cops on Trial
Type: video, color
Length: 4 volumes, 50 minutes each
Date: 1997
Cost: $129

Source: Insight Media
          2162 Broadway
          New York, NY 10024-0621
Phone: (800) 233-9910
Fax: (212) 799-5309
Website: http://www.insight-media.com

In many criminal trials, the police officers involved in the investigation and arrest of the defendant play an important role in determining his or her guilt or innocence. As a general rule, judges and juries look up to police officers who testify in court. Police officers are familiar with court scenes and procedures. They are trained how to act as credible witnesses in front of the jury or how to respond in a calm and professional manner to aggressive defense lawyers. However, when police officers are on trial as criminal defendants as presented in this four-volume video series, do we encounter a different dynamic in relation to the ultimate outcome of the case? After all, it is a known fact that it is not easy to convict experienced police officers involved in criminal activity. This video presents four trials of four police officers accused of the murder of a woman suspect in a burglary (trial 1), of tampering with evidence (trial 2), of the use of excessive force (trial 3), and of burglary and first-degree murder (trial 4). In each video a segment is devoted to interviewing the courtroom players (judges, prosecutors, defense lawyers, and jurors) so as to get an understanding of what each player thought about the trial process and the criminal defendant's conduct, rationale, and demeanor in court.

Criminal Trial Procedure
Type: video, color
Length: 19 minutes
Date: 1980
Cost: $129 (#GAA800)
Source: Insight Media
          2162 Broadway
          New York, NY 10024-0621
Phone: (800) 233-9910
Fax: (212) 799-5309
Website: http://www.insight-media.com

A U.S. criminal trial is complex, with many steps and procedures that meticulously must be adhered to in determining the guilt or innocence of a criminal defendant. In this video, a judge discusses these steps and procedures—such as how judges give preliminary instructions to the jury, how the voir dire in jury selection proceeds, and what kind of legal strategies and maneuvers the two sides utilize in court.

Evidence of Guilt: The Complexities of Jurisprudence
Type: video, color
Length: 45 minutes
Date: 2003
Cost: $129.95 (#HFU9244)
Source: Insight Media
              2162 Broadway
              New York, NY 10024-0621
Phone: (800) 233-9910
Fax: (212) 799-5309
Website: http://www.insight-media.com

Prepared by CBS News, this documentary explores the complexities of the notion of guilt in the U.S. system of criminal prosecution. This complexity stems from the fact that legal guilt is quite different from actual guilt in the U.S. legal tradition. In fact, the term *criminal justice* implies that a defendant is entitled to just treatment as he or she is going through the justice process to determine his or her legal guilt. This documentary stresses the fact that the U.S. criminal justice system puts the responsibility for proving guilt on the shoulders of the prosecution. Establishing evidence of guilt is one of the most complex and arduous processes in any criminal trial. The evidence must persuade the members of the jury that the accused has committed the alleged crime "beyond a reasonable doubt." In the documentary, the CBS News correspondent William Schlesinger investigates a murder case in which the cause of death has not been well defined and a rape case in which the victim did not see her attacker and therefore is unable to positively identify the accused as the culprit in the crime. The documentary explores how the jury goes about determining the guilt of the two criminal defendants in the two cases. Interviewing the criminal defense lawyers and members of the jury, the documentary sheds light on the complexity of the U.S. criminal trial and system of jurisprudence.

First-Degree Murder Trial
Type: video, color
Length: 4 volumes, 60 minutes each
Date: 1987
Cost: $149 (#GAA165)
Source: Insight Media
        2162 Broadway
        New York, NY 10024-0621
Phone: (800) 233-9910
Fax: (212) 799-5309
Website: http://www.insight-media.com

The trial and conviction of those criminal defendants charged with first-degree murder entails much time, energy, and expense. For a killing to be considered of the first degree, it must be an intentional and unlawful killing of a human being based on premeditation and malice. The prosecution has to prove the presence of all these factors to convict the defendant of the crime. This four-volume video follows the trial of Robert Sandoval, accused of first-degree murder and tried in the Denver District Court in 1987. The video covers how the preliminary steps of the trial are initiated and tracks the proceedings until the verdict is pronounced.

Gideon's Trumpet: The Poor Man and the Law—1964
Type: video, color
Length: 51 minutes
Date: 2003
Cost: $89.95 (#HIH11038)
Source: Films for the Humanities and Sciences
        P.O. Box 2053
        Princeton, NJ 08543-2053
Phone: (800) 257-5126
Fax: (609) 275-3767
Website: http://www.film.com

The universal right to legal counsel for noncapital offenses did not exist in the U.S. system of criminal prosecution prior to 1964. This important right was won in the landmark decision of the U.S. Supreme Court *Gideon v. Wainright*. This documentary video discusses this important right, showing how it was won. In the documentary interviews are conducted with the criminal

defendant in the case, Clarence Earl Gideon, Justice Arthur Goldberg, defense attorney Abe Fortas, and other officials of the court
involved in the case.

In Time of War: Striking the Balance between Freedom and
Security
Type: DVD, color
Length: 23 minutes
Date: 2003
Cost: $114.95 (#HIH30566-KS)
Source: Films for the Humanities and Sciences
             P.O. Box 2053
             Princeton, NJ 08543-2053
Phone: (800) 257-5126
Fax: (609) 275-3767
Website: http://www.film.com

This documentary discusses some of the negative impacts of the
11 September 2001 events on U.S. society. The basic premise of
the documentary is that in the aftermath of this tragic event, the
U.S. public has started to reevaluate the relationship between
security and privacy. Based on an ABC News poll, 64 percent of
Americans support expanding the powers of the FBI in return for
effective security measures against terrorism. However, these
measures would adversely impact the Bill of Rights and especially those parts of it that relate to law enforcement activities—
be it arrest, search, seizure, or interrogation. Legal experts, scholars, and law enforcement practitioners discuss how security
concerns may impact a criminal defendant's Fourth Amendment
rights in the aftermath of September 11.

Inside the Jury
Type: video, color
Length: 45 minutes
Date: 2003
Cost: $129.95 (#HIH10729)
Source: Films for the Humanities and Sciences
             P.O. Box 2053
             Princeton, NJ 08543-2053
Phone: (800) 257-5126
Fax: (609) 275-3767
Website: http://www.film.com

Produced by CBS News, this video addresses important questions such as how a jury is impaneled, what goes on in the jury room, and how jury members discuss a case and go about evaluating the evidence presented to them during the course of a criminal trial. The video presents how a case of armed robbery is tried in court and how the jury deliberates the case. In addition, the video includes a panel of experts who discuss different aspects of the case.

An Introduction to the Federal Court
Type: video, color
Length: 29 minutes
Date: 1991
Cost: $149 (#GAA772)
Source: Insight Media
          2162 Broadway
          New York, NY 10024-0621
Phone: (800) 233-9910
Fax: (212) 799-5309
Website: http://www.insight-media.com

How do persons charged with the commission of crime defend themselves in a federal court? How does a federal trial court operate? What is the jurisdiction of the federal courts and how are they administered? These are some of the questions that this video answers. In addition, the video discusses how federal courts handle criminal cases and appeals. It also describes the division of the system into district courts, circuit courts, and the U.S. Supreme Court and their administration.

It's the Law
Type: video, color
Length: 30 minutes
Date: 2003
Cost: $129.95 (#HIH11901-A)
Source: Films for the Humanities and Sciences
          P.O. Box 2053
          Princeton, NJ 08543-2053
Phone: (800) 257-5126
Fax: (609) 275-3767
Website: http://www.film.com

In this video a panel of judges, prosecutors, and defense lawyers discusses how laws governing different aspects of the U.S. criminal justice system are created and enforced. In addition, the panel discusses various rights that criminal defendants enjoy in the U.S. system. To this end, the panel also discusses some of these rights as enunciated in Amendments Five through Eight of the U.S. Constitution and how different categories of crime and misdemeanors are defined and enforced by the U.S. law enforcement and court systems.

Landmark American Trials
Type: video, color
Length: 4 volumes, 45 minutes each
Date: 1998–1999
Cost: $149 (#GAA1526)
Source: Insight Media
             2162 Broadway
             New York, NY 10024-0621
Phone: (800) 233-9910
Fax: (212) 799-5309
Website: http://www.insight-media.com

This four-volume documentary depicts the details of four important trials that have left everlasting impacts on the U.S. justice system. These are the trial of Nicola Sacco and Bartolomeo Vanzetti for the alleged murder of Frederick Parmenter and his guard in Massachusetts (1921); the trial of John Thomas Scopes (also known as the "Monkey Trial") in Dayton, Tennessee (1925); trial of the "Scottsboro Boys" for the alleged rape of two white girls in Alabama (1931); and the trial of Julius and Ethel Rosenberg for the alleged conspiracy to give America's atomic weapon secrets to the Soviet Union in New York (1951). These are landmark trials, according to the producer of the documentary, because they have raised important questions about nonlegal factors (e.g., social, political, or religious) that have impacted the U.S. system of defense and criminal prosecution. For example, in the case of defendants Sacco and Vanzetti, the documentary shows that it was their political radicalism that led to their conviction and execution rather than any concrete evidence proving their involvement in the alleged murder of Parmenter and his guard. In the Scopes case, it was the secular scientific views of

Scopes that got him into trouble with fundamentalist Christians in his community and ultimately with the law. In the Scottsboro case, it was the race of the criminal defendants (black) versus the race of the alleged rape victims (white) that propelled the case. In the Rosenberg case, it was a combination of ethnic and religious prejudice coupled with anticommunist hysteria in the 1950s that led the couple to their deaths, not their actual guilt.

Legal Issues of the Fifth and Sixth Amendments
Type: video, color
Length: 58 minutes
Date: 1994
Cost: $199 (#GAA1364)
Source: Insight Media
             2162 Broadway
             New York, NY 10024-0621
Phone: (800) 233-9910
Fax: (212) 799-5309
Website: http://www.insight-media.com

The Fifth and Sixth Amendments provide important legal rights for criminal defendants that we have discussed at some length in this book. This video documentary features ten self-incrimination cases brought before the U.S. Supreme Court. In addition to the legal and social facts that surround the cases, the documentary discusses the high Court's decisions in relation to each case.

Our Legal System
Type: video, color
Length: 20 minutes
Date: 1993
Cost: $219 (#GAA518)
Source: Insight Media
             2162 Broadway
             New York, NY 10024-0621
Phone: (800) 233-9910
Fax: (212) 799-5309
Website: http://www.insight-media.com

The U.S. legal system is a complex one composed of an array of legal doctrines, philosophies, structures, and rights and responsibilities. This video briefly explores the U.S. legal system, probing into some of these complexities and controversies.

Presumed Guilty: Tales of the Public Defenders
Type: video, color
Length: 120 minutes
Date: 2003
Cost: $149.95 (#HIH30757)
Source: Films for the Humanities and Sciences
          P.O. Box 2053
          Princeton, NJ 08543-2053
Phone: (800) 257-5126
Fax: (609) 275-3767
Website: http://www.film.com

Public defenders provide an important legal service to those criminal defendants who are not able to pay for the services of defense lawyers. Being represented by counsel is an important right that criminal defendants enjoy in the U.S. system of justice. This video documentary is about a public defenders office in San Francisco. The office has eighty attorneys with busy daily schedules. The video focuses on some of these attorneys as they perform their duties. The aim is to familiarize the audience with the justice process from its inception to its end, from the time of arraignment to the time of sentencing. In addition, an important part of the documentary is to shed light on the relationship between attorneys and their indigent clientele within the overall philosophy and organization of the public defenders office.

Privacy and Security
Type: video, color
Length: 57 minutes
Date: 2003
Cost: $89.95 (#HIH10469)
Source: Films for the Humanities and Sciences
          P.O. Box 2053
          Princeton, NJ 08543-2053
Phone: (800) 257-5126
Fax: (609) 275-3767
Website: http://www.film.com

This video discusses the gradual erosion of privacy in U.S. life and its adverse impacts on constitutional rights that U.S. citizens and others enjoy in this country. This erosion in daily privacy is due to the intrusion of electronic monitoring, which records many aspects of daily life. For example, every time we purchase through credit cards, check into a hotel, or are provided with services such intrusion takes place. The video raises the question as to whether such electronic monitoring of the average citizen's activities would ultimately make the constitutional notion of privacy moot or irrelevant. This question has taken on a new urgency in the aftermath of 11 September 2001. Under the guise of fighting terrorism, police are now able to conduct much more intrusive investigations of suspects, gathering more detailed information—much of it electronically—than they could in the past. In the face of these realities, the question has arisen as to whether the constitutional notion of privacy as expressed in the Fourth Amendment should be reexamined and even revised.

Rights of the Accused: Our Legal System
Type: video, color
Length: 30 minutes
Date: 1998
Cost: $139 (#GAA147)
Source: Insight Media
          2162 Broadway
          New York, NY 10024-0621
Phone: (800) 233-9910
Fax: (212) 799-5309
Website: http://www.insight-media.com

The U.S. legal tradition provides a wide range of rights for those accused of criminality. Analyzing the protective clauses of the Fourth, Fifth, Sixth, and Eighth Amendments, this video discusses whether the rights of the accused ought to be balanced against the rights of society.

Trial by Jury
Type: video, color
Length: 25 minutes
Date: 2003
Cost: $79.95 (#HIH10783-A)
Source: Films for the Humanities and Sciences
          P.O. Box 2053

Princeton, NJ 08543-2053
Phone: (800) 257-5126
Fax: (609) 275-3767
Website: http://www.film.com

It is estimated that every year around 1.5 million Americans serve as members of a jury. The right to trial by jury is one of the fundamental rights that criminal defendants enjoy in the Anglo-American system of criminal prosecution. Trial by jury is a complex undertaking that this video explores in its different dimensions. In eight segments, the video discusses the history of trial by jury, the duties of the jury, the courtroom professionals and what they do, qualifications for jury service, steps taken in jury trials, the grand jury, and advantages and disadvantages of jury trial.

The Trial Lawyer: Five Courtroom Champions Speak—1968
Type: video, black and white
Length: 52 minutes
Date: 2003
Cost: $89.95 (#HFU11039)
Source: Films for the Humanities and Sciences
P.O. Box 2053
Princeton, NJ 08543-2053
Phone: (800) 257-5126
Fax: (609) 275-3767
Website: http://www.film.com

The aim of this documentary video is to dispel the commonly held view that criminal trials resolve in a "Perry Mason" type of good triumphing over evil. Interviewing five nationally prominent criminal defense lawyers (F. Lee Bailey, Percy Foreman, Melvin Belli, Louis Nizer, and Edward Bennet Williams), the documentary sheds light on the arduous and complex legal procedures that criminal defense lawyers go through as they prepare their cases. Subjects discussed include the complex task of jury selection, the use of expert testimony, defending clients known to be guilty, and others. The commentator is Harry Reasoner of CBS News.

Index